International African Library 8
General editors: David Parkin and J. D. Y. Peel

BETWEEN GOD, THE DEAD AND THE WILD

For Bouba and Titlesime
with my thanks
and in memory of
Lawal Dura who
died in 1989

International African Library

General Editors

D. Parkin *and* J. D. Y. Peel

The *International African Library* is a major monograph series from the International African Institute
and complements its quarterly periodical *Africa*, the
premier journal in the field of African studies. Theo-
retically informed ethnographies, studies of social
relations 'on the ground' which are sensitive to local
cultural forms, have long been central to the Institute's
publications programme. The *IAL* maintains this
strength but extends it into new areas of contemporary
concern, both practical and intellectual. So it includes
works focused on problems of development, especially
on the linkages between the local and national levels
of society; studies along the interface between the
social and the environmental sciences; and historical
studies, especially those of a social, cultural or inter-
disciplinary character.

Titles in the series:
1   Sandra T. Barnes   *Patrons and power: creating a
    political community in metropolitan Lagos*★
2   Jane I. Guyer (ed.)   *Feeding African cities: essays in
    social history*★
3   Paul Spencer   *The Maasai of Matapato: a study of
    rituals of rebellion*★
4   Johan Pottier   *Migrants no more: settlement and sur-
    vival in Mambwe villages, Zambia*★
5   Günther Schlee   *Identities on the move: clanship
    and pastoralism in northern Kenya*
6   Suzette Heald   *Controlling anger: the sociology of
    Gisu violence*
7   Karin Barber   *I could speak until tomorrow:* Oriki,
    women, and the past in a Yoruba town†

★ Published in the USA by Indiana University Press
† Published in the USA by the Smithsonian Institution

BETWEEN GOD, THE DEAD AND THE WILD

CHAMBA INTERPRETATIONS OF RELIGION AND RITUAL

RICHARD FARDON

SMITHSONIAN INSTITUTION PRESS
Washington, D.C.

© Richard Fardon 1990
First published in the
United States by Smithsonian
Institution Press
Library of Congress Catalog Number 90–63714

Set in Linotron Plantin and
Printed by Redwood Press Ltd,
Melksham, Wilts

British Library Cataloguing
  in Publication Data
Fardon, Richard
Between God, the dead and the wild: Chamba
  interpretations of ritual and religion. –
  (International African library).
1. West Africa. Religion – Sociological perspectives
I. Title II. Series
306.60966

ISBN 1–56098–044–3

Contents

LIST OF ILLUSTRATIONS

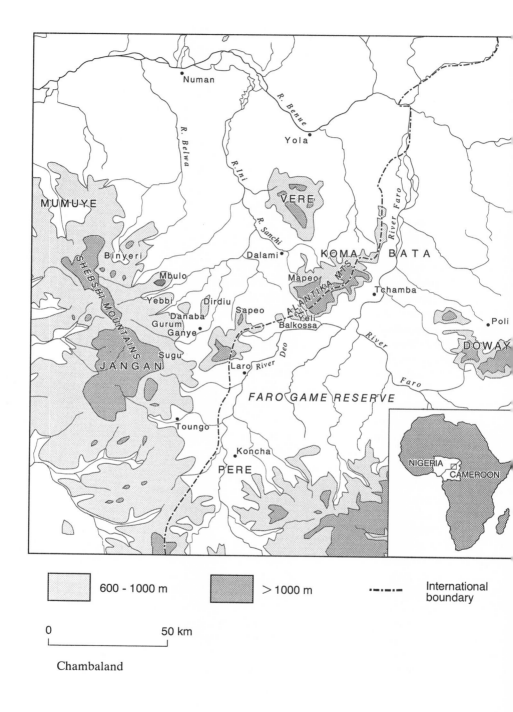

Chambaland

PREFACE

I meant to write a more accessible second book about the Chamba: one that developed arguments begun in its companion volume but could be read singly. Taking the Chamba people (defined in the most extensive terms) as its subject, *Raiders and Refugees* tried to demonstrate that an interpretative grasp of agency helped us understand in what sense Chamba made their history and ethnic identity during a period of roughly two centuries. Given the variation between myriad Chamba communities, formal typological devices were necessary to organise the materials from diverse sources (archival records, historical accounts, survey fieldwork and intensive research carried out in a few Chamba communities) that provided evidence for generalisations about trends in Chamba political development.

This volume relies less on secondary sources or survey fieldwork. Most chapters draw on evidence gathered during intensive research in only two Chamba communities. *Between God, the Dead and the Wild* is my attempt to understand Chamba ritual or, more exactly, how Chamba have tried to explain to me the way their rituals affect a world they think to inhabit. My brief reflections on the different anthropological theories of ritual and symbolism that have helped or hindered my effort to grasp Chamba apprehensions are virtually confined to the first and last chapters; the chapters between are devoted to a detailed, descriptive account of a 'traditional' (yet contemporary) West African religion.

The book's main title picks up, what I take to be, three self-evident and non-derivative categories of Chamba interpretation: God, the dead and the wild. I neither suggest that their self-evidence makes these categories obvious nor propose that they are self-evident in the same way. Close attention to Chamba expression is required to make sense of the creativity of these ideas. Together they make possible a world in which a fourth, or subject, term is conceived: 'the children of men' are between God, the dead and the wild. 'God' above is associated with the sun. The 'dead', to choose one conceivable translation of a word that cannot be rendered by a single English term, are subterranean creatures, associated with the being and relics of past and future living people; they are below. 'The wild', 'things of the bush' in Chamba terms, encompass the space occupied by the living. Imagined this way, the three categories locate forces surrounding the human individual. But the spatial ontology is only the most apparent. The surrounding agencies may also be explained, and presumably experienced, as aspects or qualities of beings and of things, akin to their qualities of gender, number, shade, heat, partibility, and openness or closure.

Children of men are not unique in this composite character; masks and cults also are explained by Chamba by analogy to the three less reducible categories of existence. Masks, 'men' and cults share properties, but not in equal proportions. Rituals, likewise, are deemed to be effective, in different ways, because they combine or realign qualities and efficacies proper to God, the dead and the wild. However personal understandings differ, terms of explanation are relatively invariant: God, the dead, and the wild are the assumed basis even for disagreement about the way they affect the living.

How and how fully do composite, interpreting human agents make sense to themselves of this situation? I introduce the book with this question and conclude with a query that stems from it. How far do they anticipate comprehensibility? What measure of understanding is supposed available to the kind of human agents they are? Between these two questions, I examine a variety of Chamba rituals and Chamba beliefs about them in order to explore a third question. How far can ethnographers impose order on the practices of others without falling foul of the fallacy of over-interpretation? If interpretation is an effort to represent the viewpoint of other people, do we have a brief to write out ignorance, doubt or uncertainty that may be central to their experience? These, otherwise too invitingly diffuse, conundrums are grounded in a contrast between Yeli and Mapeo, two Chamba places, and the different styles of exegesis found there.

Because such questions are difficult even to address from passing acquaintanceship or secondary sources, this book concentrates upon only two communities, in less historical depth, than its predecessor. By the same token, because the questions require a greater detail in local description, my research experience is foregrounded here, and not treated as a background against which to assess broader regional trends. Recent commentators have reminded us how ethnographic experience differs from accounts we afterwards write on the basis of it. Thanks to its subject matter this book is a rather more conventional ethnography than its companion—although it is based on the same research experience. Accordingly, I include information on the way I was accommodated by my hosts and how their definition of my circumstances mediated my access to their lives. None the less, the writer's persona is a professional one, which construes a complex personal experience in the terms appropriate to an ethnographic investigator. It is a presentation that contains as much (or little) of me as is likely to interest a reader I expect to have opened these pages from curiosity about Chamba. I try to satisfy that reader's demand to be told how I can claim to know things, but I do not seek to recapitulate my experience.

ACKNOWLEDGEMENTS

These two Chamba books complete a plan that has taken ten years: to contribute a history of Chamba peoples to the collective project of West African regional scholarship, and to write an account of Chamba religion, ritual and worldview. In the preface to *Raiders and Refugees*, I explained how the extensive focus of that study was cued by local interests; my concern with religion and ritual also reflects the terms on which my presence and purpose were understood by my Mapeo Chamba hosts. I began research among Chamba intending to study economics, in which I took a first degree, and marriage systems, on which I had worked as a postgraduate student. The extent of my debt to Chamba informants can be measured from the fact I have written instead on politics, history and religion.

Acknowledgements made in the Preface to the earlier book are equally pertinent to this, and I renew them collectively. Some chapters, or parts of chapters, were written initially for various audiences. The first chapter, and the tone it imparts to the volume, began as a seminar paper for the University of St Andrews Departmental Seminar and Satterthwaite Colloquium on African Religion and Ritual in spring 1985 with the same title as here. In a much revised version, the paper was read to a seminar on post-structuralism at the School of Oriental and African Studies in autumn that year. Revisions were suggested by participants on each of these occasions: Mark Hobart and James Fernandez read the paper and wrote detailed comments; Maurice Bloch and Dick Werbner responded at length during the meetings. The section of Chapter 5 dealing with Mapeo funerary rites was presented to the Satterthwaite Colloquium of 1986 as 'Death and the performance of society' and profited from Ivan Karp's comments. An early analysis of conversion was given to the West Africa seminar of University College London at the invitation of Murray Last. Another Satterthwaite Colloquium, in 1989, allowed me to present an analysis of the Chamba mask that was deeply indebted to the late Arnold Rubin. David Parkin and John Peel read the entire manuscript and suggested substantial changes between the penultimate and final versions.

Without Dick Werbner's enthusiastic, persuasive and argumentative chairmanship of the Satterthwaite Colloquium, this volume would have taken much longer to complete.

Thanks for material support during my research in 1976–78, 1984, 1985 and 1987 are due to the Social Science Research Council, the Central Research Fund of the University of London, the Carnegie Foundation for the Universities of Scotland, and the Hayter–Parry and Staff Travel Funds of the University of St Andrews. The Research Committee of the School of Oriental and African Studies provided a grant for the map of Chambaland. My colleagues during eight years at the University of St Andrews (Ladislav Holy, Sándor Hervey and David Riches) were models of collegial support and their assistances are too many to enumerate. Debts that are diffuse, personal and longstanding are owed to Sally Chilver for her generous and enthusiastic support, to Raymond Boyd for his company and collaboration during research in 1987, and to Catherine Davies for her care and understanding during the ups and downs of my scribbling.

ORTHOGRAPHY

Although they are not closely related, Chamba Daka and Chamba Leko share some feature: three level tones, as well as numerous glides, and a contrast between long and short vowels, are significant in both. I have not attempted to reproduce these complexities of vowel and tone quality here. My orthography is a simplification of that established by Phil Noss, for the Balkossa dialect of Chamba Leko, and of a provisional account of Chamba Daka for which I am indebted to Raymond Boyd. Only three special symbols are employed: ɛ, as in let; ǝ, as in earn; ɔ, as in paw. Initial ng signifies nasalisation and an initial apostrophe a glottal stop.

With few exceptions, I transcribe Leko words in Yeli dialect and Daka words in Mapeo dialect. I sometimes breach this rule by reinstating initial semi consonants which are replaced by a glottal stop in Mapeo, but no other, dialect of Chamba Daka (thus I write *wurum* and not *'urum*). Spellings of place names are those which appear on maps of the area, even where they do not correspond to my idea of a transcription close to the sound. Occasionally, I have retained letters that would be lost through elision in speech in order to maintain the internal organisation of compound terms: thus *jup kupsa* rather than *jukupsa*. As previously, I capitalise patriclan names and italicise matriclan names without an initial capital letter in order to distinguish them.

Because Raymond Boyd's transcription of Chamba Daka is more accurate than my earlier version and will be used in a future Chamba lexicon, I have changed some conventions. I do not think the reader will find words unrecognisable, but Daka nouns are now presented without the [-i] or [-ri] suffix that I had earlier retained, and for consistency I have dropped the corresponding Leko suffix. Thus matriclan, previously written as *kuni* in Daka and *kuna* in

Leko, is now written *kun* in both cases. Medial or final [p] is now preferred to [b] in contexts where they are not differentiated in Chamba Daka. A particularly frequent example of these changes is that the term for cult, previously transcribed as *jubi*, appears now as *jup*. I have allowed myself inconsistency in a few cases: thus *lera* flute may be abbreviated in context to *led* in Chamba Leko but not Chamba Daka. I have preferred to retain the same form for both languages. Occasionally I have retained a suffix in order to suggest the balanced contrast of Chamba terms (for instance, *lera* and *vɔma*).

Richard Fardon
St Andrews
December 1989

A visit to Chambaland in April/May 1990, primarily to study Chamba songs, allowed me to check and update some information. Thanks are due to the British Academy for funding, Raymond Boyd for continued collaboration, and Pius J. Hammawa and his family for their hospitality.

St Lucia
August 1990

1

PROTESTATIONS OF IGNORANCE?
OR, THINGS LEFT UNSAID?

TWO INFORMANTS

When I recall conversations and events from the two and a half years that I lived in Chamba communities, two personalities come most often to mind. I first knew both of them at the same time, more than ten years ago. Titlɛsime was my daily companion during the year I spent in Mapeo around 1977. I met Dura in the same year but knew him better in 1984 when I lived for six months in Yeli, where he was the priestly official closest to the chief of that small and impoverished chiefdom. Now in their sixties, both are adherents of traditional Chamba religion. Both are also considered exceptional men by their peers: Dura as priest to the Yeli chief; Titlɛsime because he is one of the most active and knowledgeable elders who undertake the onerous responsibilities of the Mapeo variant of Chamba religion.

In physique and temperament the two men are different. Dura is unusually tall for a Chamba, taller than my six feet, a slow moving and contemplative man, generally mild tempered, since his authority is relatively uncontested. Titlɛsime is short, that is to say of more usual Chamba stature, and restless; his gait is rapid, his speech husky, effusive and staccato. In ways I describe later, the differences between the two men recall differences between the places in which they live. Both could be described as connoisseurs of life. Men who despite poverty have great relish for what Simmel calls the playform of sociability and for the pot of good beer that accompanies it. I like both of them and admire their abilities to be both grave and playful; both I think are balanced, sane and rounded men. It is an opinion that seems to be entertained generally, and is one reason why each speaks with authority within his community. No one thought it odd that they became (what anthropologists call) principal informants to me about their different communities, especially about (what anthropologists call) ritual. Much, but not all, that I know about ritual comes from conversations with these two men, and from being around when they were in attendance at, or actually responsible for, important events in the lives of their communities.

Garum Titlɛsime (1987).

Lawal Dura (1984). On a ceremonial occasion Dura wears the 'traditional' two part kilt, and carries his *lama* over the right shoulder. Around his neck are beads as well as a stoppered medicine horn and ceremonial knives.

I begin like this because one of my concerns will be with the effects anthropologists' writings about ritual have upon their informants. I do not intend this directly, for my writing is unlikely materially to affect either of my informants, but rather in the indirect sense that composing places, people and events necessarily transfigures and displaces their particularity. The rough sketch of two particular informants is to help you, and more crucially me, keep in mind the image of two different men, glossing, interpreting and explaining. It is a reminder that rituals belong to interpretive communities.

I shall not refer to Titlesime and Dura throughout the book; to do so might be a convenient literary conceit but it would represent views general in Mapeo and Yeli as if they were the idiosyncracies of two individuals. None the less, these men imbue my recollections of fieldwork with much of their emotional tone, and this book, albeit they cannot read it, is an extension of conversations with them. Because they cannot answer back—because I am no longer on the fringes of the interpretive associations within which the rituals I describe take place—the conversation has become monologue. This makes it imperative that I clearly signal when, and how, my interpretation goes beyond what those societies might endorse. For the ethnographer, this deserves to be the principal consideration when deciding how far interpretation should be pushed.

ETHNOGRAPHIC INFORMANTS AND INFORMATION

Anthropological accounts commonly feature two varieties of informant who perform different rhetorical roles. There are the super-informants, whose names become well known: the Don Juans, Ogotemmelis and Muchonas, who are brought on stage as repositories of the accounts which anthropologists particularly admire. They crack the codes of culture through especial insight into the inner workings of systems of signs. They say what others do not realise or cannot put into words. Then there are the collective informants, the Nuer, Azande or whoever, who think, do, say particular things. These collective informants are frequently less reflective than their named counterparts, to whose superinformativeness they are a foil. Periodically, one of the unnamed multitude comes forward to offer the non explanation that is the anthropologist's despair: in response to the persistent anthropological interrogative 'why' they are quoted to respond 'Because the ancestors told us so', or 'Because it is our custom', or 'Because it has always been thus'. The temptation is to try a more subtly loaded or leading question to encourage the informant into telling us what we are sure he must know. The 'protestations of ignorance', to introduce one of the referents of my chapter heading, which run-of-the-mill informants make, is one reason why anthropologists feel at home with the touchplayers of interpretation like Muchona and his ilk. These informants appear capable of saying what remains 'unsaid' in the accounts of the mass.

In the contrast between these two types of informant, we encounter a rudimentary problem about ignorance. Once a superinformant's gloss is generalised to the status of an understanding common to members of a 'culture', we are equipped to argue that the mass, who by definition share that culture, somehow know, but cannot say, what practically speaking, they must know in order to do what they evidently do. We have produced the common anthropological model of culture as a set of propositions shared, but not statable, by all: whence the justification for anthropologists writing accounts of cultures, and the anthropologist's need for informants who are informative. But something more has happened. From participant in the conversations of one or several interpreting associations the anthropologist has turned judge. A verdict has been given on the contributions to the conversation: germane/irrelevant, informed/ignorant, admissable/inadmissable. The conversation turns out to have winner and losers; and no one writes about the losers.

Anthropologists' accounts are usually positive in tone, they deal with what people know, what they say and what they do; only by implication do they deal with the unknown, the unsaid and the undone. Quite right too, we are concerned with what 'is' not what 'is not'. I agree. But accounts of 'what is' usually paper over 'protestations of ignorance' which we once thought we heard, and fill in 'things left unsaid'. Sometimes they do one in terms of the other, so that a protestation of ignorance transpires to be something left unsaid. But our theories attribute additional ignorances and unsayabilities to our informants; in producing an account of knowledge on paper we necessarily situate subjectivities deemed capable of saying some part of what we are saying, knowing some elements of what we claim to know. Our theories imply subjects to whom they can be reattributed as conditions of experience. They depend just as crucially on particular constructs of ignorance and unsayability as they do on the paired members of these terms. We cannot create the one without the other; but we do this creating in numerous ways.

Below is a selection of ways in which we go beyond what is said arranged in a rough order of potential obscurity to informants whose statements furnish the basis for our judgements. Two notes before starting this: you will note that I am attributing crucial methodological importance to what is said. Anthropological fieldwork is rightly and necessarily garrulous. Even (indeed especially) when we read beyond what we construe as the propositional content of statements, these statements remain the most important means by which the reader can be given any critical purchase on our accounts. Secondly, my listing has a didactic purpose; I am suggesting that the views I group are similar only in the terms in which I am looking at them; looked at in other ways they make strange bedfellows.

(a) Mis-stated knowledge: purposeful concealment, for whatever reason (self interested or altruistic lies, or the protection of secrets), presupposes subjects who misrepresent knowledge they possess. In a more specialised sense, misrepresentation may presuppose a subject who voices a view that he would reject in another context. Simply in order to translate we have to know when someone is telling us, or someone else, a conscious falsehood. The borderline between falsehood and fantasy is underexplored ethnographically. Why, how and when statements are assessed as one or the other is an interesting question (Gilsenan, 1976). Misrepresentation of activity to do with cults is a normal feature of Chamba discourse—as Chamba willingly volunteer.

(b) Understated knowledge: this category subsumes numerous formulations of the old problem of people knowing practically how to do something without being used, or perhaps able, to explore verbally all the facets of knowing which go into their practical activities. A number of terms attack this from different perspectives.

(i) Tacit knowledge might be understood as knowledge 'how' acquired practically, perhaps through the imitation of others (Polanyi (1958) in the sense which Kuhn (1962) takes over when he uses paradigm to mean exemplary instance). The knowledge is visible in the doing but not statable in propositional form; perhaps the idea that it should be is symptomatic of what Feyerabend calls our ratiomania (Feyerabend, 1975).

(ii) Implicit knowledge is, as the term suggests, implied by other elements of the culture. 'The implicit is the foundation of social intercourse' (Douglas, 1975:5). This is a difficult term since it begs the questions implicit for whom and from what point of view. It is hard to know what empirical materials a notion of implicitness directs us towards. In one sense, implicit is close to the unspokenness of tacit knowledge. Both are inferred from what people are capable of doing. In another sense, it is close to a third type.

(iii) The doxic propositions, with which Bourdieu deals, are also similar to what Douglas means by implicit (Bourdieu, 1977:164), and perhaps to what an American anthropologist like Shweder means by 'cultural frames' constitutive of experience but beyond proof or disproof (Shweder, 1984). In Bourdieu's case, self- evident experience of the world presupposes doxa, which in turn is explained by socialisation into a culturally constructed world (through his idea of habitus). This view may introduce another sense, of the fragility of doxa when it becomes reflected upon, codified and examined for its implications.

In different ways doxa, tacit knowledge, implicit knowledge and cultural frames all address the problem of under-stated knowledge. Two stances can be derived from this: either informants know more than they can tell us because they take for granted what is under their noses, or else they have assimilated some knowledge as a condition of experience so that a contrastive 'could have been otherwise' case is not available to them. 'Under your nose' knowledge only needs explaining to outsiders;

'couldn't be otherwise' knowledge may resist exegesis because it is framed not as a feat of comprehension but as a direct response to the ways things are.

(iv) The three categories, or at least the general notions they presuppose, are sometimes addressed from the perspective of the attitude ascribed to the knowing subject: in this case terms like preconscious or prereflective may be employed when the possibility of development towards greater consciousness or reflection is being stressed; when the statement is more resolute writers appeal to unconscious or unreflective. 'Pre-' terms are more optimistic about the prospect of emancipation than are 'un-' terms.

These four terms of attribution allocate the disparities between people's ability to get on (with tasks or with one another) and what they say about this routine achievement. Here is an area crucial to the building of characters, whether by ethnographic or fictional writers.

(c) Unstatable knowledge: some elements of what we might consider to fall into a broad category of knowledge are elusive to statement in propositional form. The mysterious or ineffable cannot be addressed directly without losing its most essential quality, but our informants may have approximating notions of it which are diffuse in particular ways. The multivocality of symbols may be thought to demand multiple translations which disperse the force of the original (Turner, 1968). Metaphorical usages gain their force from the associations they conjure from distinct domains; examine them too closely and they don't work any more, or not in the same way (Fernandez, 1986). Artistic creations are not translatable into propositions without loss and distortion.

This category shares characteristics with the presuppositional type of implicit knowledge, but its unstatability is principled rather than situational. There never could be a set of circumstances nor a form of words with which to recapitulate some types of experience without loss.

(d) Unknowable generative schema: under this rubric I subsume a host of, very different, theories which propose rule governed subjects who follow the rules in ignorance that they do so. Possibly, knowing the rules they might no longer follow them. Foucault's pairing of episteme with a positive unconscious of knowledge, Freud's pairing of unconscious and conscious, Lévi Strauss's mentalistic ontology of representations all, admittedly in very different ways, situate subjects capable of producing particular types of acts or speech almost despite themselves. Each proposes conditions under which the unknowable would be known, which in Foucault would involve changing relations of power and knowledge, in Freud would follow from particular techniques of self awareness, and in Lévi-Strauss would involve the emergence of a particular scientific outlook on thought itself. In some cases, the newer awareness would be seen as emancipating—the truth claims of its analysis more compelling than those of the old. Other analyses are less sanguine, believing all truth claims to be relative. By and large, Freudian analyses belong to the first type and Foucauldian to the second. Lévi-Strauss's followers also tend to propose strong claims for the scientific status of their analyses, although the master's nostalgia for the sad tropics makes him more evasive.

(e) Unknowable comparative schema: anthropologists often know more about the histories of the societies in which they work, as well as the characteristics of neighbouring societies, than do their informants. This leads anthropologists to identify as problematic elements of their informants' knowledge with which the informants themselves find no problem. (As an example, Gilbert Lewis's interest in the *absence* of an explicit association between menstruation and penis bleeding among the Gnau could not constitute as urgent a problem for the Gnau 1980.)

(f) Unthought consequences: theories of latent function, by definition, and at least some versions of ideology theory, rely upon the idea that the consequences of holding to particular notions or categorisations (for instance gender categories) are unthought or even unthinkable given the resources for reflection available to our informants. Inversions, mystifications and maskings have to be submitted to analytic tearing away of masks, dispersing of mists or turning the world right side up.

When anthropologists go beyond what informants say, as they must if only to translate, there is a generous choice of levels to which to attribute the discrepancies between the anthropological account and the interpretative practices of those who do the informing. The handling of this disparity creates responsibility for what occurs. Outcomes may be construed to result from conscious intentions (which informants state, mis-state, understate or are unable to state in their accounts), or be explicable only in terms of generative notions. By reference to unavailable comparative schema and unthought consequences, anthropologists may shed doubt on the relevance of their informants' accounts to the problems at hand. I wish to make two points about this. Most anthropological accounts seem to favour one style of distributing interpretative disparity, if only by default. However, it is not always clear why a particular level has been chosen, or whether alternatives have been contemplated. By privileging one level, potential movement and tension between our informants' ways of understanding are precluded. Secondly, although I would not argue that informants' opinions are definitive as analyses, they clearly are methodologically definitive. Only by reference to what informants can and cannot say are we able to justify our own analyses. How, for instance, could I be convinced of the latency of an effect other than by bringing forward verbal evidence that it went unrecognised?

Anthropological accounts rest on the shadow side of their assertions: the absences, ignorances and unsayabilities which must exist for things to be as they are claimed. Yet systematic attention is rarely given to these ethnographic non events. To encompass the two examples with which I must deal, such an approach will not do. Too many variations can be documented for the notion of a coherent Chamba culture to be convincing. I start instead from the proposition that Chamba belong to multiple and cross-cutting interpretative and performative associations. Rituals are not simply events that occur within bracketed time and space coordinates but encompass traditions of exemplification and transmission that have institutional moorings. They are learnt by participation in one or many associations. Rather than supposing a Chamba culture, I assume instead a complex institutional context (of clans, cults, localities, gender prerogatives and so on) that only sometimes coincides with the Chamba ethnic boundary. The partiality of everyone's view is assured both by divergent individual access to communities of interpretation and by the fact that these institutional matrices of knowledge are themselves not defined uniformly in different Chamba places.

Ignorance is inherent not in opinions voiced to us but in our interpretation of them: the refusal to answer a misdirected or inappropriate question is just as amenable to glossing as wisdom. The dictionary account of the state of play in the use of the word points to related extensions of sense: ignorant of—having no knowledge of, hence unconscious of, innocent of, having no share in; to ignore—to refuse to take notice of, to leave out of consideration, shut one's eyes to (*S.O.E.D.*). Ignorance supposes an absence of knowledge which makes the subject innocent of, or not sharing in, what occurs. To ignore presupposes a refusal, for whatever reason, to take account of knowledge the subject possesses (in our attachment metaphor). The idea of selective attention encourages us to substitute something left unsaid; the sense of the description 'ignorant' is more intransigent and suggests that the substitution of an unsaid would be inappropriate (Gellner, 1970). The levels to which interpretative disparities are despatched correspond to ignorances and unsayabilities that must be attributed to informants.

The ethnographic and anthropological processes (from research to writing) can be seen as a succession of states of play in the allocation of different types of ignorance and knowledge; often the trajectories of informant and ethnographer intersect. Beginning in ignorance the ethnographer acquires knowledge; but as the informant divulges information so the ethnographer begins to see him as ignorant of his own society. Ignorance, rather like Weber's idea of charisma, masquerades as innate quality but is the precipitate of a relationship. Expansion of the circuits for the circulation of what passes as knowledge in our world presupposes a concomitant growth of ignorance; indeed the concomitance is disproportionate since each item of knowledge, in our commoditised tendency to view it, creates a larger class of all those who are not in possession of it. This effect is at its greatest wherever diverse interpretative associations are incorporated.

Taken in their own (contemporary and extensive) identity Chamba are highly diverse. Emigrant groups of Chamba left the Chamba homeland around the Nigeria/Cameroon border during the early nineteenth century and settled hundreds of miles to the south and south-west. These movements added to differences that already existed between the Chamba communities of Chambaland. For instance, Chamba have two languages, which I call Chamba Daka and Chamba Leko, following Meek's usage (Meek, 1931). Until recently, the languages were thought to belong to the same language family, but now even that degree of resemblance has been challenged (Bennett, 1983; Boyd, 1989). Despite a few shared, presumably loaned or borrowed, terms in specialised areas of common concern (kinship, ritual and some flora and fauna) the Chamba languages are mutually incomprehensible. Diversity characterises most areas of Chamba culture and organisation. Chamba, of either language group, lived in scores of political communities that once were regulated in different ways (acephelous communities, ritualised chiefships, small conquest states) and rested upon varieties of organisational devices (matriclanship, patriclanship or double clanship). Although Chamba share many ritual forms, and have rather similar ways of talking about them, even this disguises further difference. The 'same' ritual may be explained, in terms of common conventions, as something rather different in two places. Its significance is not the same. The more I learned about Chamba rituals comparatively, through further research and more conversations with practitioners, the less I was tempted to believe they intrinsically mean. Because Chamba diversity makes any notion of underlying, shared understanding of ritual implausible, it has seemed more reasonable to focus on the differences in exegesis. Pursuing different lines of reasoning, Chamba informants run out of interpretation in interestingly different ways.

THE LIMITS OF CHAMBA EXEGESIS: LOST AND HIDDEN MEANINGS

Most generally and explicitly, Chamba claims to ignorance (the literal response 'I/we do not know') rely upon two devices used singly or in combination, which I call the hidden and lost meanings. When in the Bamenda Grassfields I asked emigrant Bali Chamba why they performed particular rites in the way that they did, I was told that this knowledge had been lost in the course of their migration from the Chamba homelands. (Forebears from whom they claim descent covered a good five hundred miles in the nineteenth century as mounted raiders before settling again. The notions of the epic journey, immigration and conquest are important elements of their definition of the position they now maintain in the Bamenda Grassfields.) Since I had come from the Chamba homelands, my informants responded, would it not be more sensible for me to tell them the significance of their rite.

A great deal can be said in defence of their response. Bali Chamba lay claim to being introducers of a superior northern culture to the Grassfields, which they tend to represent as a backward region prior to their arrival (as slave raiders, a Bamenda man would want to add). The preservation of occasional, selfconsciously Chamba, 'traditions' from a previous context, and the elevation of decidedly non Chamba customs to the status of 'Bali or Chamba custom', have been strategically important in their attempts to exert an ethnic dominance over the area. This strategy was particularly successful with the German colonists who were co-opted into Bali schemes for domination and Bali notions of superiority, and slightly less successful with their British successors (Chilver, 1967).

Bali Chamba required that *their* 'customs' were not Grassfield customs (some of them were, but that is another story). Bali Chamba do not suggest by a claim to ignorance that the question is irrelevant (throughout my stay they were keen for me to answer questions of this sort). Because immigration and dominance are linked organising motifs of the past, the fact that their meaning was lost in the north is crucial to what, in another sense, rituals still mean. Bali Chamba admit that the present significance of a ritual like their *lela*, a martial display held annually, is that it is the occasion for everyone to renew allegiance to the chief, it brings them together. In another sense, the ritual still *is* what it was in the past, because it is assumed to have been kept alive by dint of faithful repetition, but it may not mean what it meant in the past.

Signs of the past are self-conscious in the Bali chiefdoms: guinea corn is grown especially for use in some rituals although the staple food is now maize; harvest celebrations occur at the time when guinea corn would be harvested—if it was grown; a single round hut is constructed in the chief's palace—although everyone now builds square huts on the Grassfield model; bamboo flutes and gourd horns are the most highly valued of musical instruments used at special occasions. Identities and discontinuities are reasoned to suggest the formal persistence of Chamba customs—whether or not they are understood as they were in Chambaland.

The lost meaning is not the prerogative of Chamba emigrants. In Mapeo, the once uncentralised community where Titlesime lives, my enquiries about some apparently symbolically informed piece of behaviour in ritual often elicited the recommendation that I should visit Yeli, the remnant of a chiefdom across the border and across the mountains. In Yeli such things had not been forgotten. When eventually I lived in Yeli, I found some questions referred up to the chief priest—Dura. He was helpful when he was able, but on other occasions he would explain apologetically that his successor died before imparting to him all that he should know, and that anyway chief priests were not what they had been. It begins to seem as if some Chamba versions of the past encourage the notion that things are always not what they used to be.

The idea of a hidden meaning is encouraged by the secrecy surrounding Chamba cults, each of which is the prerogative of a performative association to which access is restricted. Within the association members are 'shown' items of the cult apparatus as they continue to make initiation payments. Much that happens during the cult rituals appears inexplicable to most members.

Somebody is assumed to know the why and wherefore of a rite. However, it can happen that no-one has gone sufficiently far along the initiatory path to have seen the final mysteries. Perhaps, there no longer are guides to take anyone that far (a combination of lost and hidden meanings). In Mapeo some informants belonged to a cult group to which I was initiated. The final mystery of their cult was hidden under a large inverted pot. Very few initiates ever saw what was under the pot, and the last to do so had died without initiating a successor. One man had looked under the pot without knowing the proper precautions to be taken before doing so, and he had died. No-one else was keen to take the risk, and anyway the cult rites worked without enquiring too closely into their internal mechanisms. Whether this was a ploy to discourage my questioning, I can never know. But it was stated to me independently by people whom I thought to be stating what they believed.

During ethnographic enquiry these types of response accumulated as a sort of patterned sub-text, a by-product of the attempt to elicit a text of explanations. None of the responses suggested that my interlocutors and I were subscribing to wholly different canons of explanation. I was not told that my questions were daft, unanswerable or irrelevant (and I was told that my questions on other topics were some or all of these things). Mapeo and Bali elders assumed that there was an explanation, which someone somewhere else, or at some other time, knew. If they also knew that answer, it would be the reason for doing what they were doing. For the present and the foreseeable future, they would carry on doing what they were doing on the basis of a partial understanding and because there was no good reason to change. Their attitude towards ignorance was reasoned in the context of a particular account of human knowledge.

Occasionally, Chamba exponents of the lost and hidden meaning can persuade themselves that there exists a unitary account of Chamba culture to explain precisely why things are done as they are. Different people have, or had, different bits of this information: thus, Bali Chamba culture could be repaired by reference to knowledge left behind in Chambaland, and Mapeo understanding augmented by insight from Yeli. This attitude towards ignorance is shared by anthropologists who identify coherent cultures with ethnic subjects and attribute unsayabilities and ignorances to their informants on the assumption that cultures are such. On the Chamba part, the assumption of a single, ethnic culture is an interesting indication of the contemporary identity to which they sometimes subscribe. So significant is this identity that in some contexts rituals beg no explanation other than that they are done the way that Chamba do such things. In common with structural accounts of culture, Chamba informants presuppose systematic connection such that every usage entails the entire organisation of differences of which it is a part. However, this form of reasoning, must be as recent as the contemporary version of Chamba ethnicity. That, I have argued previously, has antecedents in the nineteenth century but assumed its present form during the colonial period (Fardon, 1988). The same statement, that such and such is a Chamba way of doing things, could not have had the same meaning when the sense of the term Chamba (*Sama* or *Samba*) was relativistic. Chamba understanding of their culture as an ethnic possession converged with anthropological accounts of tribal cultures as the supposition of bounded ethnic groups became common to both.

Chamba only sometimes reason this way; more frequently, I have heard accounts which draw upon perceptions of ethnic and cultural heterogeneity within the community, or between communities, to argue that the wherefore of some practice is completely outside the range of an informant's experience. 'The members of clan X are simply different, not like us at all'. When Chamba villagers argue that their communities are ethnically diverse, they let go the assumption of a potentially unitary understanding of culture. Having once conceded that the cultural boundary is not singular, it seems to be a short, and easily taken, step for Chamba informants to argue that there are boundaries almost everywhere.

MAPEO AND YELI

Before sketching the resemblances and divergences between Chamba accounts of ritual, it will be necessary to say something about the two places where my informants live.

Mapeo and Yeli lie on opposite sides of the border between Nigeria and Cameroon where it follows the watershed of two major river systems along the ridge of the Alantika Mountains. No more than a few miles separate the two places, and the journey between the mountains is not arduous. But the trip is seldom made. Yeli is generally accepted once to have been the most important place in all Chambaland: most of the larger chiefdoms to its west claim an origin for their own royal families from Yeli; and the Yeli chiefship was apparently the model for a type of ritualised chiefship that was widely diffused among central Chamba in the eighteenth century and possibly before. The royal matriclan that presently supplies the village chief of Yeli is considered to descend directly from the prestigious chiefs of the past.

Mapeo is a younger community which emerged, in its present composition, during the nineteenth century as the Fulani jihad in Adamawa forced hetero-genous sections of Chamba to seek refuge in the mountains. The Chamba of Mapeo speak Chamba Daka language, whereas the Chamba of Yeli speak Chamba Leko. In certain very specific and limited ways, Mapeo people believed the people of Yeli, and especially the chief of Yeli, exercised power over them by virtue of control over rain, smallpox and locust infestation. This sanction underwrote a small payment made by Mapeo households to Yeli on a formally annual basis. Apparently, the payment was intermittent and depended upon the visit of Yeli representatives to Mapeo. Fear was, and remains for older men, the most marked quality in Mapeo representations of Yeli. Few Mapeo Chamba, other than their representative who is drawn from a patriclan of reputed Yeli origin, were supposed to visit Yeli. The present representative had not made the trip by 1987, although he already occupied his office when I visited first in 1976. Most older men claim that they would die before reaching Yeli if they were to attempt that journey; but this belief is losing credence with the young.

Mapeo is far more populous than Yeli, perhaps by a factor of ten. Population has declined in both places since the colonial peace opened the plains to safe cultivation, but Mapeo now has a population of over two thousand whereas Yeli has only two hundred. None the less, by tradition Mapeo is chiefless; indeed the relatively high population, perhaps five thousand in the immediately precolonial period, and the chieflessness seem to be related. Despite proximity, Mapeo and Yeli are rather different places and may have become more different since the demarcation of boundaries during the colonial period.

Chamba of Yeli and Mapeo (and indeed the rest of Chambaland) share a few explicit ideas about cosmology and the differentiation of ritual forms (regardless of the language in which these are expressed). Broad categories of agent within the Chamba world include God, the dead, and a variety of creatures and forces of the wilderness. These entities, as I explained in the Preface, are most explicitly located above, below, and around the living, but can additionally be envisaged as qualities of the living: who resemble the dead in some respects, the wild in others and have God-given attributes. Rituals adjust relations between and among the living, dead, wild and God by means of special techniques. There is a measure of agreement about how particular classes of ritual should be conducted and what they are designed to achieve, but less agreement about how or why specific actions bring about their objectives.

The pre-eminent means to affect the relations between types of being are cults; what Chamba Daka call *jup* and Chamba Leko call *vɔm*. The anachronistic term 'juju' might almost be a better translation (and one often used in Nigerian and Cameroonian English). *Vɔm* and *jup*, like juju, habitually appear in the singular to denote the plurality of cults, when the speaker wishes to emphasise the unity of the cult phenomenon. The generic term is usually understood to include women's cults, although these may be distinguished by specialised terms: *jɛm* in Daka, or *vɔm ken* in Leko. Whether owned by men or women, cults both cure and cause particular afflictions. Techniques giving them this mastery were revealed to the forebears of present cult owners by the dead, or occasionally by animals. So long as initiates respect cult rules, and pay to avert cult contagion, they remain safe from the misfortunes controlled by their associations and achieve a degree of control over illness and misfortune. Signs of the cults can be used to protect property, or retrospectively to 'catch' those who have stolen or damaged the members' property, absconded with their wives, attacked them with witchcraft or otherwise caused them nuisance.

Because cults are strongly associated with their owning clans they may appear as conventional markers of clan involvement at the protracted funeral wakes which take place some time after burial. On such occasions, cults are associated with semi-public performances: songs, dances, or menacing noises off-stage.

The ambition of Chamba practitioners to exert control over their own, and others', lives through membership of such cults imparts common features to informants' experience in both Yeli and Mapeo. I shall outline a few shared problems of comprehensibility (initially from the stance of academic criteria of understanding) that are intrinsic to general Chamba conceptions, before beginning to address differences that stem from the divergent ways that human and inhuman capacities are related in Yeli and Mapeo. Explicit exegeses and frank uncertainty, incomprehension, and indeterminacy overlap in some respects but not in others. My aim is to show why this is so for two communities that are neighbours and belong to a common people.

(a) In many contexts knowledge and power are mutually referential. Rituals have proprietors and important 'things to know' are not freely available. If they were, they would not be important. Cults are joined by initiation; not everyone is entitled to be initiated into every cult, and not everyone can afford to join all the cults to which he or she is entitled. Once a person has joined a cult, there are grades of initiation; not everyone is entitled to undergo them all, or if entitled can afford to do so. In short, knowledge, conceived as a resource, is not freely available.

(b) Cult rituals are hidden. Some rituals predominantly concern the dramatisation of this unseen and undiscussed quality. Outsiders 'do not see' and insiders 'do not say'. Outsiders certainly 'do hear', because most cults have a distinctive instrumentation or threatening noise that announces the performance of hidden things. But the particular knowledge protected is less important than the idea of concealment. Cult rites are definitionally secret, in this limited sense of hidden from outsiders. The hidden things may, on initiation, transpire to be of minor importance, or much like things hidden in other cults seen by the initiate, or actually seen by no-one at all (like the final cult mystery hidden under a pot that no-one living had dared lift). Concealment, rather than what is concealed, is the value crucial to Chamba cults.

(c) Idioms relating initiates to cults are not idioms of knowledge in the sense favoured by western academic culture, although the widely initiated elder is supposed to 'know' much, in the closest sense in which I can translate the Daka verb *nyi*. Initiates are 'shown' things, they 'see', but they do not 'speak'. To 'finish' the cult is to have 'seen' it all, and to 'hold' some aspects of it. Seeing and holding are forms of knowledge to the extent thay they put the initiate into the position of being able to report what should not be spoken. A man's knowledge is the degree to which this restraint is attributed to him. But the emphasis upon not divulging observation or experience differs from our academic criterion of knowledge as demonstrable in the practical ability to instruct another, or to elucidate a topic. Chamba practitioners 'know' that which they do not freely divulge to others.

(d) Chamba knowledge of cults is partial and discontinuous because the contexts in which rituals occur are systematically insulated from one another by ownership, prerogative, difference and concealment. Given that the main criterion of knowledge is experience based upon presence and access, a panoptic vision is institutionally unavailable to individual practitioners. Even if a Chamba informant was convinced that a single comprehensible system of signs was used in all cult rituals, the insight could not be experientially tested. However, it is not obvious why an informant would work from this supposition.

I have noted that there are contexts in which Chamba argue from an extensive ethnic identity to something like the idea of a Chamba culture (and vice versa), however they may alternatively describe their local communities as pervaded by ethnic difference. Indeed, the more intense the focus on the local community the greater the likelihood of an informant emphasising difference. Such differences are anticipated to coincide with patriclan divisions to a far greater extent than matriclan divisions. Consequently, in many contexts the notion of distinct culture (translating Chamba phrases like the 'so and so way of doing things') coincides with patriclan divisions, and patriclans are represented as ethnically heterogenous. From this perspective, Chamba plausibly deny that their communities are founded on common culture. The rationale for the behaviour of members of some other clan becomes explicable only in terms of their rather curious view of the world, which results from a different origin and previous location.

In so far as a Chamba informant talks himself into this context, he lets go the assumption that a coherent explanation underlies ritual activity. Difference precludes an understanding of motivation. This same point can be extended to consider the treatment of inhuman agencies. Sometimes Chamba talk as if the motivation of the dead or animals was sufficiently assimilable to that of men as to be transparently comprehensible. But in other contexts this analogy loses its appeal, and inhuman agents are seen as unpredictable and capable of vitiating properly constructed efforts to interact with them. Looked at this way, it is impossible to understand why rituals work.

(e) Most intrinsically, Chamba knowledge is truncated by the centrality which death and relics of death play in Chamba conceptions of the world and effective action within it. Although they have some ideas about what occurs the other side of death, Chamba admit these to be speculative and my direct questions about death and the transformation of men into sprites were either disarmed ('Since I am not dead I cannot tell you') or turned back on me: European technical abilities are rationalised by traditionalists in terms of privileged access to the dead, which implies that a European should be an informant on the behaviour of the dead not a questioner. But, as we shall see throughout my description, death is the most powerful reason for the efficacy of Chamba ritual.

These five tendencies encourage a truncation of accounts of ritual. They would apply, in different degrees, to informants in both Mapeo and Yeli. Beyond these Chamba generalities I want to turn briefly to my other theme—of Chamba variations.

A TALE OF TWO INFORMANTS

I broach Chamba diversity as a tale of two informants and of the two places which figure most prominently in this book. In Mapeo, the nineteenth century witnessed a rapid escalation of population as refugees from the plains settled into a series of hamlets strung along the side of the mountains. Mapeo history reads something like a timetable of the arrivals of twenty-six patriclans which are still distinguished (and previously, one assumes, of others that have died out). Dispute about the order in which arrivals are supposed to have occurred is widespread. In comparison with other Chamba places, the people of Mapeo appear to have presided over, what I called in my earlier book, a cult involution.

As the number of named cults multiplied, so did their costs, the complexity of their multiple ownerships and the problems of arranging some time in the calendar when the cults could monopolise the attention of the villagers. Earlier immigrants apparently found their niches by, in comparative Chamba terms, drastically complicating the cult rituals of harvest into four cycles, each with numerous stages, which offered the different patriclans a chance to assert their importance. Later arrivals, finding this slot oversubscribed, annexed some month or other in which to perform the rituals associated with the assimilation of their members who had died in the previous year. Meanwhile, the number of cults in the possession of matriclans was also increasing, in part because heterogeneous elements each brought their own ritual techniques with them. Mapeo communal aetiology became highly complex, densely related to a complicated network of clan rights in cults, while other (non cult) explanations of misfortune, important in most other Chamba communities, became marginalised under the explanatory overload offered by the large number of cults. Out of this grew many circumscribed positions of power, but no hierarchy that could be recognised aside from a particular context. The proliferation of difference took place at the cost of the plausibility of a notion of underlying meaning and system. Mapeo cult performances abound with differences which tend to be viewed with great satisfaction for being what they are—just different. Any characteristic of a cult: small membership or large membership, high fees or low fees, dramatic performance or disturbing silence, frequent meeting or infrequent meeting, ownership by some or other clan official can and will be picked out by some informant at some time to show that this is the most important, authentic and powerful of Mapeo cults. Only the members of his own clan who belong to the same cult are likely to agree with him.

My companion at numerous cult initiations and convivial gatherings was Titlesime, who later told me that he had kept an eye on my progress in Chamba Daka and decided that once we could talk to one another he would like to help me record Chamba religion. Young men had grown refractory, he added, joining world religions and refusing to contribute towards cult meetings. If he did not help me they certainly could not, and other elders would simply lie to me, as was normal when it came to cults. Since his own sons fell into the category of refractory youth, I think he took pleasure in piloting the efforts of an initiate who did not have to be cajoled. He and other elders insisted that I should write down what I saw and what they told me—although their accounts often diverged. They were conscious that their particular practices (they talked of *Sama langsi*, the Chamba way of doing things) were going to disappear. If something was too secret for me to know, then they would take responsibility for my not finding it out. What I knew, unless I was expressly told I should not have known it, I should record. Otherwise it would be lost.

In this, I now believe I detect an attempt to explain themselves via me to the younger literate Chamba audience who no longer paid heed to their ideas. Titlesime derived no material benefits from companionship with me, indeed as a postgraduate student I was chronically short of funds. His only real advantage from our relationship (apart from diversion) seemed to be a late discovered penchant for riding pillion on my motorbike, which increased the range and efficiency with which he could visit gatherings in the component hamlets of Mapeo village or the more distant hamlets in the plain belonging to the Mapeo dialect area. On a return visit, six years later, he told me that his access to transport had been the envy of other elders. But his recollection may have been clouded by current accusations of witchcraft; such suspicion had always been inevitable thanks to his matrilateral relation to a late, known witch and the Chamba dogma that witchcraft is shared by close matrikin.

Titlesime was an active member of a dozen or so cults and a mine of information about who owned what, how much it cost to join, how much beer had been and should have been brewed at particular occasions and so forth. His scale of importance among these types of evidence could be gauged by the frequency with which he reminded me to write things down. He soon discovered that as a penalty of literacy I tended to forget whatever detailed information was not recorded. He, on the other hand, had a tenaciously retentive memory. Titlesime's analytic turn of mind was roughly 1960s Manchester processualism: he was good on transactionalism, well versed in network theory and had a keen eye for a latent function ('cults are men's way of making sure women and young men do not share beer and meat with us'). Had I been trained as an anthropologist only a few years earlier, I would have found my ideal informant, unhappily I had been told about other things anthropologists were supposed to find, and Mapeo Chamba appeared to have them: the use of a colour triad in ritual, the association of rituals with particular leaves and many, to my mind, symbolically informed actions. Hours spent in earnest contemplation of these matters yielded paltry results; Titlesime knew what colour should be put on the different bits of ritual paraphernalia, what leaves the paraphernalia should be placed upon and so on. He was not at all bemused by my suggestion that the uses might be consistent, but he was thoroughly unconvinced. Sometimes he would try to wean me from the idea in terms of the ethnic heterogeneity argument (there are all sorts of people in Mapeo, some were not originally Chamba—a down-to-earth variant of the argument that I was not dealing with a closed system); sometimes he would play the Popperian card by producing the instance that made nonsense of a correlation I was attempting; when most exasperated he would give me some variant of the 'that's the way we do it', 'have always done it', 'how the ancestors were shown to do it' argument. Before the reader protests there is no reason to expect informants to be able to do our symbolic analyses for us (I suspect they often have done them—or at least the best of them), rather than produce arguments of principle, I introduce my second informant.

In Yeli I put to Dura the kinds of questions that defeated Titlesime and his friends in Mapeo. His answers exploited many of, what we call, the symbolic codes which Titlesime and his friends were predisposed to downplay: associations between colour and gender, between ritual and thermal change, between the leaves used in rituals and the effects that they were supposed to have, and so on. I learned that the impartibility of the chief's body after his death related to his association with black cloth: the chief was drawn from a matriclan, matriclanship is transmitted through women and concerned with substance; in some contexts women are associated with black and the injunction against taking the chief's skull relates to the association of matriclanship with the body. (Further exegesis now volunteered . . .) he, Dura, had to take the skull of his predecessor, but then he was appointed from a patriclan. Anyway, by virtue of his association with *vɔm* cults he was hot, whereas the chief was cold, so steps had to be taken to maintain the coolness of the bodies of the past chiefs . . . and so on. I have cheated slightly by condensing accounts in both cases, but I have not misrepresented their contents. Dura explained as if he had spent a lifetime absorbing structuralism at the feet of Luc de Heusch. Why should the accounts of two acknowledged experts on ritual in their respective communities diverge so much?

The extensive answer given in this book relates the availability of accounts and their plausibility to the institutional context informants imagine for themselves. For instance, Dura could offer an expansive view of a coherent set of rituals because Yeli, with its hierarchical organisation, allowed explanations to be tied into the exemplary figures of the chief, his assistants, his priests and his smiths. In Mapeo, the analysis would simply not work. The relationship

Bouba's father, the late chief of Yeli (1984). Over his right shoulder he carries *tɔma*, the curved baton of chiefship.

between understanding the rituals and performing them was tautological. Since Dura thought he was performing symbolically informed rituals, his rituals remained symbolically informed. Mapeo elders were, by and large, performing rituals with half an eye on the rituals of competing clansmen; they also performed what they intended to—in their case, difference.

The story has a neat ending, which I did not engineer but might have encouraged had I had more foresight. Titlesime heard through market gossip that I was in Yeli, across the international border. For a time it was not wise for me to cross the border which was officially closed for political reasons, so he decided to come to visit me. On the way he asked directions from those he passed; Yeli was not far, but he had never been there. Older Mapeo men have not wholly lost the belief they will die by going to Yeli. I found him one Sunday morning sitting alone and nervous under the large locust bean tree outside the chief's compound clutching an enormous cockerel and a sack of roast groundnuts, which he remembered that I enjoyed. Yeli elders were ignoring him; I had not seen him for six years and this sight of him so far out of his depth was not that which I remembered. To calm his disquiet I invited the chief of Yeli and Dura, almost unreal figures to Titlesime I suspect, to share a pot of beer in my hut. The chief, very old and almost blind, delivered a little homily which was translated into Chamba Daka about the changing times and the fact that Yeli people no longer wanted to kill people for visiting them. Titlesime looked slightly reassured. The chief departed but Dura remained (advised of the imminent arrival of more beer in search of which cyclists had been despatched in different directions).

Since Dura could get by in Chamba Daka, he and Titlesime discovered that they were brothers in terms of the furthest reaches of matriclanship. Titlesime judiciously settled on being the younger brother. My hut was cluttered with leaves about which I had been asking Dura in the context of their use in cults and rituals. Since Titlesime asked me about them, I started to outline my understanding of the reasons they were used as they were. Dura soon took over the account. The upshot was Titlesime's discovery that Mapeo rituals were using too few leaves. Little wonder that he could not explain why particular leaves were used in particular rituals. But clearly the Yeli account was authoritative, coming as it did from his older brother, the Yeli chief priest. Mapeo elders had made a mess of their rituals. When later I returned his visit in Mapeo, the subject of leaves had evidently preoccupied him; as we walked out of the town he repeatedly pointed out leaves, noting the rituals they were used for in Mapeo, and concluding that some particular ritual, at least, made sense.

This is one of those open-ended stories that can be played for a good deal. It is also a reminder of the role of serendipity in fieldwork, and how the unrepeatable and unanticipated event, too slight to figure as a 'research method', can transform an ethnographer's perspective. Dura's description of slight aspects of Yeli rituals became for Titlesime a critical perspective on Mapeo practice. The symbolic sceptic apparently became convinced that ritual ought to be symbolically motivated and not a mere repetition of efficient means, and this leap into faith was assisted by the happy prior circumstance that Yeli had always occupied an authoritative position in Chamba versions of the past. Perhaps I witnessed the transition between pre-reflective and reflective states in an unforced circumstance. Clearly too much could be made of all this, but it does help me to ground talk of exegeses, interpretations and reflections in an image of particular people, from particular interpretative communities, talking about particular things on particular occasions.

I began this chapter by noting that attribution of knowledge on the basis of people's statements also implies attribution of either ignorance or things left unsaid. Our re-creations of, for instance, rituals on the basis of statements made to us about them presuppose agents capable of saying some things and not others. Statability is crucial to the reattribution to subjectivities of conditions of experience so that we can maintain that they are doing what we say they are doing. I proposed, on the basis of some ethnography, that Chamba informants also attribute ignorance and unsayability to themselves and others, and that there are reasons for the unknowns and unknowables clustering in Chamba accounts as they do.

Finally, I have suggested that informants from different places have diverse problems of explanation, and that the differences between their accounts are also explicable. However, it does not make sense to transpose their accounts. Dura's symbolic glosses are not relevant to Mapeo, despite the fact that in some rituals the same leaf is used in both places. Symbolically informed imitation and purely conventional imitation are both capable of, in this narrow example, maintaining associations between some leaves and some rituals in the short run. But the persistence of a general symbolic coding seems to require a conscious local appreciation of correct performance. Otherwise, the accretion of purely conventional usages, like the Mapeo leaf uses, will result in a variety of practices resistent to symbolic interpretation.

Together these points argue that we have to pay close and explicit attention to areas of practice which tend to bemuse our informants. If informants suggest that both they and their fellows are ignorant of some things, uncertain about others, and recognise some matters to be indeterminate, we have no brief to ignore their protestation in the interest of tidy and coherent presentation. By ignoring local conceptions of knowledge and its limits, we introduce closure and dogmatism into reflections that lacked those characteristics and, in the process of creating closed systems of thought, we pose ourselves insurmountable problems in explaining evident tendencies to innovation. Paulin Hountondji (1977) has claimed that by representing African systems of thought as if they were philosophies, Europeans are constantly able to rediscover that they are bad philosophies. The metaphor of translating a local text is misused in order to write our own version of African philosophy. This danger seems to me sufficiently pressing for the attempt to write against its grain to be worthwhile.

2

WAYS OF BEING: THE LIVING, THE DEAD, THE WILD AND GOD

PEOPLE AND PLACES

We can begin where the ethnographer began, with the physical appearance of a Chamba village. At first sight, there is nothing particularly Chamba about a Chamba village. Mapeo, the village where I stayed longest, consists of a string of hamlets which line a laterite road connecting the local administrative centre, Ganye, to the Gongola state capital, Yola. Around its mid-point, the road runs along the foot of the Alantika chain of mountains, which was the nineteenth century home of the Mapeo Chamba. Since the border between Nigeria and Cameroon follows the watershed of major river systems which cross the plains to either side of the mountains, the ridge of the mountain range is also the international frontier.

I first arrived in Mapeo along this road at the tail end of the rainy reason in 1976. The road was a quagmire, and a Mapeo companion and I were arriving on a small and underpowered motorcycle. Just before entering the village, we passed a small hillock on our right, which I later learned was called Mama. In Chamba Daka, Mapeo is called Dim Ma, or behind Mama, because seen from the west the hillock is especially prominent and all the hamlets are behind the hill. Some glosses hold that the repetition of the syllables of the name is explained by the echo you would hear if you were to shout 'Ma' from a particular place. But I was never able to produce the effect. Mapeo derives from the Leko Ma-peu (Ma over there). Whereas Dim-Ma makes sense if you come to Mapeo from the west, Ma-peu derives from an orientation to the south and east, perhaps from Yeli. The name of the place already begs a relational perspective which enmeshes the village in broader local orientations. Mapeo probably stuck as a name because early European naming took place from the perspective of the eastern cordon of Fulani chiefdoms which acted as mediators of European advance. Because the name was applied to them by Fulani, many Mapeo Chamba believe Mapeo to be a Fulfulde name; until told differently by Chamba Leko speaking informants, I also believed this.

We could stay with the hill a moment longer to remark the way in which it stands for the entire village; coincidentally, Yeli is similarly identified with a small hill. Stories, of dubious historicity, relate that German colonialists and Irish missionaries were at different times thwarted in their desire to build upon Mapeo hill by the dead (*wurumbu*) who live there. Chamba villagers say that they have never attempted to build on Mama, but the nominal ownership of the hill is a recurrent theme in the disputed ownership of the Mapeo village headship. If you own Mama, then you own Mapeo.

The village sprawls alongside the road for about three kilometers. In some places, considerable gaps separate concentrations of homes. But the distinctions between the named, component hamlets of Mapeo are not always immediately striking. The buildings themselves are of different styles and in various states of repair. Not until a brief visit eight years later, did I practically grasp what is obvious in principle: how quickly the style and condition of a residence adapts to the current circumstances of its occupants. The dwellings were of two main types, thatched round huts and tin roofed square huts; the enclosures surrounding them were either of mats tied to poles, which had often rooted and grown into trees, or else of mud walls, reminiscent of those I had seen built by Fulani and Chamba of the administrative centre. Some of the enclosures, of both types, were in a state of such disrepair that a few freestanding uprights, shreds of mat, or piles of collapsed mud wall did little more than mark the nominal boundary of a living space. Other compounds were securely wrapped around with a barrier of privacy. But in either case, the notional margin of a compound was not difficult to determine. I noted that the best maintained section of the enclosure was usually that by the entrance. Most, but not all, compounds were entered through a reception hut with an opening at either side. Wandering around after my arrival, I saw that some areas of settlement hugged the road in a ribbon development, while others had a greater depth stretching hundreds of meters from the road. Later still, I realised that a couple of minute collections of huts, invisible from the road during wet season when the grass was tall, clung to the hillside.

With only rudimentary Chamba from a six week stay in Ganye, I could at least begin to read these physical signs. Mapeo consisted of about a dozen hamlets, each named and nominally owned by the members of the patriclan which had first lived there. Hamlet names either referred to some natural feature of the place (prevalent trees or grasses, or perhaps a prominent stone) or directly to the name of the owning clan. Settlements had been founded in the course of a gradual descent from the hills subsequent to the cessation of slave raiding with the imposition of colonial rule. In general, the closer the compounds were to the road, which itself had been shifted from the foot of the hills, and the more their layout tended to a ribbon pattern, the more recent was the settlement. Older abandoned settlements could be recognised by hut rings, the stone foundations of the large granaries that Chamba build, and the circles of trees which had grown from the planted supports for matting enclosures. Newer hamlets tended to have more rectangular tin-roofed huts, and these were usually built by younger men who had been able to gain the cash required to purchase corrugated sheeting. Compounds that were surrounded by mud walls, especially if they belonged to older men, were usually the homes of Muslim families. The most disorderly compounds often belonged to elderly men or women who still clung to traditional Chamba religion, but lived apart from their children.

My house was a rectangular, mud-walled and tin-roofed building of three rooms shaded by a mango tree. It had been loaned to me by a friend in Ganye, who had purchased it from its previous owner, a Nigerian teacher who had been transferred away from Mapeo. The house was fairly typical of the newer style: its central room was entered by a front door which faced a door in the rear wall, thus resembling a conventional entrance hut. The right-hand room was reached from the entrance hall, while another room to the left had its own front door. My house was untypical of Chamba living spaces because it had no enclosed compound. To serve as the home of a Chamba family it would have been enclosed, however nominally, by mats or walls, and have contained a rear area for cooking and sleeping huts. If the occupant were a farmer, it would also have needed one or more of the tall granaries which hold guinea corn and soup ingredients. A traditionalist might have built an additional small hut with matting walls to keep his cult paraphernalia. Optionally, other shelters, like huts without walls, might be constructed for beer-brewing operations or to shelter women's grinding stones.

Although I was aware that some other West African people had elaborate ideas about the organisation of domestic space, I never succeeded (even after witnessing the siting and building of new ones) in finding much plan to Chamba compounds. Compounds faced either the main road or the entrances of other compounds, if they were built away from the road. They had a top (head, *ti*) and a bottom (*kin*). But top and bottom were oriented in keeping with the slope of the hamlet as a whole, rather than according to the disposition of space within the compound. Hamlets likewise had a head (the high end) and a bottom (the low end). Within the compound, areas were set aside for cooking, washing and sitting. Co-wives might or might not have their huts built in different parts of the compound; sometimes the compound was divided into areas occupied by a father and son. The master of the compound might have his own sleeping hut, but some did not. The compounds answered the needs of their inhabitants for shelter from sun and rain, a place to cook and an area to invite friends to sit and chat or drink. But they did not appear to be organised according to any symbolic schema.

My house stood in a section of the hamlet of Natup (*na tup*, among the shea butter trees) that was predominantly inhabited by Chamba Muslims. In

Chamba Daka, Muslims are called *Nɛ dɔmen Su bu*, 'people who greet/salute God'. Respectful greeting in the style Chamba consider to be traditional involves not just some appropriate variation on a litany of conventional questions about the health and welfare of an individual and his or her family, but also a posture from which the salutation is offered: head bowed while the hands accompany each phrase with a patter of clapping. Perhaps, this bodily aspect persuaded early onlookers to describe Muslims as those who greeted God. Traditionalists would not 'greet' God, but implore him through offerings (*pɔp*). A term is borrowed to describe how Christians make 'prayer' (*nak adua*) in church. Chamba Muslims accept the description of themselves, despite its implication of a familiarity at variance with more orthodox Muslim ideas.

The patriclan owning Natup, also the most populous patriclan in Mapeo, was called Yangurubu or Sirinɛpbu. The first name referred to the Yungur, a non Chamba ethnic group, but whether this notion of Yungur origin was to be taken seriously or in jest was not agreed. The alternative name is that of a type of spear grass (*siri*) used to make mats for sitting or sleeping; Natup was sometimes referred to as Nasiri because spear grass, as well as shea trees, had been abundant when the area of the present hamlet was a wild resource for the Chamba living on the hill. Sirinɛpbu might denote all the people who lived in Natup, whether Yangurubu or not, or it might be synonymous with Yangurubu. This depended upon context. Place and patriclanship tend to merge into one another.

My Mapeo sponsor not only loaned me a house but, unintentionally, gave me two statuses in Mapeo, since my hosts chose to treat me as his younger full brother and, therefore, a member of the same matriclan and patriclan as he. These were among a number of roles between which I was shifted in different circumstances: honorary clan member, stranger, European, European who speaks Chamba, student of Chamba, young male, friend, repository of certain types of knowledge, fool, and in terms of which I was given access to different types of information and confidence. In defining these roles for me, my hosts also laid down the terms on which I would get to know them and what I would learn from this.

Researchers typically begin to read the communities in which they live in terms of things which are apparently 'data', amenable to formalisation and do not make great demands upon linguistic competence. My first perceptions of my hosts were in terms of their personal names, gender, age, religious affiliations, place of residence and patriclan membership. All simple enough to grasp. At a superficial level the pieces slotted into place quite quickly. Mapeo Chamba married, lived in homes and traced family memberships through their fathers, but other elements of their formalised relations between people were more refractory.

HUMAN COMPANY: THE STRUCTURING OF SOCIALITY

Chamba call humanity the 'children of men' (*nɛ mɛmbu* plural; *nɛ mi* singular). Just as in unself-conscious English expression, the term for man in Chamba Daka is also the gender unmarked term for people. Woman is distinguished by a suffix (*nɛ ngwu*), while the masculine character of man may optionally be emphasised by using the term *lɛrum* (a compound of *nɛ* and masculine suffix *lum*).

These terms, for people and children, and to distinguish males from females, pervade speech. Shadowing their usage is one, albeit imperfect, means to gain purchase on Chamba ways of distinguishing and relating ways of being. For instance, patriclan names are conventionally suffixed in a number of ways: sometimes one of the resulting forms is preferred, in others alternatives are recognised. Mapeo patriclan names are most commonly suffixed by a simple plural (thus Yanguru + bu), or by the term for people (thus Tiran + nɛpbu). In a few cases suffix the 'children' is optional (thus either Gban + mɛmbu, or, Gban + bu). The Chamba Leko usage is the same, except there are only two suffixes available: a simple plural or a 'people' form. Such details acquire significance when we realise that the same convention can be applied to 'ethnic' groups (*Mɔmbu*, for Vere; *Kɔmbu*, for Koma; *Kambu*, for Bata, etc.) but not to matriclan divisions, which are called *kun*. People are distinguished according to their 'type' in terms of patriclan or ethnic group membership, the difference between which is only a matter of degree for Chamba. However, this idiom of distinction is inappropriate to describe maternally derived differences.

The terms I am translating as patriclan are composites of 'father's children' in both Chamba languages (*da mi*, singular, *da mɛmbu* in Daka; *ba wa*, singular, *ba yɛbbira* in Leko). Matriclan translates *kun*, which occurs in both Chamba languages without etymology. Thus, the Chamba contrast between 'father's children' and *kun* lacks the neatly symmetrical opposition suggested by our terms patriclan and matriclan.

Chamba kinship terminology can be explained in terms of the way that a limited number of distinctions are used to classify a large number of people. Basic discriminations made among immediate kin concern gender, seniority between siblings, and the distinction between lineal relations, what I call relations of parentation, and collateral relations. Other distinctions refer to the difference between kinship and affinal relation, and to generation.

The difference between membership of a 'father's children' and membership of a *kun* (matriclan) is clearest in the parental and collateral relationships within either category. Each domain of clanship contains one parental and one collateral type relationship traced between adjacent generations. The parental relation in the case of patriclanship is that between 'fathers' and 'children'; the corresponding parental relation for matriclanship is between 'mothers' and 'children'; mothers and fathers 'bear children'. All men of the father's generation in the patriclan, and all the women of the mother's generation in the matriclan, are also 'fathers' and 'mothers' of that person: they 'bore' him or her (*ngwan* in Daka, *lɛb* in Leko). Therefore, they will address that person as 'my child'. Sibling seniority, relative to a person's parents in the narrow sense, may be recognised by adding the suffixes 'big' or 'small' to the father and mother terms. The use of the terms father, mother and child, along with recourse to the idiom of birth, suggests that a translation of them as relations of parentation is more appropriate than the anthropologically more conventional ideas of lineality or descent. Chamba are barely attentive to lineal relations of great genealogical depth, instead they describe a variety of relations in terms of the immediate link between parents and children.

The verb to bear carries the major burden of this sense. In restricted use, it refers to the actual parent–child bond, but it is a potent, more general idiom for relations in which the seniority of one party normatively obliges a nurturance of the junior, dependent member. In arguing the pre-eminence of his own small matriclan in Mapeo, Malub Gudi (one of my senior classificatory fathers) would stress that all the clans of Mapeo had to come to his forebears (literally, grandfathers) in order to be given water from the all season spring on the hill which they owned. So, he reasoned, the 'people of the hill matriclan' (*nɛ kusum bɛ kun*) bore all the people in Mapeo. When I questioned this usage, he responded rhetorically, could they have children if they did not drink? Can a child live if you do not feed it? The usage was shrugged off by other informants, but demonstrates the metaphorical extension of the usage of parentation in the interest of clinching a practically salient point of argument.

Collateral relations between members of adjacent generations include those between an individual and his or her paternal aunt and maternal uncle. The term for paternal aunt (*mala*) occurs in both Chamba languages; maternal uncle is *pɔp* in Daka and *mun* in Leko. Strictly, neither of these relatives ought to say they bore the individual concerned; in a roundabout way they should state that their brother or sister bore him or her. In keeping with this, the reciprocal form of the terms for paternal aunt or maternal uncle is not 'child' but a diminutive form of the term by which the older person is addressed. A number of other terms form reciprocals in the same fashion as *mala* and *pɔp*.

mala	father's sister	*malawe*	brother's son or daughter
pɔp	mother's brother	*pɔpwe*	sister's son or daughter
ka	grandmother	*kagwe*	grandchild
kalum	grandfather	*kawe*	grandchild
gunu	mother in law	*gunuwe*	daughter in law
gulum	father in law	*gulumwe*	son in law
minu	mother's paternal half sister	*minuwe*	paternal half sister's child
pɔptəmbɛ	mother's paternal half brother	*pɔptəmwe*	paternal half sister's child

These paired terms encode seniority, and their pairing suggests them to be the halves of a single relationship constructed reciprocally by their interaction. Behaviour between paternal aunts and their nephews and nieces, maternal uncles and their nephews and nieces, and parents and children-in-law is strongly marked by respect, familiarity and avoidance in each of the three cases, even if each of the relations is realised more ambiguously than a normative account suggests (Fardon, 1988).

A further set of non reciprocal terms is used to denote seniority between people who claim siblingship in whatever context. The terms used between same sex siblings unavoidably carry information about relative seniority; between opposite sex siblings these may optionally be substituted by terms marked for gender rather than age. Birth order is particularly stressed towards same sex siblings in a person's own generation and, as noted above, towards a parent's same sex siblings. Outside these two contexts which involve parentation relations, seniority is usually marked only between generations but not within them. The only entirely reciprocal terms of Chamba kinship and affinity (unmarked for age or gender) are used between individuals in a relationship of privileged abuse; this class includes spouses of older siblings, regardless of sex and, paradigmatically, the wife of the maternal uncle. Terms for these joking affines (*mamngwɔsi*, in Daka; *mangnara* in Leko) belong to a class of particularly close others (marked in both languages by the prefix *mam-*) that I discuss below.

A polarity in emotional tone invests the relationships between Chamba individuals and their matrikin and patrikin. Mapeo Chamba normatively contrast relations of 'children' with their 'mothers' and 'fathers' in terms of 'love' and 'respect'. The polarity is more marked yet in the contrast between the latitude allowed in the mother's brother and sister's son relation (and this is all the more true for the maternal uncle's wife), and the marked deference appropriate between paternal aunt and nephew/niece, at least in Chamba theory.

As important as membership of their own clans are the relations Mapeo Chamba trace to the matriclans of their father and grandfathers and the patriclan of their mother. Although men cannot pass on full membership of their matriclans, their own children are considered by clan members to be· 'children' of the matriclan (*mɛm ngwananbu*, children born) and the 'parent–child' pair of terms is used between them. The 'children' of these 'children' of the clan will be in turn 'grandchildren' of the clan. Thus, each clan consists of its full members (who are internally differentiated according to generation and sibling seniority) and the attached categories of 'children' and 'grandchildren'. A further relationship extends an individual's affiliations to the patriclan of his or her mother, the members of which are called 'maternal uncle of the bow' or *minu*, a compound of the terms for child and woman, thus a woman who has given birth to a child.

Because the Mapeo culture and dialect area has virtually been endogamous until recently, each individual is meshed in a web of relationships to virtually every other individual that formally identifies and models the behaviour between them. The conventional anthropological approach to African societies in terms of residence and kinship statuses is enlightening because it so clearly corresponds to the ways that people model their own ideas of relationship. Introducing me to a third party, a companion never failed to specify the relationship between himself and the person being introduced; and when senior people were introduced by their juniors it was invariably through relationship rather than name. That all anthropologists of African villages discover the centrality of kin statuses strikes me as a convergence between anthropological methodology, with its roots in jurisprudence, and African ideas of personal status (Strathern, 1985). The danger of the legalistic model is to make the different kinship positions seem to share an ontological grounding just because all are named and normatively defined.

For Mapeo Chamba, the two spheres of clan relationships are strongly contrastive. The unifying theme of the complex associations of matriclanship is consubstantiality—the sharing of substance. This is explicit in Chamba ideas of procreation (Fardon, 1985, 1988). Children share substance with their mother, because pregnancy results from the retention of blood (*nyɛng*, Daka) and nurturance and growth are sustained by the mother's milk (*nya 'esa*). Sometimes an analogy with the potter's art is made, and the creation of a child is imaged in the act of God as a potter forming a child from the claylike substance of the mother. The analogy is carried through in the conceptualisation of the newborn child as wet, soft and red. A child shares this common substantiality with other members of his or her matriclan. The idiom can be extended or contracted, according to context, argument and the interests of the speaker at the time, so as to apply to siblings from a single mother, at one extreme, or to all matriclan members, whether Chamba or not, at the other.

Common substance entails joint interest in the condition of matriclan bodies. There are numerous indications of this preoccupation, and many involve the maternal uncle as the (albeit ambiguous) figure of the authority of the matriclan so far as the child is concerned. He rather than the father at least ought to inflict physical punishment on the child, and his is the responsibility to assure that the child's physical development lacks the features of animality associated with breech births and children who cut upper milk teeth before lower (see Chapter 5). The maternal uncle is responsible for organising payments to cults which have 'caught' junior matrikin and might continue to 'follow' the matriclan were no reparation made to the cult owners. Matriclans people are collectively vulnerable. For his part, the sister's son has rights of privileged use of his uncle's property. Because he inherits this moveable property at his uncle's death, the two men have a common interest in such substantial properties. Witchcraft may also be conceived as a substantial property, so that the conviction of a single member of the matriclan implies the guilt also of the co-descendants of a common grandmother, of a matriclan section, or of the entire matriclan according to the circumstances. Similar bodily associations are foregrounded in Chamba notions of the transference of people. Blood debts between matriclans may be settled by the transference of a bodily equivalent of the member lost, but this is not possible in the patriclan. Slavery also is a bodily status: children transferred to settle blood debts are slaves of the matriclan, as were individuals seized in the bush or bought.

The consubstantiality of matriclanship is double edged. The nurturance of a person by his or her mother forms the closest relation of lasting common concern that Chamba recognise, and the privileged familiarity with the mother's brother and his wives is unique in relations with members of the senior adjacent generation. But matriclanship also concerns sickness, witchcraft, slavery, control over the body's development and the coercion that others can exert over the body's behaviour. In matriclan chiefdoms, such as Yeli, the bodies of the royal matrikin are charged with significance for the community as a whole, and negligence of their ritual care and placement after death menace collective welfare. Matriclanship concerns continuities between humanity and animality, for matrikin share what people more generally share with animals: flesh and blood. Many matriclan ancestresses were animals; matrikin may be witches, and witches may transmute into abominable creatures of the bush. Control over and the preservation of substance is the dominant motif of matriclan culture.

If by no means a mirror image of matriclanship, none the less patriclanship is conceived in strongly contrastive terms. Although the verb 'to bear' is used of the father's relation to his child, as it is between mother and child, Chamba are not dogmatic about the nature of the physiological link between father and son. Sperm is sometimes likened to seed, such that a patriclan can alternatively be called the line of seed (*gbi*). But more frequent reference is made to reincarnation which, in Mapeo at least, is considered to occur invariably in the patriclan. According to all accounts one of the dead (*wurum*) returns to his or her patrikin and should be recognised and named as in its previous life. Exactly how this occurs is not altogether clear, but most aver that God (*Su*) not only forms the child from the mother's claylike substance but also adds the personality which the child will assume through incarnation and the breath (*gɔngsi*) which gives life to all sentient, moving things, both human and animal. Forebears who died at peace with their kin and were content with their funerary observances will be reincarnated within the clan they left, often among their own grandchildren. A forebear who felt slighted could choose reincarnation into a distant part of the patriclan so as to avoid further insult and maltreatment. Reincarnation is not really a relation between father and child but a supposition of continuing identity between the discrete, self-sustaining cultural unit which is the patriclan, and the personalities which populate it.

As with the matriclan, patriclan values seem most strongly to inform relations between members of adjacent generations. The father/child and father's sister/brother's child relations are normatively authoritarian, but this authority should not extend to disciplining the body, which is the preserve of the mother's brother. The common interests of patrikin tend towards their relations with their forebears, their prestige among other patriclans, and the defence of their male members' rights in women, in property and to remain unmolested. So patrikin are responsible for the passage of the individual through life: from birth rites which begin the slow return to humanity, through circumcision which gives a man entry to adulthood, and tooth evulsion which once had the same significance for women of some patriclans, until the rituals surrounding burial, mourning, skull taking and remembrance (see Chapter 5). If the practical concerns of matrikin involve management of affairs at the borderline between animality and humanity, the patrikin are oriented to that other margin between the living and the dead.

Sociality is pervasively sorted between the contrasted terms of the two clan domains of culture and a third domain, to which I turn below, that overlaps them both. Themes of shared long term identity in the patriclan, and shared substance in the matriclan, summarise much of the diversity. This contrast makes comprehensible the different temporal constructions of the clan domains: patriclanship is discussed in a historical idiom which suggests that these clans are experienced as the result of unique histories which make them finally incomparable. Matriclanship tends, in the absence of the duresses of competition for office or avoidance of witchcraft accusations, to be mythologised. Quintessential matriclan origin tales claim shape-changing animals as ancestresses. But patriclanship consistently eschews animal associations and emphasises the succession of its incarnated members. If matriclanship concerns bodily substance, patriclanship eventually fixes upon the skull as the enduring vessel of the spirit. Whereas the interest of matrikin in bodily well-being encourages a conserving and retentive attitude towards individual bodies, the patrikin entertain a longer term view, in which the alliance of patriclan identity with matriclan substance is temporary and death will restore the skull, removed from its bodily trappings, to its patriclan owners. Patriclanship is inscribed in the partibility of the body at skull taking and also at circumcision.

A third type of sociality cuts across the institutional moorings of clanship. Behaviour that is, at the least, indulgent and, at the most, teasing is expected in a range of kinship relations. There is the mutual tolerance between grandchildren and grandparents; the petty theft and mild disrespect an individual may visit upon his or her maternal uncle, and perhaps also on matrisiblings. But aside from this, there exists a type of behaviour that begins where tolerable behaviour towards familiar kin ends: relations of privileged physical abuse and verbal insult in which no extreme of behaviour ought discernibly be taken as falling outside the parameters of fun. Many of the terms for these relations, in both Chamba languages, share a single prefix *mam* or *man*. At least in Chamba Daka, *man* may stand independently as a term for person, if the speaker wishes to underline a closeness felt towards that individual (as, perhaps, in the case of a co-resident). Those to whom such latitude is permitted are the closest of non kin.

Statutory insulting relations exist with particular affines: the wife of a maternal uncle, or the spouse of an older sibling. The term used reciprocally in these relations for one another is *mamngwɔsi*, in Daka, or *mangnara*, in Leko. When the joking partners are of opposite sex, their play often has a bawdy and physical character. Informants always volunteer the right of the nephew to marry the widow of his maternal uncle in explanation of the behaviour in this paramount example of a joking relation. However, I have been unable to document a case in which such a marriage occurred (which is not to say that none exists) and the explanation would have to treat the case of sibling's spouses, predominantly unmarriageable, as an extension.

Insulting relationships do not tally well with a class of potential marriage partners, but they are susceptible to being seen as variations on a notion of extreme proximity that lacks a basis in clanship. In Chamba Daka, the diagnostic *man-* prefix, for close others, occurs in the term for friend, *mana*, and a special friend may be singled out as the friend for whom the goat's ears would be reserved in a soup, *mana vin ta*. Although the Chamba Leko term for friend, *'ɔtzera*, does not belong to the *mam* class, in other respects the range of the lexically marked category of close others is similar in the two languages. Age mates, born so closely in time that relative seniority between them is disputed, are called *mankasi* in Chamba Daka, or *mankasa* in Chamba Leko. Their jokes dispute unwearyingly their right to the deference due to age. These age mates, usually lifelong friends, receive special gifts at the funeral distributions of one of their number. Their equality is maintained even after death, since the children of the age mates dying earliest inherit the right to receive their father's portion at the death of his age mates.

Additional relations of privileged abuse are enjoined between categories of people. Matriclans and patriclans each recognise conventional insulting relations with other like units. The Chamba Leko term for these relations is a member of the *mam* group: *manzala*; although the Daka term is *kpɔm*, behaviour is explicitly seen as cognate with that appropriate to individual joking relations. Members of the categories linked in this way frequently tax one another's patience sorely. And this is at least one of the points of the relation. Insults may be reciprocated, petty theft repaid in kind, but the relation is 'spoiled' should one party ever fail to take a slight, however maliciously weighted, in the spirit of jest. 'Even if your *kpɔm* stole your wife,' a Mapeo man told me, 'you could not fight him; everyone would simply laugh at you'. Thanks to immunity from aggrieved response, joking partners are often able to voice delicate criticisms (especially concerning sexuality or witchcraft) that others dare not raise. Joking partners can censure behaviour because the victim can never admit to certainty that the jibe was not in jest.

Abusive relations between groupings extend beyond what anthropologists would identity as patriclans to a scale they might prefer to call ethnic groups. For Chamba, this distinction corresponds only to a matter of degree of difference. In Mapeo, the pre-eminent example of ethnic joking relations is played out with Bata and Bachama (both called *Kam*). Yeli Chamba claim they also would joke with Bata and Bachama, but tend to see more of Pere, their southern neighbours and joking relations. In different parts of Chambaland, additional ethnic groups are selected as joking mates.

Putting the individual and categorical joking relations together, it is apparent that many relations in Chamba societies are acted between parentheses that frame behaviour as play. Such relations develop readily. In Mapeo, there were circumstances in which members of the higher and lower ends of the village treated one another as joking partners. Some of my new friends also found the play format the most convenient way in which to treat my intrusive presence. When unsure how to behave with some new acquaintance, it was often safest to joke. Jokes (*pɛn yaksin*, 'thing playing') and laughter (*jɔn*) are, despite their attribution to animals in tales (*tit jɔn*), pre-eminently human characteristics. Together they constitute a third domain of human sociality encompassed by neither of the clan domains.

If the roster of relations in these small communities already seems crowded then we have hardly touched on the relations which derive from the recognition of common parentation between clans or from co-residence. In the discussion of funeral wakes, Chapter 5, we shall encounter a set of circumstances under which all these different human relations are given some practical content, when people are made to live up to the ideals in terms of which the ties are defined.

INHUMAN COMPANY: THE DEAD

To learn more about the 'children of men' we must pose questions which elicit relational answers. What are not people? On the face of it the answer is simple: animals are not people, and the dead are not people. But this is too simple: humanity shares characteristics with both animality and the dead. Resemblances are clearest within the clan domains: matrilateral connection implies consubstantiation, and substance is shared by people and animals; patrilateral connection draws upon conceptions of identity and incarnation which are associated with the skull, the relic of the dead.

In different contexts, ancestor, forebear, spirit, sprite or some combination of these are each possible translations of the term for the dead. I have equivocated over these senses in other publications. Rather than defending the choice made here, I need to explain why no single English term has the range and connotations of the Chamba original.

The Chamba Daka *wurum* is apparently a composite of two particles: *wut*, skull, and *lum* the masculine suffix (we could compare the term *lerum*, male person, a composite of *nɛ*, person, and *lum*). The term incorporates a masculine suffix although it refers to the dead of both sexes. Moreover, the male bias is stronger than in the case of the living: *nɛ*, particularly in the plural, is either masculine or unmarked. The dead are male in a marked sense. The dead are also associated with the skull or, more broadly, with relics of which the skull is exemplar. *Wut* can also be a nail paring, tooth, grave soil, or fragment of the garment in which a person died. Literally, *wurum* could be translated as 'skull man', but this gloss would be unrecognisable to an English speaking Chamba. I toyed with the coinage ghommid (Soyinka, 1981: 7), the single term is composite, has a human suffix with masculine bias, and evokes the ideas of ghost and thus death. To my English ear, it comes closest to having the effect that *wurum* has in Chamba. However, a reader suggested this sympathy between sounds and ideas muddled rather than clarified. He is right but, since it works for me, I cannot quite let the idea go and would encourage any reader who cares to hear ghommid wherever the dead appears on the page.

Given the very distant relation between the two Chamba languages, it is noteworthy how similar are the associations of the Chamba Leko term for the dead. *Vunɛd* (plural *vunɛpbira*) is a composite of the person suffix (*nɛng*, singular, *nɛpbira* plural) and a term meaning skull, *vad*, or death, *val*. The term for the dead meshes into the same set of related terms and ideas in either language; informants volunteer that they are 'one thing'.

	skull	death	to die	the dead/forebears/spider
LEKO	*vad*	*val*	*vad*	*vunɛd*
DAKA	*wut*	*we*	*wu*	*wurum*

Terms belonging to these clusters are pervasive in Chamba exegeses of ritual. Moreover, each term connotes the others, so that the substitutions we shall find in comparing Daka and Leko usage—the fact that a memorial 'dead pot' in one language is a 'skull pot' in the other—seem no more than a difference of focus within a shared vision.

While lexical indications support identification of *wurum*/*vunɛd* with dead people, this is over-simple. From the perspective of the life cycle, *wurum* is one stage in a process of incarnation. Newborn children and the senile share resemblances to *wurumbu*. I have written elsewhere how a 'conversation', to my ear only a coincidence of noises, between a baby and a senile, dying man was decribed to me by Titlɛsime as a conversation in *wurum mum*, *wurum* language. From the perspective of reincarnation, the very aged are childlike: 'child' can be added to the term for an old person to designate this resemblance (*danga mi*, old man child; *wɔ mi*, old woman child). Substantially the states of childhood and old age are contrasted, in terms of the wetness of the newborn and the dryness and tautness of the old. Deaths of the very old and the very young are both anticipated. Very young children are buried outside the patriclan graveyard; they are said not to die but to return (*pɛ*) refusing to rejoin the human company. The funerals of the very old are celebratory, since their breath has been used up rather than destroyed or cut short. Their deaths are due to God, or the nature of life itself, rather than to cult contagion or human malevolence.

However, the entity *wurum* is not entirely assimilable either to conceptions like that of ancestor or to the idea of a fund of spirit either incarnate or awaiting incarnation. When the recently dead are addressed as clan members kin terms are applied to them. More distant ancestors are called *kalum sasanbu*, retaining the kinship sense of the term for grandfather. *Wurum* is used only to describe the dead who are without individuality. *Wurum* is not equivalent to ancestor.

A translation of *wurum* as spirit suffers from the fact that *wurum* is not seen as a component of the person. Instead, people are said to become *wurum*, and *wurum* to become people. The verb specifying mutation (*bit*) is used also in stories to describe the instantaneous transformation of animals into people, or witches into diabolic black creatures.

The cyclic sense, in which the 'children of men' and *wurumbu* are transmutations of one another, is most appropriate to the domain of patriclanship. Name, incarnation, facial appearance, the skull and its equivalents—in short identity—are the historical property of the patriclan. However, when *wurumbu* are invoked in ritual, reference to this cyclical relation of identity is absent. *Su an tɛ, wurumbu bɛn sɔ*; 'God is present, the *wurumbu* below the ground'. The formula with which cult meetings are conventionally opened locates beings in space rather than time. For this purpose, the fact of reincarnation is not relevant.

To direct questions about *wurumbu*, informants respond that they are under the ground where their lifestyle is much like that of humans: they live in houses, have livestock, follow certain paths on their way to market and so on. They are richer, wiser and more powerful than humans. Evidence for their behaviour has to be put together piecemeal, since direct experience of *wurumbu* is normally restricted to a category of specially gifted people: seers (literally 'person with eyes', *nɛ tug an*). The sighted may be recognised when babies because their crying presages a death. Nowadays they make outstanding school students; traditionally they had special aptitudes for divination or priesthood. Seers may see the future; a Chamba friend in Ganye told how his grandfather had seen the things to come with Europeans: houses with shining metal roofs and aeroplanes. Europeans themselves only had such things because they had seen them in the underworld of the dead. All Europeans are seers.

Stories about seers and the riches and extraordinary aptitudes of the dead are commonplace. One account is told most often. I have heard it on many occasions—usually as a general account of the self-regarding behaviour of seers, but once in explanation of the indisposition of the priest of Mapeo's sister settlement of Tisayeli. Because seers are able to see the riches of the *wurumbu*, they cannot resist the attempt to steal them. But if the *wurumbu* detect the thief, and their superior knowledge suggests they always will, they will continue to beat him until he releases whatever he has grasped. Ordinary people, those who 'do not see', cannot witness the anger of the *wurumbu*; they see only the body of the seer convulsed as if under a hail of blows. The seer's firmly clenched fist must be forced open to release the stolen object, which is also invisible to the unsighted. If this is not done, the seer will certainly die.

Things that have been associated with the *wurumbu* continue to be imbued with their power. This makes their possessions especially desirable. Their crops are said to yield more heavily than those of the living. Occasionally, in the past, *wurumbu* freely gave things to humans that became elements of the apparatuses of the cults. Even today, men sometimes come into possession of things the sprites have negligently abandoned, and these curious objects should be added to a cult paraphernalia.

Seen from this perspective, *wurumbu* appear less like forebears of the living and more akin to the beings of a parallel and more powerful underworld. A variety of anecdotes may suggest why this more common representation is also more malleable. The rains of 1977 were of insufficient duration to secure a good harvest and, to make matters worse, a few rain storms were of particular intensity. One night, the heaviest storm of the year brought a massive black rock crashing down the hillside behind Mapeo. In the morning, the priest leader of the adjacent hamlet summoned a *lera* flute band to play around the rock where it lay at the foot of the hill. A young Chamba friend dropped by to tell me in English that the *ngwan* (priest) had been playing flutes to the spirit of the stone. I thought such an account unlikely, but missed the performance. Later, *ngwan Jambum*, priest leader of the event, explained—to my relief and his amusement—how the flutes were played, not to the boulder, but to calm the *wurumbu* living under it who would have been angered by the disturbance to their home. The flute music and a spray of water flicked from a bunch of the small leaves of the locust bean tree would cool them.

Months later, during a cult meeting we attended together, Titlesime pointed to a sculptured stone among a collection of cult paraphernalia plastered with beer and lees. The stone resembled a face (just like an Easter Island statue), but it had been found in the bush. The face was sculpted by *wurumbu*; so when someone chanced upon it, it had been brought to the cult place to be added to the cult 'things'. Everyone seemed to agree. 'So *wurumbu* make things in stone?' Certainly, my uncle added helpfully, and small stones are like the chippings from their workshops. Our audience looked unconvinced by this statement which stretched the point too far.

Titlesime also showed me the pot shrine of his maternal grandmother's patriclan, which was in his care because the owning clan had virtually become extinct in Mapeo. Among the pots were a number of round stones. I assumed that these were substitutes for skulls, since the two are sometimes interchangeable. 'No', he answered, 'these stones were vomited by the chief of snakes' (*ye gang*; usually identified with the python). From previous conversation with a priest whose power was linked to his special familiarity with pythons, I knew the python and *wurumbu* were associated because both lived under the ground. The successor to his priestship, so my informant had claimed, was chosen by the python's wish revealed by holes that would appear in the floor of his compound. The python's burrowing efforts were also held responsible for the annual erosion of an earth culvert built across a local river. Pythons and *wurumbu* were associated with deep water as well as the dry underworld. A young boy's drowning during my stay had been attributed to the negligence of his parents who allowed him to play near deep water while they were occupied with their farm work. *Wurumbu* grabbed his ankle and drew him under the water. This was predictable since *wurumbu* constantly attempt to draw humans who disturb them into their realm. Moreover they are tenacious; only special techniques release their grip.

Close by a river on the hill behind Mapeo was a path known to be frequented by *wurumbu*. Should anyone fall there, it was necessary to call for a *ngwan*, priest, to lift him by passing the sickle shaped emblem of his office under the prone body in order to release the grip of the *wurumbu*. Were this not done, although the person might feel fine and reach home safely, he would carry the *wurum* back home clinging to his back, and later he would die. My maternal uncle, Dɔngwe, told me this story one day when we had gone to look at the hillside place once inhabited by members of his patriclan before the twentieth century descent to the plain. Others knew the place, but took exception to the idea that these *wurumbu* belonged exclusively to Dɔngwe's patriclan. How, they asked, could anyone know the patriclan affiliation of *wurumbu*?

Priests, and office holders more generally, have particularly close relations with *wurumbu*. The priest's emblem called *lama*, most examples of which resemble an ordinary wooden hafted sickle (*gbɔmsa*) but embellished with an undulating iron tip, is supposed to bring him into closer association with the *wurumbu*. Some claimed *ngwanbu* became seers when they grasped their ceremonial sickles, but I was unable to find a priest willing to confirm this. Priests did concur in the popular opinion that they raised ridges on the ground simply by pointing these *lama*. Although we could not see these ridges, when *ngwanbu* danced together they attempted to trip one another by means of them. The fallen *ngwan*, though I never saw one fall, would have to admit defeat by asking his vanquisher to release the grip of the *wurumbu* on him, or else he could not stand again without dying.

Mapeo stories are quite typical of those recounted elsewhere. In Yeli, my friend Bouba told me of a man who died after felling a large tree which was home to some *vunɛpbira*, the Yeli equivalent of *wurumbu*. *Vunɛpbira* often sat in the shade of large trees at the edge of the village, and you had to be careful not to tread on the calabashes from which they drank beer. Entering a place populated by *vunɛpbira* you would shout, 'Here we come stepping as carelessly as cockerels', so as not to take them unawares. In Sapeo, when I visited the royal graves on the hilltop, our guides threw pebbles towards the grave site to forewarn the spirits of our arrival.

Anecdotal evidence of this kind could be multiplied, but a sample is sufficient to indicate the type of information on which any generalisations are based. Although the subterranean beings have human qualities—and are potential and past humans—they are not human. Their preference for dark, cool, places—on the margins of human habitation or around abandoned hamlets—is reminiscent of the location of graveyards and the grave. Burial of the dead is indeed the moment that the guises of patriclan forebears and underworld inhabitants are briefly coordinate. Because they are the dead, close association with *wurumbu* invites death for the living. They are beyond such danger, associated with hard persistent qualities: stone and the ground itself, the skulls of the dead. Although they can be entreated, by analogy with humans, through respectful behaviour and the gift of beer, *wurumbu* are highly irascible and sensitive to disturbance. Signs of life seem to disturb them most. There is no evidence of sexuality in the world of the dead; by implication they are entirely masculine. They dislike heat, especially the heat generated by sexuality and blood shed upon the ground by menstruation or circumcision. Not only do reincarnation, skull taking and funerary observance associate the dead with the sociality of patriclanship, by abjuring warmth, substance, and sexuality they suggest an antithesis to the sociality of the matriclan.

Putting together the implications of observations and anecdotes suggested at different times (as no informant would) reveals how the notion of *wurum* or *vunɛd* in the parsimonious Chamba ontology is to perform intellectual work that elsewhere in West Africa might be distributed between nature sprites, ancestors and a notion of spirit incarnate in people. Context often makes clear the particular aspect of *wurum* character to which a speaker means an utterance to refer. But use of a single term means that in thinking out loud, a speaker can pursue associations to different parts of its semantic range. A sparse ontology spawns a discourse rich in ambiguities.

INHUMAN COMPANY: ANIMALS AND ANIMALITY

If *wurum* connotes human characteristics that are prominent values of patriclan sociality, then animals, especially the larger animals of the bush, connote an animality in humankind most readily associated with matriclan sociality. A detailed account of human relations with the wilderness is the subject of Chapter 7, my brief introduction here is intended as a counterpoint to discussion of the dead. Anomalous or aberrant humanity offers a way into the animal characteristics of the living: Chamba feel compelled to evict some classes of human from their community and to discard the corpses of others, as a sort of eviction after the event. The individuals and their bodies evoke the immediate judgement that they are simply bad (*vɛ*), but in either case further exegesis involves connotations of animality.

In common with Pere, their southern neighbours, Chamba evince a marked fear and abhorrence of breech births. A breech delivery should be disposed of, placed in a calabash which is left in the bush or swept away on the flowing water of a river. Rituals which must be performed to purify both the compound and the parents involve the special powers of a cleansing cult (*jup dagan*, Daka, or *vɔm dagan*, Leko; derived from the Daka verb *dag*, to make light). If allowed to live, the child would bring disasters. Wild animals would enter the village, and tornadoes destroy houses. The rain would not fall. Then deaths would follow, beginning with the child's parents. A child entering the world feet first challenges the sequence proper to events and brings a dislocation of order.

The terms for breech born child are identical in the two Chamba languages (*mi su*, Chamba Daka; *wa su*, Chamba Leko). However, local etymologies of the terms are at variance. Some Mapeo informants thought the term to mean that God (*Su*) was somehow responsible for sending the child, though how this squared with such extreme human aversion to the child could not be explained. Etymologically, the gloss is unconvincing since the particles (*su*) have different tones in the two cases. Alternatively, this time with appropriate tone, informants drew on a metaphoric sense in which a breech born child could be compared with the cylindrical gourd container for seeds (also *su*) which stands with its mouth upwards. The Chamba Leko gloss suggested by Dura in Yeli draws on another metaphor. *Su*, the term for the forked tail of a bird, is claimed to be a euphemism for the appearance of the child's legs at the moment of birth. The term is also used of a tree (*wa su nyia*; *nyia* trunk), the bark of which is one component of the 'medicine' (*gan*) used to cleanse the compound and its occupants.

To judge by their accounts, Chamba aversion to children whose dentition they considered anomalous was less extreme. Children should produce their lower before their upper teeth; once it cuts milk teeth a child must be shown to its maternal uncles who are responsible for bodily development. An upper tooth cutter was sold or given away outside the community; or failing this killed. Should the child remain within the community, wild animals would enter the village. The hunting companions of a youth who cut upper before lower milk teeth would risk being killed by wild animals in his company. Mapeo terms for an upper tooth cutter (*'in bak tu*, one whose teeth have stuck, or *'in daran tu*, one whose teeth have erred or missed) both convey the sense of anomalous development. Informants attribute a wilful desire for such abnormality to the child. The Yeli term, *nɔgɔl vɔga*, is composed of the term for tooth and one that may derive from the verb to cut, *vǝd*. An explicit animal analogy is made with the bush pig whose fearsome tusks earn it the epithet of the 'tooth cutter'.

Breech births and upper teeth cutters menace the community with disturbances in the order of the wild: animals that enter the village, the deaths of hunters, winds that destroy villages. The conditions involve the proper priority and development of the head. One is tempted, in terms of the preceding analysis, to detect a failure on the part of the matriclan to discharge its responsibilities towards the development of the unique incarnated individual identified with the head. However, it would be premature to move so far beyond informants' exegeses.

Witchcraft can be envisaged as a phenomenon similar to anomalous childhood development but affecting adults. Chamba dogma holds that witches (*nɔran*, Daka; *dǝra*, Leko) transmit their powers within the matriclan. It is less certain in what the witches' powers consist. Some informants describe witchcraft as innate, a matter of the witch's ability to change shape and prowl at night in the form of an owl, black baboon or hybrid black animal which discharges fire from its anus. These animals dig up the graves of their victims in order to eat their flesh. Other informants envisage witchcraft as a technical art that employs poisons, or iron needles thrown into a victim's body or ingested in beer. The accounts need not be mutually exclusive. Matrikin convicted of witchcraft were once, so it is recalled, beaten to death with staves, and their bodies thrown into the bush without proper burial. To the best of my knowledge, monkeys are the only other creatures killed in this manner, and monkeys are explicitly recognised as the most humanlike among animals. Despite their depredation of crops, they are portrayed as well disposed to men in Chamba stories. That witches and monkeys should be treated analogously in death seems appropriate given that witches often adopt the guise of baboons for their nocturnal activities.

Breech birth, anomalous dentition and witchcraft demonstrate the conceptual link between anomalous humanity and excessive animality. Each case predominantly concerns the matrikin: as those responsible for remedying the intrusion from the wild (since the father's matrikin dispose of breech births and the maternal uncle of upper teeth cutters), or those sharing in the anomalous condition (as in witchcraft). Two forms of bad death show how pervasive are these associations.

Chamba abhorrence is strongest for ways of dying which destroy the body in life; leprosy and burning are the pre-eminent examples of 'bad deaths' (*we vɛ*, Daka; in Leko also *val tigǝlu*, death of the night, referring to secret burial). Although such corpses are buried, they are not properly interred in their clan graveyards; accounts claim that the tomb is filled rather than covered with a stone or pot. There is no intention to open the grave at a later time to take the skull or any other relic of the deceased. Earth is simply pushed in by the grave

party who face away from the grave and this act, along with the unceremonious
way in which they run out of the village with the corpse, is designed to prevent
the reincarnation of the dead person. The corpse is simply thrown into the
bush 'like a dead animal'. No celebration is permitted to 'cry the death'. In so
far as possible, the deceased is expunged from the community's memory.

Animal associations of leprosy are more precise: one of the leprosy-causing
cults in Mapeo, and the only one such in Yeli, are called elephant (*kɔngla*,
Daka; *dɔna*, Leko). Elephant's skin is thought to resemble that of a leper,
moreover elephant's meat is greasy and lepers are considered to suffer from an
excess of bodily grease. On account of this, some Chamba refuse to eat goat's
meat which they suspect makes the body greasy and, thereby, predisposed to
leprosy.

Anomalous people suffer from animal characteristics: wildness, excess of
substance, appetite for human flesh and so on. However, animality in controlled proportion is the portion that matrikin share in the human condition
(see Chapter 7). Excessive animality, at one extreme, and death, at the other,
are the polar conditions of either type of clanship unconstrained by the other.

METAMORPHOSIS: THE LIVING, THE DEAD AND THE WILD

Chamba rituals can now be construed as means to manage relations between
humanity, the dead and the wild that are crucial to well-being. These types of
being may be envisaged as discrete classes or as aspects of human subjects.
People are constantly liable to slip out of their human frame by lapsing into
animality, and eventually they must slip out of this frame the same way as they
entered it: by rejoining the dead. Chamba languages share a verb to express
these changes: *bit* or *bid*—suddenly to become, or to metamorphose into.
Numerous stories, like the origin tales of the bushcow and elephant clans, or
the story of the metamorphosis of people into the nightjar and touraco (see
Chapter 7) hinge on the moment when the protagonists change life forms. The
shape changing capacity of witches is a source of fear, and *wurumbu* also have
assumed human guise in order to stay with Chamba forebears—instructing
them in new methods of divination, or revealing cults to control disease and
enhance the prestige of their owners.

Metamorphosis crucially informs Chamba expectations of the possible.
While endorsing the boundaries of categories, metamorphosis questions the
stability of category membership. Humanity, the first of three terms—men,
cults and masks—that I have suggested to be analogously constructed, is
defined by the relatively stable concatenation of features of the dead, the wild
and the uniquely human. These features parallel institutionalised forms of
sociality particular to patriclanship, matriclanship and privileged abuse. The
next chapter moves to the second term: the cult.

3

JUP: THE MAPEO VARIANT OF CULT

THE ETHNOGRAPHER AS INITIATE

Initiates to Mapeo Chamba cults (*jup*) are offered little explanation of the mysteries revealed to them. The lexicon of initiation and advancement consists of 'seeing', 'seeing all' and 'holding' or 'owning' the *jup*, in order to 'make' and 'repair' it. These terms are conventional ways of speaking, but also literal descriptions of activities they label. Initiates are shown how, not told why. Properties of the world are demonstrated and discovered anew in the practical attempt to mould it to human interests. Exemplification and participation more appropriately describe this process than do elucidation or instruction. Knowledge is passed on by example with the transmission of technique. However, when we contemplate the experience of *jup* created by such exemplification, it is difficult to ignore an analogy between the way in which Chamba construe the composite natures of their cults and themselves. I want to argue that it is by virtue of this assimilation of the less to the better known, that practitioners are persuaded to see cults as agents, beings with volition, akin in respects to themselves. The ethnographer's compressed experience, albeit deviant in many respects from that of a true neophyte, can assist in grasping this.

My awareness of Chamba channels for influencing their world accrued piecemeal. More philosophical concerns tended periodically to recede in the face of practical questions of ways and means, times and places, debts and payments, memberships and exclusions. Residence in Natup as honorary junior brother to Dominic opened doors on some domains of sociality and by the same token closed others. Membership of Sirinɛpbu (the residents of Natup) and the Yangurubu patriclan bestowed privileges and obligations. I could not be patrikin and co-resident in two places simultaneously: my exclusion from some activities was taken as seriously as my inclusion in others. Matriclan affiliation to *ngwana kun* (dog matriclan) brought the discovery of siblings, 'children' and an invaluable maternal uncle. Because my new matrikin, unlike my patrikin, were not localised, they took longer to identify. Later, I was given a father's matriclan (*yɛt kun*, the bushcow clan), in recognition of the interest shown in me by the oldest man in the village. The adoption of a European may have been unprecedented in Mapeo, but the distribution of a stranger's loyalties between clans must have been a regular means to find accommodation for incomers in the domains of sociality.

While my patrikin lived in Natup, among the people who lived 'down' (*nɛ daranbu*), a majority of my active matrikin lived 'up' across a small river a few hundred yards away (*nɛ garanbu*). Like many relationships in Mapeo, that between up and down people was handled by analogy with a more fully institutionalised joking relationship. I had to recognise other such relationships with a patriclan (Sanbu) and a matriclan (*gang van ji kun*, the chief of the red rock clan) and with affines who had married my matrikin or patrikin (though my seniority was never clear). I had neither mother's patriclan, nor grandfather's matriclan, nor wife, nor circumcision age mates (although a few individuals, particularly a blacksmith friend, and his peers on account of him, chose to treat me as an age mate). As time went by, I was also known to have some special friends and one quasi-institutionalised friendship. Thus a third sphere of sociality was created by and for me; these parameters allowed most people, and myself most of the time, to know what I ought to be doing and whom I could trouble with my questions. In relation to the cults, this network determined what I could and could not see.

Villagers to whom I talked often fell into one of a number of categories: initially, I talked to the people whose compounds surrounded mine, predominantly the Chamba Muslim community of Natup; next, I got to know the Natup traditionalists whose compounds tended to be located away from the road where mine was; through my matrikin, I came to know the people who lived just across the river; and by going to matrikin *jup* I met a range of people who were involved with the cults of various matriclans: *ngwana kun*, *yɛt kun*, *dəng kun* and *kɔm kun*. Contacts with younger English-speaking Mapeo Chamba formed a less localised network of people who would drop in to help me with Chamba words which I could not understand or remembered conversations I had not fully grasped. I fitted into the margins of a pre-existing network of dispensers, teachers and absent workers who returned periodically to the village and sought out one another's company to celebrate Independence Day, Christmas, Easter or simply to drink beer and chat. These people tended to be known by their jobs.

As my interest fixed on Chamba religion, I spent more time with the 'traditionalists' in my network of contacts. The available social worlds in Mapeo were relatively insulated in many contexts; *jup* was said to be the reason for the separation of traditionalists' interests and activities (Chapter 9). The differences between my socialisation, enculturation, or adoption and that of a Chamba bear upon the use to which a fieldworker's experience can be put. The partiality of my knowledge about Chamba cults, a necessary corollary of having been adopted as a clansman, would be shared, from their different positions, by all Chamba practitioners. However, my initial problems in apprehending *jup* probably bear slight resemblance to those of a cultural neophyte. Our experiences are marked by different sorts of likely anxiety in the face of the contrast between infancy and adulthood for the neophyte and in that between understandings for the ethnographer. A residue of both anxieties is liable to invest later attitudes towards the object of disquiet: Chamba men never, I think, completely shed the image of cults which they absorb as children. Most ethnographers, at least privately, admit to fear that they entirely misunderstood the societies they studied.

My initial apprehension of *jup* as a class of ritual practice was in the course of a first visit to Mapeo that coincided with the major harvest *jup* called *jup kupsa*. I saw the festival again in its entirety in 1977 and in part in 1984. Within a matting enclosure erected for the purpose, three men play different kinds of drum: a tall standing drum, with a schematic relief carving of a man, a large tom tom, like the first hand beaten, and a third drum, a smaller version of the second, vigorously beaten with a stick, providing a pulse for the overall orchestration. Seven other men circle the drummers swaying, bobbing and playing a tuned set of gourd horns, that range from something under a foot to about five feet in length. The sounds of the horns are, according to length, between that made blowing through a comb covered with tissue paper and the lower end of the range of brass instruments. Two of the horn players shake rattle bags of basketry with inverted calabashes as bases. Small fruit seeds inside the bags create a shuffling, scudding rhythm to accompany the drums and horns. While men play instruments inside, women dance in concentric circles and sing outside the enclosure. The performance in its entirety is described as *jup kupsa dɔp sɔn*, dancing to *jup kupsa* music.

I am told that the enclosure is built so that women cannot see the *jup*, of which they are supposed to be afraid. But, in swaying back on their heels, the musicians often, and apparently purposefully, raise their gourd horns above the matting walls; moreover, the enclosures in which the *jup* performs on some nights are in less than perfect repair. Although the women fix their eyes upon the ground while dancing, the source of the music can be no mystery to them. 'It is not good for women to see the *jup*; this spoils the *jup*'. However, '*jup kupsa* is not *giran*'; 'it does not catch anyone'; '*jup kupsa* is just for dancing'. By implication, other cults are something more or something else.

What, then, is *jup*? The performance, or something behind the performance that the performance demonstrates? I never answered the essentialist question, and no Chamba could answer it for me. The question is inappropriate, un-informed. Rather than being something, *jup* now seems to me a field of different attributes among which relevant aspects are accentuated according to circumstances. For children, *jup* is something controlled by the elders: either a bush animal or the dead issued from their graves. For women, *jup* is the preserve of men, about which, by definition, they are supposed to know nothing. But their ignorance is only conventional: arriving to collect Titlesime on the way to a cult rite some months later, his wife let me know he had already departed by raising her right arm, hand curved downwards, to the level of her mouth, shaking the left hand at her side, as if she held the cult rattle, and performing a very passable imitation of the shuffling dance of the cult players. Through this mime, she barely observed the injunction against women speaking about hidden aspects of *jup*.

For men, connotations of *jup* increase in complexity since initiation, and ownership or custodianship of them defines the worth of the man in terms of the obligations he is able to discharge to his own status and that of his clansmen. For all concerned, though for different reasons, *jup* do not seem to be entirely knowable.

JUP

Cults appear rather different from within and from outside their organisations. The outsider might infer some characteristics from ways that *jup* are recurrently discussed. It would be apparent that each type of *jup* has a name, although frequently these names are either devoid of meaning or have a sense that bears no ready relation to the attributes of the cult. Named *jup* are owned by named patriclans, matriclans or both. Some *jup* are said to be patriclan *jup* (*jup da bɛ*, father's cults), others are matriclan *jup* (*jup kunan*), while those that remain are owned by both sorts of clan (*da i kun*). Clans, most especially patriclans, are identified with the *jup* they own as one name with another (thus Yangurubu, or other clans owning the same cult, may alternatively be called *bɔntɔng tu bu*). Some cults are owned by many clans; others occur just once in Mapeo village.

Most *jup* are associated with a disease or misfortune of which they are both cause and cure. The range of diseases is comprehensive (the Appendix indicates how comprehensive); however, some complaints attract more attention than others. In Mapeo, cults concerned with bad deaths (by leprosy or epilepsy and burning) and with snake bite are particulary numerous. Only one named cult is devoted to other diseases Mapeo Chamba distinguish. Cult contagion, the way '*jup* catch (*gut*) people', is never random; *jup* are moral, rule-governed forces, though sometimes ambiguously so.

Members pay to 'see *jup*'; grades of initiation range from 'seeing a little' to 'seeing all'. All those who go to the cult meeting place (*jup bum*) may be called *jup tu bu* (*tu* being a particle that associates people with things or attributes; *bu* simply a plural). In Mapeo, members of the world religions may use this form to describe adherents of Chamba cults (or they may prefer the pejorative *dɔ*). Between cult practitioners, *jup tu* refers especially to those who have seen many *jup*.

Members of any cult periodically meet to make gifts of newly ripening crops to their *jup*. One or more crops is taboo (*giran*) to members of every cult before such offerings are made. Failure to observe this prohibition is one of many circumstances which provoke *jup* to afflict people with their particular form of distress. Payment must be made on behalf of an afflicted person by his or her matrikin, in order that appropriate ritual can be performed and *jup* medicine (*jup gɔn*) applied (*sɔ*) to the patient. All other things being equal (which they frequently are not) the affliction should end.

Membership of *jup* is prestigious in terms of the traditional life cycles of both men and women (who have their own cults called *jɛm*). Traditionally, people who have livestock and guinea corn with which to make beer should give that wealth to *jup* in order to be 'shown' (*'isi*) and 'see' (*nyɛn*) *jup*. Chickens dedicated to the *jup* become *jup kpa*, beer given becomes *jup sim*, and so on for other items. Once something belongs to the *jup*, with a few precise exceptions, it cannot safely be eaten, drunk, or in the case of cult apparatus, handled, by non-initiates.

Jup appear publicly on many different occasions, not only at the harvest festivals (of which Mapeo has four), but also at different stages of funerary celebrations, and when *jup* 'shuts the road' in order to drive out diseases. On these occasions some *jup* are associated with songs and dances (*jup* are said to dance, sing, eat and drink). Women and children should fear and respect men's *jup* (*lat lari*), and men should fear *jup* of which they are not members.

Seen from the outside in terms of such attributes, *jup* are potentially danger-ous agents that have to be managed, usually by men. They are differentiated by the diseases they cause, the manner of their public performances and the categories of clan members who own them. Outsiders know little about the internal organisation of *jup*. Attributes are loaded onto the name *jup*: *jup* are anthropomorphised (*jup* dances, sings, drinks beer, eats, catches people, comes to the death compound, shuts the roads and so forth) and explicitly likened both to animals of the bush that roar, and the dead who speak. The pervasiveness of the term *jup*—prefixed to practitioners, places, livestock, beer, and performances—spins an impenetrable lexical web. Outsiders ac-quire the more fetishised version of what *jup* is.

To know much more than this about *jup*, it is necessary to be a member. Although the hiatus is not absolute, insiders' accounts present *jup* as something closer to technologies than fetishised agencies. Much that appears unclear from the outside becomes clearer to the insider, but this knowledge generates fresh areas in which ignorance may prevail.

Jup are highly individualised; each type of named *jup* has an apparatus, a performance, and a set of rules which affect: commensality, eligibility for membership, the cost of admission, the stages of admission, the way in which rites are carried out, and the times at which rites are obligatory. Although *jup* have generic features, such particularity makes knowledge of *jup* a true specialism. Those who can be said to 'know things about *jup*' (*nyi jup pɛn*) have committed to memory a considerable body of particulars—not least because this knowledge is their only means to avoid inadvertently breaking the rules and turning *jup*'s capacity for affliction upon themselves.

Payment to 'see' *jup* is justified by the danger posed to non-initiates by things associated with the cult (its paraphernalia, the leaves on which it is made, the beer and animals consecrated to it and so on); all *'jup* things' are *giran*, dangerous, and will cause affliction to anyone who improperly comes into contact with them. The scale of payment is only loosely related to the severity of distress the cult controls. A more direct relation may be traced between expense and ownership of the cult. Since membership of their major cults is virtually obligatory for patriclan members, who traditionally began their induction at circumcision, payment is low, usually no more than a couple of chicken. This contemporary fact is related by informants to a historical circumstance: patriclan cults, unlike those of the matriclan, were not sold to their present owners but shared as a token of alliance ('one father', *da nonsi*).

The level of entrance payment does not affect the standard reparation the matrikin of anyone caught by a cult must make in order to gain relief from distress. Payment consists of a goat, chicken, dried meat, basket of guinea corn, calabash of guinea corn flour, bambara groundnuts (both raw and roasted), salt and soup ingredients—in short, all the foodstuffs which Chamba reckon traditionally to be their own. To be exhaustive the reparation includes the fruits of both male and female labour, not only by virtue of the donation of guinea corn and bambara groundnuts, traditionally the staple crops cultivated by men and women, but also because of the requirement for processed foods (guinea corn flour and roasted bambara groundnuts) which require additional inputs of female labour. In addition to the foodstuffs, contributions of beer, in both thin and thick varieties, have to be made in order to complete the inventory of Chamba gastronomy. The payment to repair the cult is, in cultural terms, a total payment.

Cults in which membership is optional, reflecting personal prestige, rather than effectively statutory, like major patriclan cults, have the greatest entrance payments. Failure of members to pay entrance fees, or to make contributions to regular meetings, or failure of matrikin to pay reparation when a cult has caught one of them, are the most common explanations for the afflictions that cults visit on their victims. But they are not the sole reasons: disrespectful behaviour in the cult place is also a sufficient cause for a person to be caught by the cult. So is failure to observe the injunction against sexual intercourse on the night before a practitioner knows that he will have to handle the cult objects. These cases, predominantly of omission or inattentiveness, and not closely related to standards of morality outside the cult system, are augmented by other reasons directly concerned with everyday life. Properties may be protected by leaving a symbol of a cult by them; a thief will automatically fall victim to the *jup*. Even after the event, the power of *jup* may be invoked to catch thieves or witches. Some specialised cults automatically punish deviation from ideal behaviour: *jup dagan* catches parents of breech born children, or the children of adulterous women, if their husbands are cult members; *jup ya* apprehends the lovers of the widows of its members. In both cases, payment may be made and ritual performed to avert the misfortune and 'repair' the cult. Danger, payment and contagion are mutually entailed.

Materially, *jup* consist of 'things' (*jup pɛn*) and performances directed towards such things (especially libations and sacrifices) or achieved with them (dances, songs or noise more generally). Gourd horns, rattle sacks of basketry, iron rattles and bullroarers are the most common instruments of the cults. Other things (coloured stones, figurative statues, shells, animal skulls, animal figures, to mention only the most common), are hidden, usually under pots, and somehow affect the potency of the *jup*, albeit they appear passively to accept offerings rather than being used in dance or music making.

Many of the instruments, differing only in form and combination, occur in most of the cults. Explanations of their functions have to appeal to generalities relating cult efficacy to the capacities of the dead and the wild. More unusual apparatuses, when they can be explained, elicit accounts in terms more specific to the cult in which they occur.

Cults are associated with leaves and medicines. Cult instruments are lain upon a specific kind of leaf during rituals, and leaves are occasionally used in other ways during cult performance. Given the variety of those potentially available (Chapter 7), an extremely limited range of leaves is put to such uses. Cults also have medicines, the basic ingredients of which are commonly 'female medicine' (*gɔn nu*, an onion shaped bulb), and 'male medicine' (*gɔn lum*, a type of common succulent that is quadrangular in cross section). Medicine plants are grown both in the cult places (*jup bum*) and in the compounds of traditionalists, especially to the side of the entrance to the home (Chapter 7). Features common to many cults include the use, in part or in its entirety, of a red–white–black colour triad (Chapter 8).

The social organisation of *jup* affairs is shared to an even greater extent than apparatus. Meetings of *jup* members are serious yet highly convivial occasions when numerous pots of beer are drunk and large quantities of meat consumed. How much beer is brought, and of what type (thick, *sim 'im*, or thin, 'beer water', *sim 'og*), what animals are offered, and how they are killed, depends upon the *jup* being made and the occasion for which rites are performed. In general, by virtue of their higher entrance payments, as well as the more relaxed domain of clanship of which they are part, matriclan *jup* meetings often come closer to being gastronomic blow outs, while patriclan meetings tend to be more serious and less self-indulgent. But *jup* in general, and matriclan *jup* especially, are enjoyable occasions, and part of the fun comes from knowing that others have been excluded from the goings on.

Within each group of men who meet to 'make' *jup* is a rough ranking of owners, custodians and those who have seen more or less of the *jup*. Owners are usually members of the clan which originated, bought, or otherwise came into possession of the cult. They have 'seen all' the *jup*, or 'finished it' and may alternatively be called 'fathers of the cult' (*jup da*). Responsibility for organising the meetings, brewing the beer and summoning the members, devolves on 'children' of the cult 'fathers'. In matriclan *jup*, this means those classificatory 'children' whose fathers were matriclan members, and who may themselves be elders. 'Children' in patriclan cults are the younger elders of the owning patriclan, roughly those in the next to senior generation. These men are said to seize the *jup* in hand (*gut wa*). Owners and holders are together responsible for carrying out the formal procedures of making offerings to the cult (*be jup*), or releasing the power of the *jup* to seek out such offenders as thieves or witches (in general, *jup ngwangan*, or, *ngwɔk kpa ti* when referring to the particular action of piling [a stone on] the head of a chick), or speaking appropriately during the *jup* meeting (*balin jup mum*).

Those who attend other than as owners or holders of the cults are there because they have paid for initiation either into the version of the cult being held or into a comparable cult owned by some other grouping. Most *jup* are owned by several Mapeo clans. Once he has joined one version of the *jup* a man may, if he wishes, attend to drink beer at other versions. Sometimes cult groupings in different clans enjoy formalised relations of co-operation and attendance at each others' rituals. Such arrangements are supposed to have originated when one clan purchased the cult from another, or from a recognition of a 'one father' or 'one mother' relation between the owning clans, or simply because men found one another's company congenial at some time in the past. Apart from all these people (owners, holders, members who trace extended clanship to the owning clan, initiates to identical cults, and members of co-operating cult groups) *jup* meetings, particularly those of matriclan cults, are usually attended by initiates belonging to the clan's joking partners, who can be guaranteed to enliven proceedings. The group of men encountered at any particular meeting has assembled for diverse reasons.

In describing, as I have been, how *jup* is spoken about in different circumstances, or what people do in situations defined as *jup* performances, the question of what *jup* is recedes from attention. Direct quesions about the nature of *jup* only elicit answers like: it is something our grandfathers left us, or, something the *wurumbu* gave us, or, it is our 'big thing', or, it is something for the elders. Questions about the particularities of a *jup*: its entrance cost, the number of times it is 'made' each year and when, the people who may join or attend it and so forth, if they are asked at an appropriate place and time, elicit much more direct answers. *Jup* is active, singular, and in some contexts treated as a form of being, but above all it has a given quality. Its conceptual status, as composite of attributes of the dead and the wild with a leaven of human sociality, is closely akin to that of the human subject itself.

My initiation to membership began with two *jup* to which my clan affiliations entitled me: the major patriclan *jup* of the Yangur, called *bəntəng*, and a version of the important matriclan *jup* called *karbang*, belonging to *ngwana kun*. Both *jup* were owned by other clans: patriclans in the first case and matriclans in the second. In both cases co-ownership of *jup* was a source both of co-operation and competition. Later, I 'saw' a number of other *jup* in varying degrees of completeness. Like Chamba elders in Mapeo, my knowledge of different cults is uneven: in some I 'saw everything', in others I 'saw a little', and in others I 'saw nothing' but knew of the cult only by name and in terms of certain of its attributes and ownerships.

This patchiness is evident in the many omissions from the Appendix. Since *jup* are concealed, everyone's knowledge is partial and related to their clan and local affiliations and to various exigencies of the path through the network of affiliations that they choose to follow. Some men enter a few *jup* belonging to their closest clans and attempt to see these through to the end. Others operate in a more diffuse manner, becoming members of most of the *jup* to which they have some entitlement but 'finishing' few of them. Each cult, on close inspection, has its own history and miniature culture—its personality. This can be demonstrated only by looking at a few examples in the sort of detail that practitioners find fascinating.

JUP OF THE FATHER

Cult of the father (*jup da bɛ*) is one arm of the three-pronged classification Mapeo Chamba make of cult ownership; cult of the matrikin (*jup kunan*) constitutes a second arm leaving *jup da i kun pɛ*, cult of the father and the matrikin also, as an unmarked and residual third. Cults owned by a single type of clan tend to share characteristics.

Common ownership of a patriclan *jup* (*jup da bɛ*) is cited by informants to explain why members of the co-owning patriclans claim to have 'one father' (*da nonsi*). Occasionally, the relation may be explained the other way around: by virtue of a common origin the clans share the *jup*. Regardless of imputed causation, on the basis of this nexus between common descent and cult ownership Mapeo patriclans can be classified into a very few clusters. Compared to other Chamba places, this facet of organisation is uniquely important in Mapeo.

Yangurubu (the author's adopted clan) and Liranɛpbu are the most populous members of a cluster of Mapeo patriclans that shares the *jup* called *bəntəng*. Another cluster of patriclans, which shares the name Yambu with different distinguishing suffixes, owns a *jup* called *yaguman*. *Yaguman* and *bəntəng* are the paradigmatic examples to which informants refer when they speak of father's cults. Both are *jup* to which access is relatively restricted: only patriclansmen and the sons of patriclan women are usually allowed to join. Non-members can only guess at the precise nature of the rituals carried out by cult members, which are known to involve the treatment of the bodies of deceased patrikin. This uncertainty is expressed in a Mapeo aphorism cum joke: *Yambu kut ya i wu tari* (Yambu defecate in the entrance hut), i.e. something unpleasant is happening out of sight.

The most important rituals of the two *jup* overtly concern annual collective remembrance of their clan dead. Both performances are sufficiently dramatic to occupy the attention of the entire Mapeo community, if only through avoidance. There appear to be historical reasons for the timing of these annual rites, which in comparative Chamba terms are atypical.

Yangurubu and Liranɛpbu, both reputedly clans of northern origin, arrived relatively late in Mapeo and settled together at the eastern end of the village by the river called Da Lira. The Liranɛpbu, commonly supposed to be of Bachama or Bata origin, are believed to have taken their name from the river (or given their name to it). Not having been Chamba from their beginnings, both clans became Chamba. Which clan owned the *jup* in the first place is itself part of their current dispute, but for years they apparently performed rituals together until the outbreak of a dispute led them into a state of armed confrontation followed by a latent antagonism, at least in matters concerning *bǝntǝng*, which has lasted over a half century.

Yambu are also ethnically distinct in origin. The main body of their patrikin lives far to the west of Mapeo in the northern Shebshi Mountains, where they rule over a number of small conquest chiefdoms founded during the nineteenth century. Their Mapeo contingent settled initially at the western end of the village. On their arrival, according to all accounts, they found patriclans of predominantly eastern, that is Chamba Leko, origin in occupation of the village. These Leko clans had put in place the Mapeo harvest festival of *jup nyɛm*, the initiating, and politically most important, cycle of a four cycle series of harvest rites. The festival is set in motion by Gbanmɛmbu (who claim to have arrived in Mapeo as emissaries of the chief of Yeli) and then continued by versions of the same *jup* belonging to the priests (*ngwan*) of Sanbu and Jangbu patriclans that trace origins from Chamba Leko areas further north than Yeli. In recognition of the Leko origins of Gbanmɛmbu, Sanbu and Jangbu, dancing *jup* of the type that appears around harvest time, and also at funerals, may be called *jup Jang*, the cult of Chamba Leko. Finding the harvest cycle fully subscribed, the new immigrants established their patriclan *jup* at other times in the calendar. The *bǝntǝng tu bu* (people of that cult) hold their death beer (*we sim*) at the end of the dry season, around late February or March, while the *yaguman tu bu* hold their death beer between the first and second cycle of harvest festivals. A fourth cluster of patriclans, predominantly claiming western origins (including Tirannɛpbu and Dagabu), share another father's cult called *jarɔ*; their major rituals coincide with the first of the harvest cycles.

The association between four blocs of patriclans and their different father's cults is a telling sign for Mapeo Chamba of the diversity of patriclan cultures. Other ritual markers accentuate the distinctiveness: thus patriclans that own *jup Jang* gourd horns tend not to possess *lera* bamboo flutes; some patriclans have, while others lack, *nam gbalang* masks (Chapter 7), funerary customs differ and so on. These differences persuade Mapeo Chamba that separate ethnic origins imply differing and probably incommensurate practices. From this perspective, the rituals of others communicate only as markers of events and the identities involved in them. There is no underlying system on which to draw. As I noted earlier, this perspective is not the only one open to Chamba exegesists, but it is a particularly influential consideration in the context of patriclan performances.

Of the four father's cults, I know most about *bantang*, by virtue of my honorary membership of the Yangurubu patriclan. The *jup* makes public appearances on three occasions concerned with funeral observances: at the wake (*we kpan*, crying the death, or *we 'og*, death water; water in this case referring to clear beer, *sim 'og*), at the collective ritual of remembrance (*we sim*, death beer) and at 'gathering up the dead' (*we 'ɔsin da*, bringing the death up). Variants on a distinctive cult performance are prescribed for the three occasions.

A story is told of an ingenious forebear who shinned up a tree beneath which witches gathered in the bush. While they danced under the tree, he sprinkled them with guinea corn paste. Continuing to dance they shouted 'Oh, a little bird has shat on us'. Next morning the ancestor called on villagers before they had time to wash and demanded payment from each who bore the tell-tale signs of corn paste on pain of denunciation as a witch. The dance which he had witnessed was incorporated into the *bantang* ritual.

Distinctive to *bantang* is a dance rhythm—struck on the two mouths of an iron double bell, and echoed by a single drummer on two drums of different pitch—that accompanies the tom tom and *lera* flutes. Informants aware of any etymology for the cult name say that *ban* and *tang* are ideophones of the distinct tones of the two bells or two drums. I first saw the cult dance, also a unique feature, during the wake of a Yangur woman. Two phases alternate. The musicians are led by the striker of the bell. Behind him comes a man attired in women's dress, traditionally consisting of two bunches of leaves. (He wears them over his man's kilt, were this a man's wake he would wear the kilt only.) He has hooked a hoe—blade downwards— over his shoulder, an image of women's work, and the calabash on his head is covered with the clan's war shield. Behind him come the *lera* players, while in an outer ring two men, carrying a spear and pestle respectively, circle the assembly in opposite directions. Each time they meet they raise the rights arms holding the objects distinctive to men and women as if in salutation and turn back in the direction from which they came. Initially, the dance is performed with a rather jaunty and strutting gait, but when the tempo changes the dancers hurl themselves around at breakneck speed executing side kicks and waving their knives at onlookers who venture too close. As the percussionists relax the beat, so the dance subsides into its earlier phase.

Like their dance, the most important element of the *bɔntɔng* apparatus came into the possession of the clansmen from the bush. This time the benefactor was not a human with animal-like qualities, but a human-like animal. My version of the story is from a Liranɛpbu source.

A forebear went into the bush to cut grass. As he was cutting he heard a noise and, dropping his sickle, climbed up a tree to hide. From the tree he saw a lion kill an antelope with a strange type of throwing weapon. After he killed the antelope the lion could not find his weapon; he took off his animal skin to become a man and wandered around looking for it. The lion heard a noise as the man shifted position in the tree, he had already seen the sickle dropped in the grass and wanted to warn its owner to reveal nothing of what he had seen—how lions could change into men, or about the special weapon used for hunting. He called the man to come down from the tree and, fearing that otherwise the lion would climb the tree and kill him, the man did so.

The lion man asked where the weapon had landed and the man replied, 'Over there, under the leaves'. The lion told him that he could keep two of the tools, which were hard like iron and yet not iron, and that he should keep them as a secret thing. Everyone he showed them should give him a goat or a chicken. But he should never tell how he found the weapons. If people did not want to see the weapons, then the lion would call the man into the bush and give him meat to eat.

But our forebear ignored the lion's wish and gave the weapons to his father. Neither did he keep their origin a secret. Often the lion would call to him from the bush to come and receive meat. One day he was sitting with friends when the lion called him to come and receive meat. 'This lion is really bothering me', he said to his friends, and left to the bush. The lion heard the conversation and was angry that the source of the meat had been revealed and warned the man not to approach him. But the man wanted to receive his meat, so the lion killed him. However, the lion could not recover the *bɔntɔng*, as the forebear's father had hidden them.

I have not seen the objects to which the story refers; they are claimed not to be throwing knives but kidney shaped discs. The last custodian of the *bɔntɔng* died before he initiated a successor. One man dared to look under the pot which concealed the *bɔntɔng*, and he died. Since then, no one has looked at the *bɔntɔng*. I do not know whether indeed no one has seen the most important element of the cult lately; the story is certainly believed by some with whom I have talked about it, and there is scope in Chamba practices for such a situation to occur.

The *bəntəng* dance and cult objects both have a source in the bush and, more immediately, from forms of life that are ambiguously animal and human. However, the connotations of danger and power are diffuse rather than specific. *Bəntəng* is held responsible for malformed births, death in childbirth and broken bones, especially when caused by falling. None of these maladies relate directly to the stories of origin, unless we choose to associate the dangers of falling with the fact that both ancestors observed events in the bush from trees—not a parallel that any informant has drawn to my attention. Whenever stories of the origin of cults can be recalled, and not all have them, ambiguously human sources are involved: witches, the dead, or shape changing animals.

The stories about *bəntəng* also share the narrative device of human ingenuity: in observing the witches dance in the first tale, and in concealing the *bəntəng*. Artful deception is a human asset: one *lera* song is a homily that says if an elder (*nɛ wari*) does not know how to deceive (*nyi yira sɔ*), he will surely sit alone. However, human cleverness can land the over ingenious in mortal danger: for instance, seers are liable to be beaten to death for their thefts from *wurumbu* (described in the last chapter), and the husband of the bushcow ancestress, like the man who gained possession of the lion's weapon, was killed by his animal familiar when he revealed to companions (in circumstances a Chamba listener would certainly construe as a convivial beer drink) the animal identity of that other.

Craving for meat is a more obvious theme of the stories: *jup* provides meat to men that they cannot share with non members. The meat eating propensity of *jup* (*jup tan kaka*, the cult eats meat) evokes the association between *jup* and the flesh eating animals of the bush. Finally, we may note that the theme of concealment appears in both stories. The elder in the first story conceals the identities of the witches because he receives payment; in the second story, failure to conceal the identity of the lion leads to the protagonist's death— although the consequences of his death are ameliorated by his ingenuity and by his gift of the valuable object to his father. The stories appear to evoke not so much properties particular to the cult they are supposed to explain, but more general characteristics of cults: that they are dangerous, related to the animal forces of the wild, secret, restricted in access and yet enticing because of the possibility they hold out of meat.

The symbolism of *bəntəng* rituals also resonates with the general properties of *jup* rather than with the specific symptoms of *bəntəng*. The largest scale annual performance of *bəntəng* takes place at the 'death beer' of the clan (*we sim*). During the night preceding the public phase of the ritual an object, known simply as *bəntəng*, is prepared. A calabash of large diameter is filled

Titlesime leading the Lira clan's *bɔnɔŋ* (1977)). Note the spear and glimpse of *lera* players. The photograph is of the semi-public stage of the ritual.

with alternate layers of earth and sand (*sə* and *gɛra*), which in Chamba colour terminology are respectively black and red. Towards the top of the assemblage, a blacksmith's hammer (*jɔ*) is wedged upright. The hammer represents the *bəntəng* hunting weapons referred to in the tale of origin. To each side of the hammer is placed a relic of the dead, which was removed at the end of the burial ceremony once the mourners have left the graveside; some earth is also taken from the grave. There is dispute over the identity of these relics, and I have not witnessed the making of the assemblage. They are called *wut*, which has the primary sense of skull. However, despite an earlier report to the contrary (Cullen MS), there is agreement that the skull can form no part of the *bəntəng* assemblage, since it is not removed until the flesh has rotted. I have been variously told that the *wut* is a stone put in the mouth of the deceased and removed at burial, a paring of fingernail from the middle finger (this relic is certainly used in another rite of *sɔri pɛn*), or an incisor tooth.

Soil camouflages the shape of the *bəntəng* contents, and the entire package is covered with tightly stitched bands of local cloth coloured blue and white so that it resembles a gigantic egg in shape. Into its top are stuck long white feathers and iron pins. These feathers recall those stuck into the headdresses of boys undergoing circumcision. Iron pins suggest an association with women's head ornamentation. Symbolically, the entire parcel apparently conjures up the idea of the skull. Secondary associations might (for informants offered only the skull referent) cluster around the iron elements inside and outside the parcel, or else pursue the associations of the feathers and coloured cloth to recall the analogy between skull taking and circumcision.

Elders of the patriclan owning the *jup* sleep with the parcel for the night in the 'death compound' of the hamlet (*we ya*, the compound in which the deaths of outmarrying women, or emigrant men, are mourned if they have no immediate kin in the hamlet). This compound becomes the focus of activity for the duration of the cult.

Provisions for the 'death beer' are supplied by the relatives of the deceased. A levy of two pots of beer is made on every resident male member of the patriclan. Two pots are also given by wives of the men who died during the year and as many as eight by each husband to whom a woman bore children or with whom she remained for long. Just as at the wake or death crying (*we kpan*, *we 'og*), *bəntəng* will not perform unless animals are donated to its owners. A goat and an unblemished large white cockerel are given by the matrikin of the deceased; these donors are usually her sons if the deceased is a woman. Wing feathers of the cockerels are stuck into the *bəntəng* bundle and, before the dance can take place, some of the down from the chest of the bird is thrown onto the cult object. Only if it adheres can the ritual continue, if not there has to be discussion of possible impediments and disagreements followed by further attempts to secure a propitious response. The test is said to test the approval of the *wurumbu*. When all is well, the public phases of the ritual begin.

Playing the *lera* flutes inaugurates this, as all other death celebrations. People gather at the death compound in the morning: the success of the event will depend not only upon correct execution of the prescribed ritual, but also on satisfying visitors' thirst for beer—in so far as this is ever possible. Once the *lera* players complete their performance, they give way to *jup dagan*, the cult that 'lightens', or makes clean. Aetiologically, this is a cult concerned with women's adulterous liasons, and the pollution of breech births. *Jup dagan* performs with gourd horns and rattles in similar fashion to the harvest cults. The performance includes no curative ritual on this occasion, since the cult attends to 'help' rather than 'cleanse'. Sanbu bring their *jup dagan* to help their joking partners Yangurubu; Liranɛpbu are assisted by their co-residents Dagabu. While this is going on, the final preparations for *bəntəng* are made in the test of sticking chicken down to the skull-like bundle.

Goats are sacrificed and divided in different customary ways. Yangur donate a leg to each of four patriclans with which they share their cult; the head of the goat is given to the man who carries the *bəntəng*; he is always the son of a Yangur woman. The back, cut into two sections (the male upper back, *kum lum*, and the female, lower back, *kum nu*), is given to the two drummers, both Yangur, while the chest and innards are said to belong to the *jup*, which is to say that they are consumed by the owners of the cult. The Liranɛpbu distribution of meat reflects the co-operation of two matriclans in their per-formance. The head of the goat is given to the member of the elephant matriclan (*kɔngla kun*) who beats the gong for them. One leg is given to members of the mist matriclan (*jam kun*), and the other to the Dagabu patriclansmen, who brought *jup dagan*. What remains is consumed by the cult owners.

The main performance begins in the early afternoon. The drummer strikes out low and high notes on his two drums: *bən tung tung, tung tung tung*; the theme is repeated on a double ended drum (*mum bara*, two mouth) which has been upended, and on the double hand bell. The bell player is followed by the headloader of the *bəntəng* bundle who now carries the sickle of the cult over his shoulder. Behind him is the bearer of the war shield, followed by men with the spear and pestle of the cult. Other men and boys cut sticks or brandish knives. The circling dance begins with a mincing step to the six-beat riff of the drums and gong. As the momentum increases the younger men perform high side-kicks stirring up the dry season dust in an increasingly agitated circling. The holders of the spear and pestle continue their stately procession around the outside of the dance. As the drumming slows, and a back beat is introduced, the dancers organise themselves into a stately file once more until the fast tempo returns and they throw themselves into a yet more energetic version of the dance waving their weapons at bystanders who, on coming too close to the *jup*, fail to remove their caps and upper clothes as a sign of respect. Old women, past childbearing, may join the later phase of the dance; but younger women, especially if they are pregnant or have a child at the breast, should not even catch sight of the cult for fear that their children may suffer. A young friend refused any longer to carry the *bəntəng* bundle once he knew that his wife was pregnant.

Shortly after nightfall, the two groups of *bəntəng tu bu* arm in recollection of their old conflict. Led by the bell players and singing war songs of their clans, they carry the *bəntəng* assemblage into the dry bed (*ləng*) of a river by Natup. The elders descend into the river bed to empty the contents of the *bəntəng* and smooth the place where they have left the earth and sand. The cult objects are concealed in their clothing. First Lirancpbu and then Yangurubu descend into the river bed, timing their arrivals so as not to meet.

The following day is taken up with dances. Yangurubu perform a dance called *gang dəp sən*, chief dance music, which celebrates their chiefship: clan members deck themselves out in turbans and umbrellas, the accoutrements of chiefship copied from the Fulani. The following day, the third of the celebration, the Yangurubu chief, *wut gang* or skull chief, leaves to repair the shrine of the clan dead, where skulls of the dead are kept along with small beer pots to receive periodic offerings of beer. A new pot is added to the collection for each of the deceased, and a small offering is made to each of the pots. Apart from a virginal boy, who takes responsibility for handling some of the apparatus, the skull chief carries out this ritual alone. *We sim* is completed. The events have occupied three days, just as for the wake of a man. Periodically, such as at the accession of a new chief, the ritual must be more elaborate: then every clansman brings a chicken to be sacrificed at the skull shrine.

A last observance occurs months later, during the wet season. I know only by report that this involves a reversal of the final stage of the *we sim* when the death (*we*) is brought back up to the village (*we 'əsi(n) da*). What is actually returned is a relic of the dead, possibly a part of the clothes in which the person died.

In many respects, *bəntəng* is directly comparable to *yaguman*, the cult of the Yambu. Both are patriclan cults, from which non-patrikin are largely excluded. Only Yambu, or men with Yambu mothers, may be initiated into the cult, and the initiation begins after circumcision, when the boys give a head of guinea corn and an arrow to be shown the leaves on which the cult is made. Like *bəntəng*, the final cost of the cult is not high, only two chickens. But various abstentions make initiation onerous in Chamba eyes: during the final stage the initiate has to cut himself off from the community—carrying his own sleeping mat, and his own calabashes in which to take food and beer, and abstaining from sexual intercourse for three months.

Both patriclan cults hold annual death celebrations: in mid dry season for the *bəntəng tu bu* and mid wet season for the *yaguman tu bu*. Both rituals are as intimately related to patriclan sponsored rites of passage as they are with the symptoms and medical functions of the cults. *Yaguman* is associated with painful, pus-filled swellings which must be lanced with an arrow head before the medicine of the cult is applied. The initial initiation payment of an arrow refers directly to this lancing. More generally, the cure associated with the cult evokes a violence against the body that informants readily relate both to the martial reputation of the Yambu (especially in their carving out of chiefdoms in western Chambaland) and to the enactments of aggression that form part of their collective death rituals.

Yambu practices are considered the most anomalous (unChamba) of the death observances found in Mapeo. Bodies of dead Yambu are seen only by those initiated into the patriclan cult; they are said to become a *jup* thing and therefore dangerous (*pɛn giran*). Whereas other Chamba are interred in shaft and niche graves, into which their flexed bodies are placed lying on their left sides, Yambu dead are apparently interred on their backs with their hands raised to cover their eyes. Instead of the grave mouth being sealed with a stone or inverted pot, the entrance is overlaid with branches and a grave mound of earth about two feet high is built. At burial, the gourd horn of the *yaguman* cult is sounded within the grave, and a relic of the deceased is taken from the grave: said to be the broken mouthpiece of a gourd horn for the men, and for women a small stone, earlier placed in the corpse's mouth. These relics, like those of *bɔntɔng* called skull (*wut*), are added to the apparatus of the cult.

The Yambu 'death beer' occurs during a lull in agricultural activity. The elders meet on the night before the ritual and remain in a hut with the cult apparatus. They eat heartily and apparently sacrifice at least three chickens; their esoteric activities must include preparation of such cult objects as the collection of stones coloured red and white (possibly grave relics) which remain covered under an upturned pot during performance of the cult. During the night, these cult emblems are moved out of the hut to a cleared space on the edge of the hamlet. In the early morning, elders and young initiates sit around the upturned pot with their caps, upper dress and shoes removed out of respect for the *jup*. Periodically, the boys leave the 'place of the *jup*' (*jup bum*) and swagger back into the hamlet to the front of the hut in which the elders passed the night. They are accompanied by two older men: one of whom plays a gourd horn, and the other the mouthpiece from such a horn (reminiscent of the male grave relic or an actual example) which accompanies the booming of the former with a high pitched whistling. The boys whistle and swagger, periodically squaring up to wrestle in pairs grasping opponents around the waist or shoulders and attempting to fling them to the ground. The horn players act as umpires, intervening to stop the wrestling from getting out of hand, since bloodshed would spoil the celebration. Their interventions usually prevent boys actually being thrown to the ground. Although the event lacks superficial order, wrestling partners are usually age mates or members of the clans of joking partners. At a signal from the horn players, the boys return to the cult space with the same show of swaggering aggression. Onlookers taking no part in the ritual observe events from a safe distance.

Later in the afternoon, the initiation of youths is undertaken. Each recently circumcised youth is laid on his face after presenting a head of guinea corn to the older youth who will act as his instructor. His mentor lifts him from behind and he is shown the leaf (*ya*) on which the '*jup* is made'. An elder approaches and taking one of the arrows makes as if to incise a line down the centre of the boy's forehead. The boy responds by emitting a loud 'raspberry' between his lips. These actions mimic the lancing of a swelling and eruption of pus from the wound. Once all the boys have been treated this way they run off for another session of grass-pelting and wrestling, while the elders devote themselves to beer drinking. When they leave at evening, they take with them the necks of broken beer pots which will be added to the pot shrine devoted to the clan's dead. As in the *bəntəng* rites, the cleansing cult of *jup dagan* is brought to play its gourd horns. But in this case the performance occurs on the succeeding day, when the ritual is closed.

The death beer rituals of these two patriclan alliances are among the more dramatic events of the Mapeo calendar. As public spectacles they share characteristics. Both encode violence. The performers monopolise the village space and make it dangerous to non-members of their cults, both through the threat of contagion and through more overt physical threat. Both sets of rituals are understood to be violent; they display the relation between *jup* and death. More particularly, they assert the rights of patrikin to assimilate the memory of their dead. To have suffered deaths during the preceding year is, in a sense, prestigious. An elder, commenting on the fact that a small patriclan would not need to perform death rituals that year, posed the rhetorical question, 'Does an empty space meet with death?'. If you are numerous, then some of you will die during the year. Since *jup* maintain their efficacy through association with death, and thereby with the *wurumbu*, the deaths of clan members paradoxically enhance the power of the clan. By performing their cultural particularity, clansmen of these two alliances assert their special rights over their dead and concomitantly exclude others' clans (especially matriclans) from this source of power. *Bəntəng* and *yaguman* respectively threaten the bones and flesh of the living.

JUP OF THE MATRIKIN

The Mapeo Chamba distinction between cults of the father and cults of the matrikin is not unambiguous (for instance, *jarɔ*, a cult of patriclan alliance, is also owned by a matriclan), but the distinction is clear in the majority of cases. *Jup kunan*, cults of the matrikin, unambiguously include all the cults concerned with snake bites (most importantly, *jup lum, karbang, ngwan ji*), the cult responsible for most stomach disorders (*nɔga*), the cult which causes eyesight disorders (*langa*) and all but one of the cults associated with 'bad deaths' through epilepsy and leprosy (kɔngla, la gənsɛn, tɔlɔng; gina has one patriclan and one matriclan owner). Matriclan cults are numerous, and each follows a cycle of meetings dictated by the necessity to offer the *jup*, as it ripens, every crop that is *giran*, or forbidden to cult members. Additional meetings may be called to carry out curative rituals, to receive reparation from the matrikin of an individual caught by the cult or, in the cases of *jup* which 'cry a death', to attend a cult member's wake.

The typical meeting of a matriclan cult lasts about a day, but it has to be planned ahead of this time, since corn must be levied for beer brewing and the beer itself prepared. Most of the *jup* have a place (*jup bum*) outside the village, frequently on the hillside, where some of the cult objects are concealed under inverted pots and where meetings take place. A gathering typically begins in the compound of the cult holder, which the members leave to make their way to the *jup* place carrying the beer and food which they will consume. The day is spent away from the village until dusk, when the members return to the cult holder's compound. The cult instruments enter the compound under cover of darkness announcing their arrival with the blowings and rattlings distinctive of the *jup*. Further beer drinking takes place at the holder's compound, where some members remain to sleep until the following morning when more beer drinking closes the meeting.

The cost of full initiation to matriclan *jup* varies greatly (see Appendix) but is usually more onerous than its patriclan counterpart. All men should belong to their patriclan *jup*, but participation in matriclan cults depends upon a man's means. Apart from numerous chickens and pots of beer, matriclan *jup* initiation may call for sheep and goats, once scarcer than they are now. Most matriclan *jup* have also been transacted between matriclans. While the histories of these transactions, who had the cult first and gave it to whom, are frequently disputed, their cost is not. Slaves and large dyed gowns (equivalent in value to slaves) are said to have been paid for the *jup*. In other cases, cults were acquired by theft from their rightful owners, or as a substitute for a person in settlement of a blood debt.

Informants' efforts to classify matriclan cults usually take as point of departure the misfortune associated with the cult. This is the classification I used to enumerate the named examples above. Both in informants' use of it, and my own, it is readily apparent that, while helpful, the classification leaves a large residual class.

The most numerous class of cults of the matrikin is sometimes called *ngwan ji*, locally glossed as 'gives birth to redness', after one of its members. *Jup* of this type primarily cause snake bite which is accompanied by secondary symptoms that allow the *jup* concerned to be identified: red blotches of blood near the surface of the skin explain the name of *ngwan ji* itself; headache or backache distinguish the actions of other *jup*. Cults of snake bite tend consistently to be associated with the leaf of the shea butter tree; a bunch of such leaves may be left to show that the *jup* is protecting property or crops.

Another class of *jup* causes swollen stomachs, *nɔga*, and is also subdivided according to secondary symptoms, in this case the colour of the excrement of the sufferer. The remaining cults are less amenable to classification.

Some informants group cults that cause leprosy or falling into fires, a symptom of epilepsy, and thereby 'bad deaths'. A variety of other *jup*, to do with enlargement of the genitals, collapsed rectum, eyesight problems, itching, emaciation, lightning strikes and so on are less widely distributed than those I have mentioned, and in some cases less consistently associated with patriclans or matriclans. The cultures of matriclan cults, like those of their patriclan counterparts, are amalgams of shared and particular features.

Nɔga, held responsible for stomach distension accompanied by sharp pain, has two distinct forms distinguished by suffixes: the male, or owl, and the white (*nɔga disa*, owl; *nɔga lum*, male; *nɔga burgi*, white). For Mapeo informants, the term *nɔga* is without etymology. The first of the two cults is owned by at least six, roughly half, of the Mapeo matriclans, the second by three matriclans, two of which have both versions. Both *jup* require an entrance payment of four chickens, but the second type additionally demands a goat; no beer payments are made to either cult.

Owl (in *nɔga disa*) evokes two relations that also occurred in *bəntəng*: with creatures of the bush and with witches. According to different informants, the witch/owl relation is based either on owls being witches' familiars or on their being one of the mutations of witches. The cult apparatus includes a short, straight gourd horn claimed either to be used by witches or to produce a sound like the hooting of an owl. Alternatively, the cult may be distinguished as male: an element in pervasive gender distinctions that Chamba make. White *nɔga*, the second form, is motivated by the observation that victims of this cult excrete white stools. Yeli informants share the names but propose different explanations of them (Chapter 4).

The apparatus of the cult consists of an assortment of *jup* 'things'. There is a pair of iron rattles with variously shaped clappers hung from iron rings: *tɔlɔng* (an open clapper with rings at either end) is said to cause neck pains; *nɔga* (a solid flaring clapper) is responsible for stomach pains; *ban mi* (a small gong) adds resonance to the rattlings. The term *tɔlɔng* refers both to another *jup* and to a creature, a large antelope for some, a unicorn for others, credited with the ability to cause the death of its hunter. The *tɔlɔng* clapper is found only in *nɔga disa*, so the coincidence of neck pains with stomach ache confirms diagnosis that this version of *nɔga* is responsible for the affliction. Rattle *tɔlɔng* are referred to as children of terracotta *tɔlɔng* which, in one version, took the form of small clay tortoises (*fən tɔlɔng*) with bent neck and tail said to cause the neck pains. Other terracotta tortoises, called *fən nɔga*, were claimed to 'grind' (*gɔg*, as for grinding corn) the stomach. A further *jup*, called *vara*, was represented by a knobbly clay stick, said to cause pains in the knees. This borrowing of elements from other cults serves to distinguish the effects of the different *jup*. The defining symptom of the cult, belly distension and stabbing pain, is represented by a calabash pierced with porcupine quills.

Additional objects complete the *jup* apparatus without being symptomatic: calabash horns, a bull roarer (*langa*), stick figures coloured red and representing the *wurumbu*, stones, and a varied assortment of curious objects like 'twin' palm kernels (a pair grown together). Virtually every cult is also associated with a leaf: in this case *bəng*, the leaf of the ironwood or false shea tree, and with a medicine: here, male medicine (*gən lum*), one type of the quadrangular succulent. Although all the items are laid out when initiates are present, during a process of initiation only some of them would be shown to the neophyte while the remainder was concealed in a large pot (*bay*, the type of pot used for beer brewing).

Comparison between *nəga* and *karbang* helps to distinguish relatively invariant from particular elements in the matriclan *jup* assemblages. Although there are no criteria on which Mapeo Chamba could agree to a ranking of cults, they constantly propose, and argue about, such rankings. *Karbang* is the matriclan cult most often cited among the pre-eminent *jup* of the community. It is also the most widely owned matriclan cult: six (half) of the Mapeo matriclans own one version of it, and one of these clans has two versions vested in different sections. The original owners of the cult are supposed to have been the members of the sun clan (*su kun*), whose forebears were instructed by the *wurumbu*.

In *karbang* the medicines and parts of the apparatus of twelve other cults are claimed to have been combined (see Appendix). This is considered to explain why the cult is the most expensive of the matriclan *jup*—costing twenty pots of beer, twelve chickens, two goats and three sheep to 'finish'. However, only the chickens, beer and one of the goats (the goat for finishing, *vin 'agan*) have to be furnished by the candidate alone, while the sheep and first goat may be offered by a number of initiates together. Even after payment of the entire amount, an initiate may have to await the death of a fully initiated member before he is able to see the most secret 'things' of the *jup*. *Karbang* is not one the cults which boys begin to 'see' after circumcision. Even the youngest members of the cult group have to be independent compound owners; and the owners and holders of the cult are usually elders.

The cult instruments of *karbang* consist of a single gourd horn and one bullroarer. No special song or dance is associated with *karbang* and, although (unlike *nəga*) the cult is brought to wakes to be given beer ('it cries deaths'), the observance involves only a private meeting of cult members. This reticence is interpreted as a sign of potency. In the past, I was told, whenever the horn of *karbang* was sounded from the hill, women would rush to stop beer pots with leaves and cover food containers for fear that the contagion of the *jup* would enter the food and drink.

The pre-eminence of *karbang* is reflected in its apparatus as well as the annual schedule of its meetings. In addition to the horn and bullroarer instruments, *karbang* has its own metal rattles, stones coloured red and a central cult mystery normally kept hidden in a pot. This has two elements: a small brass statue of a very old woman (made by Vere) and a collection of bones belonging to past masters of the cult. Only two types of bones are kept: arm bones, which are tightly lashed with fibres to prevent their splitting, and the bones from the lower, female, part of the back (*kum nu*). All are liberally coated with a red mixture of kaolin and oil (*kut*). Deterioration of the bones would result in the entire community suffering from back ache. However, the symptom pre-eminently associated with *karbang* is snake bite and, as with most cults of this class, *karbang* is 'made' upon the leaves of the shea tree (*tup*). Various other leaves are included for diverse reasons. The leaves of a plant called *buri* are included because their stem is red, evoking the redness of the site of a snake's bite. A flowering grass, called *jup ya 'isi* (flowers of *jup ya*), is included because *jup ya* is one of the cults whose medicine is supposed to be included in the cult. On account of this combination, *karbang* causes not only snake bite but also head and back ache.

Every year, *karbang* members hold up to nine meetings to make offerings to the *jup*. Most of these are linked to the ripening of particular crops, and the rituals required on each occasion differ slightly. The meetings are also designed to secure an adequate supply of medicine, which in this case includes both masculine and feminine forms of the common cult medicines, as well as chicken blood, kaolin paste and the scent gland of the civet cat (*mɘt*). The latter is included on account of its smell, but I was unable to elicit more specific explanation.

Snake bite cults are numerous in Mapeo: *ngwan ji* (part of the apparatus of which, consisting of gourd horn mouthpieces (*jup lɘ*), is included in *karbang*), *ngwan kɔblin* (apparently a variant of *ngwan ji*), *jup lum* (male cult), *ngwɔm* and *sunsun*. These cults are associated with the leaf of the shea tree (some with other leaves also) and where I have seen their apparatuses, these seem to consist of various instruments (horns, iron rattles, rattle sacks) statues, and stones. So far as I know, none includes the bone relics of the dead distinctive of *karbang*. Unlike *karbang*, these other cults hold meetings to coincide with the harvest festivals.

Another class of matriclan cults concern 'bad deaths', from leprosy (*kinan*, leper) and epilepsy (*do viri*, to have an epileptic fit; *do* is the verb to fall, *viri* is related by informants to the idea of black (*virgi*) or to blacken (*vit*) although the tones differ). The most important of these cults are called *gina* (from *kinan* leper), *kɔngla* (elephant), *la gɘnsɛn* and *tɔlɔng* (large antelope or unicorn). The first name, directly derived from the term for leper, is self-explanatory.

Elephant cult has a literal Leko equivalent (*dɔna*). Two reasons for the association suggest themselves to informants. Elephant skin is claimed to have a surface texture similar to that of the leper's. Alternatively, or additionally, leprosy is a disease of excessive grease or fat (*'um*), and the elephant is said to be a fatty animal. Most Mapeo informants would claim *la gɔnsɛn* either to have no etymology or to derive from a Leko term (this is possible; the Yeli equivalent is *la gbira*). *Tɔlɔng* is also the term for an animal considered particularly dangerous by Chamba hunters (Chapter 7).

I cannot comment in detail on the rituals of any of these cults. Traditionally, some of their apparatuses would have contained wooden statues. Gourd horns and iron rattles occur in the apparatuses of these as of other *jup*. The leaves used in the *jup* associated with animal species (*kɔngla* and *tɔlɔng*) are from the ironwood tree (*bɔng*); *la gɔnsɛn* is associated with the shea leaf (*tup*). In the cases of *gina* and *la gɔnsɛn* the cult is also associated with a substance called *nibri*, a mixture of honeycomb and soot which has a number of uses: to add resonance to drum skins, and to seal together the different sections of gourd horns. In this context, its referents involve its colour (which evokes the sense of blackness in epilepsy) and its greasy texture (evocative of the grease of leprosy).

The remainder of matriclan cults concern a variety of symptoms that I note, in so far as I know them, in the Appendix. A particularly clearly motivated example is that of *langa*, concerned with disorders of sight. This *jup* is pre-eminently associated with the iron bullroarer. Unlike the foregoing matriclan cults, its leaf is neither shea nor ironwood, but that of the silk cotton tree. A thorny protrusion from the bark of the same tree is kept inside a silk cotton pod. The pod apparently stands for the eye, which it resembles in shape, and the thorn for the pains suffered by the cult's victim. The whiteness of the cotton-like contents of the pod also evokes explicit association with the whiteness of casts in the eye. An eyewash of 'male medicine' is used to heal the cult's patients.

JUP AND SEXUALITY

Jup pervasively bear on relations between the sexes, and sexuality is uniformly excluded from contact with *jup* on pain of being caught by the cult. Control over sexuality is a condition of the efficacy of all cult rituals; it is additionally the avowed purpose of some: *jup nu* (female cult) causes impotence in men; *jup dagan* (lightening or cleansing cult) removes the pollution of breech births and forces confession from adulterous wives by the affliction it visits on their children; *jup ya* (leaf cult) receives payment before widows may resume sexual activities; *jɛm*, the women's cult, is concerned with fertility, hunting and a variety of other matters. Although an outsider's categorisation, these cults do share certain attributes: all are relatively widely owned by patriclans and matriclans, and the practices of each are marked in ways which differentiate them from cults concerned with other types of sickness.

A man knows he has been caught by *jup nu* when he cannot maintain an erection. The cult symbol, displayed prominently to protect property and warn off thieves, is a wooden baton with a fibre binding around its upper end. It explicitly represents the erect, circumcised penis. The cult is joined only by older men with adult children. Three matriclans and two patriclans own versions of it in Mapeo, and membership is gained for the modest, but specific, payment of four chickens, a worn out hoe (*ban nuran*, in which *nuran* might contain the female form *nu*), a strainer (*kasi*, made of fine grass and usually for straining beer), and a new calabash (*bum pasi*). The latter three elements are associated with women; the worn out hoe is a parodic echo of the insignium of the women's cult, *jɛm*, that I discuss below.

Cult members meet only once a year, during the wet season, to perform a ritual considered to have its funny side by those who take part in it. Entirely naked, two men face one another in a crouching position, holding a pierced, otherwise entire, gourd of medicine and a worn hoe. Bobbing slightly on his heels one of the partners then drops the hoe and passes the gourd to his partner. The action is repeated by the partner who hands back the gourd to the ritual's initiator. After the hoe has been dropped a third time, medicine is poured into the hands of the participants and they slap it onto their chest and back. Then they fill their mouths with medicine from the gourd, before grasping one another and spurting the liquid from their mouths over one another's shoulder's. Finally, they wash in a nearby stream.

The dropped hoe represents the abrogation of femininity (impotence); squatting (as Frobenius recorded in 1911) is the culturally normative position for sexual intercourse. The vigorous spitting of medicine is described as *waksi*, to fertilise, impregnate—therefore, to ejaculate. Washing, in a nearby mountain river, cleanses the pollution which attaches normally to sexual intercourse (*wa liga*, hand dirt) but most especially in the *jup bum*, or cult place. The pierced gourd container appears to represent a vagina and the medicine evokes semen. *Jup nu* has a secret cult apparatus kept under stones and known to a very few initiates; an early report suggests that this might consist of brass male and female sexual organs. The offering made to it, secretly on the day before the main party arrives to perform the rite, apparently consists of crushed snails (probably to connote semen, but I have no local statement to confirm this). The ritual of the main day of the performance involves sacrifices directed to the batons of the cult, which are brought by all the members and asperged with beer and chicken blood in which down is stuck. *Jup nu*, female cult, is concerned in short with control over the feminisation of men which makes them impotent.

Jup dagan has two distinct concerns: with the regulation of women's sexuality and with the health and normality of children. At least five Mapeo patriclans own versions of the cult, as do several of the matriclans although I lack details in this respect. Various other performances are considered somehow related to *jup dagan*, for instance the *jup ka* cult of the priests particularly concerned with breech births, and the cult of *sɛndu* which leads the cults which 'close the road' to drive out disease (*jup bin bono*). A variety of children's illnesses may be attributed to the cult: all have internal symptoms like pains in the chest, belly ache and vomiting. A woman, under pain of the death successively of all her children, must confess the names of her previous lovers. In their turn, they must pay a goat to the husband (as cult member) under threat of being held responsible for the children's deaths by their matrikin and thereby incurring a blood debt.

This cleansing cult takes part in several public events. Matriclan versions perform at funeral wakes. Patriclan variants appear at the annual 'death beers' of the patriclans. Only patriclan versions are able to *pɔp Su*, beg God, in order to remove the pollution of breech birth. The apparatus of the cult consists of the usual instruments (gourd horns and iron rattles) as well as (in the past) double male and female figurines on a single pedestal kept in the cult place. The esoteric details of the performance are not known to me. The cult is pre-eminently associated with the leaf of the locust bean tree. Switches of these small leaves are used during rituals when the intention is to cool participants with a spray of water like gentle rain. Additionally, the cult is associated with *gɛsi*, a leaf apparently restricted to cults causing vomiting.

Jup ya (*ya*, leaf) is pre-eminently associated with the payments that must be made in order to marry or have sexual relations with a widow of any of its members. It is presently owned by at least four matriclans and five patriclans in Mapeo; informants claim its popularity to have grown during the first half of the twentieth century, apparently a period of marked marital instability (Fardon, forthcoming, a). The initiation fee is relatively high: separate payments of a goat, chicken and five pots of beer, followed by a goat, chicken and six pots of beer, purchase the right to 'take in hand' (*gut wa*) two coloured staffs (*jup kusi*) which form part of the cult's apparatus. I have not seen it done, but I am told that members may grasp these staffs in order to swear to the truth of their statements. Other apparatus includes large versions of the iron rattles, a collection of stones coloured red, white and black, a ritual sickle used in the cult's dance (*lama*), and a particularly large beer jar, called a 'five pot' (*du tuna*), because its capacity is five times that of a standard pot.

This 'leaf cult' is especially associated with the harvest festival of *jup kupsa*. For reasons no one could explain to me, *jup ya* members cook large quantities of yams at the harvest ritual and these, as well as beer, may be given to any non member, so long as they eat and drink without offering thanks—simply leaving 'like a dog'. The yams of *jup ya* are almost always mentioned in the same breath as the fried seeds of *jɛm*, the women's cult, prepared for distribution at the same harvest festival. Although it is not concerned with snake bite, the leaves of the cult are those of the shea tree (*tup*), as well as a type of prolifically flowering grass called *jup ya 'isi*. At the harvest festival, a performance of the cult is danced (I describe its Yeli counterpart in Chapter 6).

The other distinctive performance of *jup ya* occurs at wakes. The cult normally appears outside the death compound twice: first at dead of night, then in the following afternoon. A dance accompanied on horns, rattles and drums involves the cult staffs and 'five pot'. The staffs are thrust along the ground towards the pot (with an action that resembles sweeping with a long handled broom); simultaneously, a man who straddles the five pot grasping its neck backs away from the oncoming staffs. The mouth of the pot points towards the staffs, but only at the end of the dance is one staff planted into the pot mouth. The pot represents the widow's vagina, entrance to which is under the control of the *jup*. Perhaps the choice of an unusually large type of beer pot evokes the mature female qualities of widows with children. Evidently enough, the staffs represent the efforts of men to penetrate the female container. These specific references to the sexual act are only part of a more general sense in which *jup ya* evokes fecundity: by virtue of the coincidence of its annual ritual with the harvest festival, by the distribution of food to initiates and non initiates alike in, what informants always stress to be, extravagant quantities, and with the 'planting' of the grass of *jup ya* during the annual rite (see Chapter 6).

Jɛm, and women's cults more generally, cannot be researched adequately by a male fieldworker. My account is limited to a few things known generally to men. Rather like *jup ya*, the rites of *jɛm* are associated with two occasions: funeral wakes, in this case for women, and the harvest festival of *jup kupsa*. The pre-eminent symbol of the cult is the miniature iron hoe (*jɛm ban*). Pairs of these are rubbed together to accompany the *jɛm* songs during the nights of a woman's funeral wake. Large hoes with metal handles, a foot or more in length, called *ban daga*, are the insignia of the chiefs of women's cults, *jɛm gang*.

All clans, so far as I know, have *jɛm*, although only some have *jɛm* chiefs. Women traditionally became members of the cult after marriage. The cult has two forms: the public type, such as the performance at wakes, and a 'hidden' form (*jɛm 'oran*). The hidden form is rather similar to a man's cult. Its apparatus includes very small versions of iron rattles designed like those in the men's cults, and it has its own sickle. Chicken are sacrificed at the cult meetings, but sacrifice has to be carried out by a man. Various symptoms are attributed to the action of the cult. In women these concern reproductive disorders. Non initiated women who see the cult may find that their periods cease, or that children die in the womb. But *jɛm* may also affect men. Blood in men's urine is supposed to show that they have been caught by *jɛm*, since bleeding from the sexual organ is a female rather than male characteristic. Continuous failure in the hunt is also attributed to *jɛm*. A final symptom of *jɛm*

A meeting of *jɛm* practitioners during *jup kupsa* (1976). The *jɛm gang* shows the hoes of the cult to the neophyte anthropologist.

is said to involve a black smut forming on the guinea corn. In each case, reparation consists of a single chicken, substantially less than the corresponding payment to a man's cult.

The symptoms caused by *jɛm* either involve women's reproduction or else the intrusion of female qualities where they should be absent. Blood in the urine, a symbolic menstruation, is a clear example. But failure in the hunt is similarly related to too close contact with women; hunters routinely avoid sexual intercourse on the night before they intend to hunt or else they know that nothing will be caught. The black smut on guinea corn seems not to belong to this general associative matrix, but we shall see later in how many contexts black is associated with female characteristics.

INTERPRETING THE CULTS

Each cult has a culture of which the most particular features are simplest to interpret. Item x (say a dog's skull in the apparatus of *jup lum*) is related to symptom y (say a snake bite) through some perception of the similarity between the two (in this case biting; for Chamba, like us, dogs and snakes both 'bite', *lɔm*). Instances of this type of resemblance are too numerous to recap, but predominantly they involve perceptible qualities: of sharp things that penetrate the body, round things that grind the body and so forth. Chamba would not attribute effect to such resemblance except within the cult setting, or some similar circumstance.

Other things that cults share, or of which they share variants (leaves, medicines, rattles, horns, colours and so forth), are more difficult for informants to motivate. They depend less upon external motivations than upon sets of internal contrasts. We shall understand these better in the following chapters.

The general associations, between *jup*, animals of the bush, and relics of the dead, are the most difficult to make explicit. Whereas the particular elements are amenable to explanation in technical terms, pervasive associations are difficult to identify with any distinct purpose and tend to be seen as constitutive of the phenomenon, and thereby outside the reach of explication. The contrasting cases that facilitate exegesis are lacking to explain the most fundamental presuppositions of *jup* as an institution.

All cults draw diffusely as well as particularly upon the powers of the dead and the wild. This is clearest in those cases where relics of the heads of the dead are assimilated to the patriclan cult and relics of their bodies to a matriclan cult like *karbang*. But associations with death are more pervasive than this suggests. Many, but not all, matriclan cults attend the funeral wakes of their members in order to 'cry the death'. And at intervals of about ten years, there is said to occur a ceremony, which I have not seen, that involves particular matriclan cults mourning all their dead members during the period (*jup kpa wari*, the cult cries the greats). A more specific link is forged via the iron implements of the cults. Metal cult rattles are called cult hands (*jup wa*); by analogy the individual elements are finger bones (*jup nina*, cult bone). At the burial of a cult master, either an element from one of the iron cult rattles is removed for burial with the corpse, or else an iron tool is left by the body to serve as the material for a *jup* bone. In either case, the iron that is retrieved when the individual's skull is removed is returned to the cult directly or after the smiths have forged a new piece of apparatus from it. In their persistence, iron elements offer a functional analogue of human bones.

Another association, this time with the deceased as *wurumbu*, is represented in the wood or brass figurative sculptures that occur in the cult apparatuses. During cult rituals, the dead are believed actually to be present in the cult place, and their co-operation is one of the reasons that informants give both for certain forms of behaviour indicative of respect (removing upper clothing, clapping) and for the efficacy of rituals. *Wurumbu* were, in many cases, the original donors of cult practices to men.

A different set of associations involves animals of the wild. In the course of my description, I have mentioned by name the lion, owl, civet cat, elephant, antelope, and tortoise; other cults contain the skulls of biting dogs (*jup lum*), and terracotta models of a variety of other animals (e.g. bow-legged sheep in *təmsi gam*). *Jup* itself can be assimilated, at least sometimes, to an animal of the wild (see the description of circumcision in Chapter 5); moreover, the danger of *jup*, as well as its use of techniques that are hidden (literally, 'in the dark'), make it analogous to the activities of witchcraft, the activity of animal-like humans (explicit in *bəntəng* and *nɔga disa*).

In addition to motivation via unique practices and with reference to the agencies of the dead and the wild, *jup* also harness the qualities of the world: colour, gender, number, heat and coldness, partibility and impartibility, and of things in the world: leaves, roots, blood, guinea corn, caolin and so on (Chapters 7 and 8). The difficulties informants face in explaining quite what *jup* is, or why it happens to work, become comprehensible when we take account of these many potential layers of motivation.

Mapeo Chamba tend to favour explanation from an altogether different perspective: that of the social organisation of the cult. Ownership, timing, payment, and the hundred mundane matters of making a cult work preoccupy participants to a far greater extent than the reasons why the cult works as it does. Their acephelous organisation renders co-ordination of cult activities (such as that achieved at harvest time) a small miracle of diplomacy. No agreed framework conceptually assembles the cults relative to one another or relative to other forms of ritual. There is no vantage from which an overall view can be had. That matters could have been otherwise becomes evident when we are able to think about Mapeo in contrast to Yeli.

4

LERA AND *VƆMA*: THE YELI VARIANT

A DIFFERENT SETTING

Separated by a few miles, in many ways Mapeo and Yeli are worlds apart. The modern international boundary has placed the two villages in different countries: Nigeria and Cameroon, the former officially anglophone and the latter practically francophone, the linguae francae respectively Hausa and Fulfulde, at least in the areas where these Chamba live. But the differences are older than that.

The later years of British trusteeship administration, from the mid 1950s onwards, largely removed the Chamba of Ganye Division (later Local Government Area), including those of Mapeo, from the administrative control of Fulani to which they had been consigned by earlier policy (Fardon, 1988, Chapter 9); French administration left Fulani control largely intact. Going back to a yet earlier period, while Mapeo assumed something like its present composition as a hill refuge during the early nineteenth century, Yeli is the relic of one of the oldest of Chamba chiefdoms, which was once recognised as ritual hegemonist by many of the Chamba to its west, including those of Mapeo. During the nineteenth century, the Yeli Chamba appear to have been at once subjected to raids and exactions by the Fulani while clinging to some aspects of their earlier prestige and ritual authority in the eyes of other Chamba communities.

There is also a difference of Chamba language. Whereas Mapeo Chamba speak a dialect of Chamba Daka, the western Chamba language, Yeli Chamba speak a dialect of Chamba Leko, the eastern Chamba language. Cut off from the rest of Cameroon by the Rivers Deo and Faro, the population of Yeli has slumped to about two hundred. Mapeo, as part of the more vibrant local economy of Ganye Local Government Area, with its Chamba chief, has maintained a population of around two thousand. The historical accretion of these layers of difference made the experience of living in the two places dissimilar, and it was easy, on first impressions, to underrate the similarities between them.

However, the connections between the two places are also important.

Traditions relate that the chiefly founders of Yeli arrived from the west and were speakers of Chamba Daka, the language of Mapeo.

The *gang kun*, royal matriclan, were chiefs of Sugu, but their *vɔm* (the Leko equivalent of *jup*) called *sugɛn kin* (Sugu woman) made the rain fall incessantly, so that women could not dry leaves for soup. It was suggested that *sugɛn kin* be removed from Sugu and taken to Yeli. There, the *gang kun* met the matriclans of the red rock chiefs (*gad bəng yɛl kun*) and (in some versions) the baboon clan (*za b[c]ngal kun*). The *gang kun* had salt (*mum yɛba*) which the other clans lacked, and so they were made chiefs.

Elements similar to those in this widely known version of the foundation of Yeli occur in many Chamba traditions of the installation of matriclan chiefly families. Sugu chiefs claim an origin from even further west, in territories associated with peoples who speak Jukunoid languages. In a scene rather similar to that recounted above, they envisage the pre-eminence of the royal matriclan to have been accepted by indigenous patriclansmen (known generically as Jangan) when the newcomers were able to provide salt to offer to the *jup*. A variant of the Yeli story also relates the acceptance of matriclan chiefs by indigenous patriclansmen (in this case the Nyɛmnɛbba). Several other western chiefdoms (Gurum, Yebbi, Danaba, Kiri among the more important) are (or were) governed by royal matriclans supposed to have departed from Yeli subsequent to the establishment of *gang kun* chiefs there. The invitation to remain among them extended to members of a royal matriclan by indigenous patriclansmen is a motif of many of these stories. The variations worked on this relatively limited set of narrative themes invoked to explain the origin of a particular type of chiefship suggest a shared sense of what is appropriate to this sort of account. Elsewhere, I have interpreted such shared elements in terms of a regional network of ritual- and clan-based relations which predated the Fulani jihad, and in which Jukun associations appear to have been prestigious. Vicissitudes of the histories of the individual chiefdoms appear as variants or divergences from the shared conventions (Fardon, 1988).

Some versions of Mapeo foundation also refer to an erstwhile chiefly matriclan that lost its pre-eminence. Like the matriclan in the Yeli story, this was named the 'chief of the red rock matriclan' (*gang van ji kun*). Quite what should be made of these indications, that appear only in some versions of foundation, of the dispossession of a previous chiefly clan is likely to remain unclear. In the Mapeo case, the episode appears to be related to the extension of the authority of the Yeli Chamba over certain specific aspects of communal well-being, especially smallpox, locust infestations and rain. Mapeo Chamba recognised the authority of the chief of Yeli over these but no other matters, and one patriclan that lays claim to an origin from Yeli (Gbanmɛmbu) was entrusted with the duty of forwarding payments from Mapeo in order that such misfortunes be avoided. Apart from corn and fowl, it is recalled that worn out hoes were sent to the chief of Yeli, and Mapeo elders believe that these hoes were used to block the hole from which locusts would otherwise emerge to ravage their crops.

Occasionally, a delegation of Yeli Chamba would visit Mapeo; to the accompaniment of a gourd horn, they would process along the paths within the hamlets collecting any stray animals or people who remained out of doors. All would be taken away under suspicion of carrying contagion. Such visits are recalled to have occurred during the 1950s, and the tradition of a Yeli visit to collect a goat and sack of guinea corn (but not to 'close the paths') continued during the period when I carried out my research. Mapeo Chamba, with the exception of their delegated representatives, did not visit Yeli. As I noted in my description of Titlesime's visit to me in Yeli, the common belief was that they would die before reaching there.

Like their Mapeo counterparts, Yeli Chamba suggest that much of their culture, especially in its ritual aspects, came from elsewhere. This is memorialised in various ways. On his accession to office the chief, drawn from the royal matriclan, changes his patriclan affiliation to that of the people claimed to be indigenous to the mountains on which Sugu had been founded, the Jangan. He becomes a member of the Lumnɛbba patriclan, glossed as a section of Jangan; regardless of his previous patriclan membership, all his subsequent children will be members of this clan. The custom is vaguely claimed to reflect the Jangan origins of chiefship.

The area surrounding Yeli, particularly the hillock aside from the main mountain range upon which Yeli village used to stand, is said to have belonged to the Nyɛmnɛbba, who gave later-arriving clans land on which to build hamlets and bury their dead. The small Yeli hill has a significance in relation to ownership of the land akin to that played by Mama in Mapeo conceptions of territorial rights. In recognition of their ownership of the land, the Nyɛmnɛbba are entitled to appoint most of the priests (*ngwan*) of Yeli. They are responsible also for the performance of the major harvest festivals which coincide with the *jup nyɛm* and *jup kupsa* cycles in Mapeo.

Seen in this light, the Yeli chiefdom is ruled by immigrants of western origin, who were originally Daka speakers, but the land is owned by indigenous people who have always been Leko speakers. The 'Daka-ness' of the royal matrikin is emphasised by the use of particular Daka language terms: the chief is properly called *gang* Yeli, not *gad* Yeli; Daka terms are used for twins born in the royal matriclan; the royal *lera* songs are in Daka language. The chief himself is supposed to be doubly related to the Daka-speaking people of Sugu by his clan affiliations on both maternal and paternal sides.

Modifications to the simple scheme relating incoming chiefs and indigenous priests are explained by stories about the arrival of other patriclans. The most significant change proposed in the stories involved the appointment of a head priest to perform rituals on the chief's behalf. Titled *dura*, the chief's head priest is drawn from a patriclan of northern origin, said to originate either from the Chambaisation of people who were originally Bata or Bachama, or from the close relations entertained with Bata or Bachama by Chamba clans once settled on their borders. The Yeli people discovered, with the arrival of these strangers, that beer used in rituals turned sour and meat became bad; the rituals were spoilt. When the chief asked the immigrants why they did this, they replied because they also wanted to eat something during the rites. So, a member of this clan (the Sambira patriclan) was appointed to be the chief's personal priest.

A member of another patriclan, Jɛngnɛbba which is supposed to be equivalent to the Yambu of Mapeo and other Daka-speaking areas, once retrieved a Yeli chief's stolen hat by changing himself into a small hawk. In recognition of this feat, the Jɛngnɛbba became the chief's bodyguards. Another clan (Gbannɛbba) became the custodians of the chief's *lera* flutes, while a further clan provided the chief's blacksmith. Together, these stories present the image of a small chiefdom evolving over time as the aptitudes of newly arriving clansmen were recognised by the chief who incorporated them as his functionaries, thus overlaying the basic distinction (between an immigrant chiefly matriclan and indigenous priestly, and land-owning, patriclan) that had existed since the inception of the matriclan chiefship.

To what extent the stories mirror events which may have occurred is difficult to tell. It does seem to be the case that Bata/Bachama southward movements, or movements of Chamba from around their borders, took place in the years preceding the jihad. It also seems appropriate that Yambu clansmen, noted for their forceful chiefdom-building activities elswhere in Chambaland during the nineteenth century, should be cast in the role of the chief's bodyguard. More to the present point, the suppositions of foundation and subsequent modification establish the terms in which contemporary Yeli informants outline the development of their chiefdom. The position of the royal clan in these narrations establishes a core value around which history can be recalled to have been made. A narrative device of this type is lacking in the subverted hierarchy of Mapeo. Regardless of the historical indications that might be argued to exist in the stories, the self-image that members of the Yeli community entertain of their chiefdom involves a synthesis of differences—initially reconciled dualistically and later modified by accretions—that represent contributions to a collective culture by clans with different endowments.

The other aspect of the image that Yeli informants entertain of their chiefdom, and which needs to be stressed at the outset, is their sense of its historical importance. The present reduced extent of Yeli makes it appear little more than the impress left upon the place where greatness once was. Again, there are two sides to this. On the one hand, it simply is the case not only that Yeli informants see matters this way, but that they are supported in their vision by Chamba living elsewhere. On the other hand, there is the historical question of the type and extent of the authority once enjoyed and of the period when it was recognised. The ritual relation has continued, as I have noted, to be recognised by Mapeo Chamba. The relation with Sugu is still alive, though with somewhat antiquarian overtones at least from the Sugu perspective. During my stay in Yeli, Sugu officials arrived to beg rain (necessarily called dew) from the Yeli chief. In other places, like Gurum, it appears that the ritual relation has had no significance, outside recollection of it, at any recent period, perhaps since the ruling family there changed around the middle of the nineteenth century. The case that some kind of ritual hegemony did exist in the eighteenth century, albeit we cannot be very sure what it was like, seems highly likely. But for present purposes, it is the sense that Yeli people have of their importance, rather than the historical basis to it, that is germane to my argument.

AN ETHNOGRAPHER'S CONTINUING EDUCATION

The Yeli population is so small that I talked to most of the adult men and many of the women at some or other time. However, my major informants on Yeli history and ritual were the chief himself and his head priest, Dura. During several visits made in 1977, I had come to know the chief and his son Bouba Bernard, who lived in a compound which adjoined his father's. When I returned to Yeli in 1984, Bouba immediately suggested that I should move into his compound. Even had there been anywhere else to live, which there was not, the arrangement would have appealed to me. Bouba had made astonishing strides in French, despite receiving little more than a year's schooling. By virtue of his literacy he was able to act as his father's administrative proxy to the satisfaction of the very small population under his charge. Moreover, Bouba understood some Chamba Daka and volunteered to teach me Chamba Leko. During a stay of six months I could not achieve speaking competence in the language, but thanks to Bouba's translations, and to the fact that many Yeli elders spoke Chamba Daka, I was able to conduct interviews in a mixture of languages or else to understand some of what was being said when Bouba interpreted for me.

Dura's was the next compound to that of the chief's, some thirty yards away, and so it was inevitable that Bouba, his father and brother, along with Dura and his son should be the people whom I saw most often. This suited me well, since I was interested to compare the Mapeo account of ritual with the view from the centre in Yeli. My earlier work had led me to suppose that the Yeli view of ritual would be symbolically more coherent than its Mapeo counterpart. I have had to rethink what I meant by this hunch, but the broad idea preceded my return to Africa.

A number of factors led to my supposition. The most obvious was simply that I was told so: Mapeo elders repeatedly emphasised the special status of Yeli as the source of much Chamba culture. When they did not know the reason for something, they tended to assume that this reason would be known at Yeli. Since they had not been to Yeli, the article was one of faith, or tautology. If Yeli was the source of Chamba culture, then someone at Yeli must know how things fitted together. I was interested to find out whether their views were born out in practice, especially since the accounts I had learned of Mapeo ritual were so wanting in symbolic exegesis.

Prima facie, there seemed to be grounds to suppose that the presence of ritual officers would be likely to enhance the symbolic coherence of ritual exegesis, after all such people had a specialist interest in the comprehension of ritual performance. Other, more specific, factors also transpired to be significant to explaining the differences between the two places. Some of these are better dealt with later: for instance the differences that seem to be attributable to the fact that Leko-speaking Chamba (including those at Yeli) have a colour system with three basic terms, while Daka-speaking Chamba (including Mapeo) have four basic colour terms. Colour associations simply cannot be chained together in Chamba Daka as they can in Chamba Leko (Chapter 8). More generally, there was a dynamic element to the argument that I had overlooked. If Yeli Chamba envisaged their rituals as symbolic performances, they would be able to explain them in terms of a symbolic groundplan. This groundplan, or set of suppositions, ought to help them to keep their symbolic house in order. In other words, their ritual activities would be consistent with the symbolic categories they thought them to enact. The upshot of this should be that most elements of Yeli rituals were amenable to explanation in terms of a few rules. Mapeo rituals could not be glossed this way to the same extent because the practitioners lacked the sense of performing according to general rules.

Hypothetically, if you perform a set of rituals long enough without worrying about their symbolic cogency, ritual codings will become more and more difficult to apply to them. There will be exceptions to any rule you care to think of. Something like this appears to have happened in Mapeo, and it explains why Mapeo Chamba were, in fact, wrong about the status of the rules I would discover in Yeli. These rules could not explain Mapeo rituals, unless it was admitted that Mapeo Chamba were making numerous 'mistakes' in applying them. In order for the rules to 'work', Mapeo practitioners would need to have been following them in the first place.

Yeli exegesis of ritual worked in the way it did, because relations between social categories and between ritual forms were similarly motivated. The same terms could be used of both. The hierarchical organisation of Yeli, crucially expressed by counterposing the composite terms of indigenous, priestly patriclanship against immigrant, chiefly matriclanship, fixed the ideal relations between social categories in a vocabulary that was also used to explain ritual (heat and coldness, *vɔma* and *lera*, head and substance, partibility and impartibility, etc.). Yeli ritual and social classifications drew repetitively upon the same contrasting pairs of terms, and the internal articulations of the categories predisposed people to group terms consistently (indigenous, patriclan priests go with head/skull, heat, partibility and *vɔm*; immigrant, matriclan chiefs go with substance, coolness, wholeness and *lera*). In the absence of conceptually fixed relations between categories of people, even in theory, this assimilation was impossible in Mapeo. Mapeo informants reasoned either that clans were really very similar, or that basically they were very different. Clans could be grouped or contrasted in various particular ways, but they could not be interrelated in a stable fashion between different contexts: the crucial criteria of resemblance and dissimilarity only crystallised around immediate and momentary activities or interests.

Yeli institutional organisation made rituals more amenable to symbolic understanding because ritual moves could be referenced to the different qualities believed intrinsic to those who carried them out. A second point follows from the success of this exercise in comprehension. To the extent that practitioners imagined their ritual to be performed in accordance with a symbolic groundplan, their exegeses were likely to be successful. Yeli practitioners intended to perform actions that were cosmologically *and* sociologically motivated, and they did so. Conversely, when Mapeo practitioners located their activities sociologically, they did not simultaneously solve their cosmological sense. The social order and the order of the world were not coincident. Three examples will clarify the point.

CONSTITUTIVE CONTRASTS IN YELI

1. *Lera* and *vɔma*: a contrast of sound and performance

Mapeo Chamba also possess the complexes that Yeli Chamba call *vɔm* and *lera*. *Lera* flutes are known by the same name in both Chamba languages, while *vɔm* is simply the Leko equivalent of *jup*. When contrasted as sound performances, *lera* refers to flute music and *vɔm* to the music of the gourd horns that is part of the ritual of most Chamba cults. Mapeo Chamba explain the possession of flutes or horns with which to perform at funeral wakes as part of the patrimony of the patriclans. Some patriclans have horns, others flutes and some have both. Conventionalised relations of co-operation require that the owners of flutes assist the wakes of horn-owning patriclans and vice versa. No consistent relations can be drawn between this element of the patrimony and other elements, albeit the priestly clans of Mapeo invariably possess horn bands which are seen to tally with their Jang (Leko) origins.

In Yeli, the associations are more exact. *Lera* flutes are pre-eminently the possession of the chief, who is actually the custodian of the most important flutes of the community. The *vɔm* horns are the property of the priestly clans. In the language of structuralism, which seems accurate in this case, the royal clan stands in the same relation to *lera* flutes as the priestly patriclans do to *vɔm* horns. Furthermore, while *vɔm* is definitionally secret, and its performance cannot be witnessed by women, *lera* is performed publicly. Priestly rites are concealed because they are potentially dangerous. Gourd horns evoke cries of the wilderness, voices of the dead, or the gruffness of male shouting; flutes mimic the sweeter tones of human, especially women's, voices. Association between *lera* and *vɔma* and the positions of the chief and his priests is one of a number of performative contrasts between these statuses. Starting from this, or any other, point in the associations, it is possible to develop a skein of related contrasts which together establish an oppositional structure of feeling at the heart of the chiefdom.

2. Heat and coolness: a thermodynamic contrast

In common with many African peoples, Yeli Chamba draw upon what Luc de Heusch has called a thermodynamic code when they describe features of their cosmos. In this coding, the statuses of chiefs and priests are opposed. As the custodians of *vɔm*, in the broad sense of cults rather than musical performances, the priests of the community are said to be hot (*vɛ'kea*). Heat is synonymous with danger and illness in this context. One local etymology of the term for priest (*ngwan*) derives the term from the verb, *ngwan*, to cook. Priests 'cook' *vɔm*. Regardless of the standing a linguist might give this etymology, it is indicative that to motivate a term appropriately local commentators seize upon a thermal contrast with the chief, who should be cool (*tɛbkea*). When he, or his compound, is considered to have become heated, appropriate cooling rituals are required. *Lera* and *vɔma* as performances are contrasted in the same terms: the cool, soothing music of *lera* may supplicate God or the dead to bring rain; the hot, agitating music of *vɔm* menaces with illness.

The ramifications of this distinction are broadly inscribed, both in characterisation of chiefs and priests, and in the dynamic of the relationship between them. Since sheep are cool animals, sacrifices to cool royal graves should involve them. By preference sacrificial victims should be male and black, both characteristics which connote coolness in this context. Neither menstruating women nor pregnant women, both of whom are hot, should enter the royal compound for fear of heating it. Sexuality and blood are both hot, thus menacing to men and repugnant to the dead. The hut in which a woman sleeps during her menstruation may euphemistically be called the cold place, *zɔng tɛbkea*, since it is designed to cool her and protect her husband from contact with her heat. Traditionally, but no longer, menstruation huts were built outside the compound, exploiting a gradation of heat that Chamba find greatest at the hearth and less as one enters the bush. The feverishly sick were taken into the bush, away from the compound, to cool them.

In Mapeo and Yeli, elders explain that their cults are not as effective as they were because women no longer take precautions to protect their husbands from pollution. Once they took alternative paths in and out of the village, and had others draw water from rivers for them. Unprotected from their wives' menstrual heat, men have become less acceptable to the subterranean beings who make the cults effective. The blood of circumcision is also hot, so it needs to be doused with cooling water to prevent the chief becoming ill (a belief also recorded by Frobenius during his trip of 1911).

Illness (*mara*) is virtually synonymous with heat, while health may be called coolness. Conjunctions of heat and coldness are liable to produce sickness and so the dead must be insulated from contact with sexuality. Men who have had sexual intercourse during the previous night do not handle cult apparatus. The chief is permanently under threat from the heat of sexual contagion; outside his compound he never sits upon a mat in case intercourse has taken place upon it. Heating the royal compound risks an outbreak of smallpox; indeed, heating royal clansfolk more generally is associated with smallpox. Traditions of the foundation of the southern chiefdoms neighbouring Yeli attribute an outbreak of smallpox to the marriage between a woman of the royal matriclan and a boy from a priestly patriclan. The dynamic interplay of heat and coolness is powerful and dangerous.

The coolness of the chief resembles the coldness of the subterranean dead, in Yeli dialect the *vunɛpbira*. The chief is like the dead in so far as the ritual of his accession moves him into close and permanent association with *vunɛpbira*. Henceforth the chief has to be treated, to some extent, analogously with the beings of the underworld. To enter his compound men remove their upper clothing, while women ought to untress their hair and wear only the bundles of leaves which were the traditional dress of Chamba women. Non-Chamba should not enter his compound at all.

3. Bodily integrity and partibility

Yeli beliefs do not encompass chief killing, as in the Chamba chiefdom of Gurum where some accounts of the past do recall such practices, but they predict that the deaths of chiefs will coincide with the circumcision of boys, and this belief may be related to the more general thermodynamic relation proposed between the vitality of the chief's body and the fecundity and health of his people. But this would not be a sufficient explanation of the beliefs and practices which focus upon the body of the chief. These play also on values intrinsic to Chamba matriclanship and contrast with values of patriclanship which the priests personify.

The most evident feature of this contrast involves the treatment of royal and priestly bodies. The chief's body is buried secretly, and his death is officially announced only when the new chief is ready to be enthroned. The chief's 'burial', which then takes place, involves the bodily substitute of a log attired in white gown and long red hat. But the royal grave is already closed definitively. The slightest crack in its seal requires repair and cooling sacrifice of a black ram if misfortune is to be averted. The treatment of the priest's body is diametrically opposed. The successor to the patriclan priest should take his predecessor's skull at his burial, without waiting for the flesh to rot which is the

Chamba norm. Only by taking his skull does the new priest become his rightful heir and develop the capacity of sightedness required for his duties. While the power of the priests revolves around the skull line, and may be localised through the removal of the head, which is to say the separation of the patriclan skull from the matriclan body, the power of the chiefly line seems to presuppose the impartibility of chiefly bodies. The distinction correlates with another. For while the chief is the source of the welfare of his people, the priest is believed to have to kill his kin before assuming his status. To a degree, priests are witchlike, but chiefs are never witches themselves and are responsible for the periodic organisation of witch finding.

The scope of these associations may be demonstrated by a number of other beliefs and observances. The bodies of all royal matrikin from Yeli must be returned to Yeli for burial; this view is endorsed both positively—by the belief of Chamba in places like Mapeo and Balkossa, who assert it to be the case—as well as negatively—by informants in the Leko chiefdoms to the north of Yeli, who give it as the reason that they do not allow intermarriage with members of the Yeli royal matriclan. Not only the corpses, but any detachable parts of royal bodies have to be returned to Yeli, including the foreskins of boys circumcised elsewhere and the teeth of girls who have undergone tooth evulsion. Elaborate precautions must be taken to prevent the blood of these royal initiates from falling upon the ground, and sacrifice must be carried out by Yeli representatives should precautions prove unavailing. The sanction which all informants believe to underwrite these observances is the outbreak of smallpox which is feared more than either of the other two powers attributed to the Yeli chief: control over rain and over locust infestation.

The imperative of impartibility applies to the bodies of all the royal matrikin of Yeli. Moreover, the lien exercised by the royal matriclan over the body in its entirety appears to outweigh that which the patriclan would normally exercise over the skull. Like those of other Chamba of the central area, Yeli graveyards are normally owned by patriclans. The original owners of the land, Nyɛmnɛbba, allotted to each of the arriving patriclans a place to bury their dead. But there is a single significant exception made in the case of the royal matriclan which has its own graveyard. The royal matriclan is localised in a way that enacts the generally presupposed relation between matriclanship and corporeality. Although the sanctions to ensure the localisation of royal bodies are designed to instil fear, once localised the royal bodies become the source of welfare and fecundity which is made available to the community through rites which also channel representative goods from the living to the royal dead. The integrity of chiefly bodies becomes a counter in communal welfare, whereas the skulls of the priestly dead are responsive only to the welfare of their own clansmen.

The culture of Yeli chiefship and priestship elaborates upon general suppositions that distinguish matriclanship and patriclanship in places such as Mapeo. There is additional consistency between the manner of these exemplary human deaths and the differing manners of death of sacrificial animals—according to their partibility or impartibility, and whether blood is retained or allowed to flow freely (Chapter 7). The management of death is critical to attempts the living make to control the capacities of the dead; and its limiting case, expressed upon human bodies in Yeli but not Mapeo, contrasts complete impartibility to abrupt and brutal severance. Both procedures, according to those who carry them out, are fraught with mortal danger.

DEATH, POLLUTION AND ACTIVITY

Maintaining the royal clan in a condition fit to confer fertility upon the community requires that they are kept apart from processes which bring about pollution and death. Conversely, the community must also protect itself against the dangers which are potential in any conjunction between pollution or death and the royal clan. The burden of these precautions devolves upon the chief himself, who is rendered passive in the interests of maintaining his coolness. The royal matrikin are submitted to similar injunctions on a lesser scale: they cannot carry out the burials of their clansmen, and it is even said to be forbidden for them to see corpses. Funerary observances are more onerous for them than for others, since spouses of members of deceased royals are confined to their huts for several days. Because the royal clan is the only exogamous matriclan in Yeli, the dangers of royal deaths are dispersed within the community.

Protracted rites follow the announcement of the chief's death, when mourning continues not for the three days of a man's wake, but for four days—as for a woman's death. By convention, the death of the chief is initially not announced to his people, although they would certainly know of it: the death of a clan chief in Mapeo was vociferously not announced by a messenger mounted on a bicycle who visited relatives of the deceased and shouted that the chief, who had been confined to his sleeping mat for weeks, had just departed on a trip. A chief's corpse is buried at dead of night, and the overt royal ritual of internment, when it eventually takes place after the choice of a new chief has been made, involves a 'dry corpse' (*val wadkea*) made from a log dressed in the white robes and long red cap which are the prerogatives of chiefship. Funerary observances for the royal dead are carried out by the priests assisted by the smiths.

The chief of the blacksmiths (*gad lama*) is like a shadow image of the chief. The smith chief is a patriclan appointee, whereas the chief is a matriclan appointee. The royal clan is exogamous, but the smith's clan is not only endogamous but also denied commensality with the other members of the community. Although the smiths may drink with other Chamba, they may not eat with them. The chief is the quintessential Chamba, whereas smiths are frequently said not to be Chamba at all; albeit, this statement has to be understood contextually since, in a sense explained below, smiths are also the source of Chamba culture. Whereas the chief is susceptible to pollution, the chief of smiths is permanently polluted without being endangered; and while the chief's vulnerability to contagion through heating circumscribes his activities rendering him physically passive, the smith is always characterised as the most active of agents: not only does he beat metal into shape in order to fabricate all Chamba require for their livelihoods, he is also the royal drummer and the digger of royal graves. His wives manufacture the pots and terracotta wares used in every household. Paradoxically, at first sight, Yeli Chamba say that the smith like the chief is cool, and this explains why he alone may sit together with the chief on the same mat. For, they reason, if he was not cool by nature he would be unable to support an occupation which constantly brings him into contact with heat. Like good empiricists they remark the extraordinary capacity of the smiths to handle heated metal that no ordinary person could touch without being burned. Whereas the chief's coolness has constantly to be safeguarded by the behaviour of the community, the smith is secure in his given coldness which neither pollution nor physical heat can affect. For this reason, chickens dedicated to the cults, which are too hot for non-members to eat safely, are safe for the smith whose presence intrinsically cools them.

Smiths transcend the limits of human capacity (see Fardon, 1988; Frobenius, 1925). The most important elements of Chamba culture, knowledge of human procreation and birth, the ability to manufacture basic items of material culture, the technique of making fire, were revealed to Chamba by smiths. Without smiths there would be no Chamba culture. But metal-working activities pollute; the smith and his products are dirty (*lira*). Products of the forge, especially if they are to be used in rituals, have to brushed with burned chicken feathers to 'remove the smith's footmarks'. This action, according to one informant, mimics the smith's own recurrent brushing with a bunch of chicken feathers of the stone anvil upon which metal is beaten. Pursuing the smith's involvement with heating processes, with physical exertion, with darkness and with pollution, and his wives' involvement with the making of pottery, a common metaphor for the making of children, Chamba discover witchlike connotations of smith-hood and infer an unrestrained sexuality to the smiths and their wives. Smiths are also the accomplices of witches because they furnish them with the iron needles used to attack their victims. Since the smiths' products were traditionally exchanged for foodstuffs, and conventionally important items had to paid for in livestock, informants reason that witches pay the smiths in human flesh. By contrast, the welfare of the community depends upon the chief performing ordeals to detect witchcraft, definitionally the chief cannot be a witch. But the chief lacks the physical vigour of the smith: in contrast to the smith's mobility and activity, the chief remains within the village and adjacent farms. Traditionally he would not travel outside Yeli and, when modern administrative concerns force him to do so, his food must be carried along for the journey.

The chief, priests and smiths represent relatively stable exemplars of states which are temporary for the remainder of the population. Ritual practices involving these key figures can therefore be indexed to their existential statuses, so that they become chiefly or priestly types of activity. By virtue of their association with particular agents, the actions can be related to one another. Thus, *lera* and *vɔma*, to take one example only, may suggest to Yeli informants a rich contrast—between all the aptitudes of chiefs and priests—which is unavailable to Mapeo commentators. In Mapeo, different aptitudes connote discrete patrimonies.

Even in terms of sociological register, Yeli and Mapeo rituals evince differing senses of scale and scope. Yeli rituals are performed with an eye to the prerogatives they represent for local clans in relation both to the local hierarchy of functions within Yeli and to their importance for the notional hegemony which Yeli was once able to exercise over the neighbouring Chamba. Mapeo rituals are sociologically glossed solely in terms of local precedences, but Yeli rituals tend to be interpreted in terms of a world of relations they are intended to affect. The difference involves the self-conscious sense entertained by Yeli Chamba of their place as exemplary among Chamba communities.

VƆM AND *VAD* IN YELI

In common with their Mapeo counterparts, Yeli Chamba solicit the powers of the dead in two ways: through cults (*vɔm*) which invoke the beings of the underworld, and by direct recourse to the dead via such relics as graves, pot shrines and skulls. The terms for the entities and practices involved in these rituals are remarkably similar given the mutual incomprehensibility of the languages spoken in the two places (Chapter 2). However, extensions of the series—death, skull, corpse, the dead, spider, etc.—are not quite identical. For both Leko and Daka speakers, small white spiders are believed to token the presence of the dead when offerings are made at graves. In Daka, the spider is called *wurum*, the term for underworld being, while in Leko it is called *vad*, the term for skull. Similarly, while Daka speaking Chamba usually call small pots to commemorate the dead *wurum du*, and the composite *wut du*, relic or skull pot, is rare, these receptacles are invariably called *vad nyin wa*, skull pot small, by Chamba Leko. The funeral wake which Mapeo Chamba call *we kpan* or *we 'og*, death crying or death water, is called *val batna*, death beer, in Leko; while the annual commemoration which is *we sim*, death beer, in Mapeo, is called *vad batna*, skull beer, in Yeli. There is room for substitution among terms in the death/skull complex, and the Yeli predilection is consistently to favour skull where Mapeo prefers the dead. However, in both languages, the name of the dead—a composite of a person term and the word for skull or death—seems to be responsible for the pervasive, difficult to articulate, sense of coherence Chamba find in the series.

In common with its Mapeo counterpart, the Yeli ritual calendar specifies occasions for donations of ripening crops. Before such offerings are made, foodstuffs are forbidden to cult members on pain of affliction by the misfortune associated with their cult. The term *gidna*, used in this and other contexts, is a precise counterpart of the Daka *giran*, taboo, discussed earlier, and like that term is also related to the term for menstruation (*girba*). In Leko, menstruation may euphemistically be referred to as *nɔga*, also the term for a cult which bears the same name in Mapeo and Yeli. In both places, *nɔga* is held responsible for distension of the stomach and for symptoms that correspond to those of hepatitis. Only in the Yeli case is the association between stomach distension and menstruation available to explain the cult's name. This and other examples support the assertion of Mapeo elders that some of their terms for cults derive from Leko language and, therefore, make no sense other than as marking the Leko origin of their practices. There is some traffic in the other direction, at least two cults in Yeli are glossed as Daka terms, but the perception of influence overwhelmingly sees Mapeo ritual as derivative of Yeli forms rather than vice versa.

Judging by the vocabulary used to describe it (for there is much I have not seen) cult practice in Yeli is in many respects identical to Mapeo. Differences are less notable in the forms themselves than in apprehensions of their significance. Yeli *vɔm* cults are described in terms identical to their *jup* counterparts in Mapeo. But, unlike the Mapeo *jup*, Yeli *vɔm* are collectively contrasted to *lera* as part of the priest/chief and other contrasts. Although I have seen little of the esoteric stages of cults in Yeli, I doubt whether what occurs during them differs greatly from what is done in Mapeo.

Most named cults in Mapeo and Yeli can be paired: either because they have exactly the same name, or because they are translations of one another, or because they are conventionally stated to be equivalent—usually because they induce similar symptoms in their victims/patients. Judging by the numbers of cults concerned with these matters, Mapeo Chamba have been especially vexed by snake bites, bad deaths and the control of sexual and marital affairs. Other cults, which fall under none of these headings, were classified by Mapeo Chamba according to ownership or the timing of cult meetings. Looking at Yeli cults under the same broad aetiological headings, an overall perspective on the degree of resemblance between cults of the two places can be suggested.

One of the Yeli snake bite cults is found under its Mapeo name of *ngwan ji*. Yeli commentators propose a Daka origin for the cult, the name of which they gloss, like Mapeo informants, as 'bears redness'. The other Yeli snake bite cult, called *vɔm van*, the male cult, is literally equivalent to the Mapeo cult of *jup lum*. Both cults are associated, as in Mapeo, with the leaf of the shea tree (here called *kɔla*, rather than *tup*). This pair of examples suggests extremely strong convergence between the two places; the most immediate difference involves the number of cults: Mapeo Chamba have come by several other snake bite cults which to the best of my knowledge are absent from Yeli.

Similarities are also striking in the cults supposed to cause 'bad deaths' (the same phrase may be used in both languages, *val vaksa*; alternatively the Leko idiom can be *val tigɛlu bea*, a death of the night). The major leprosy cult of Yeli is called elephant (dɔna, equivalent to the Mapeo kɔngla). Its leaf is that of the false shea or ironwood tree (sana, equivalent to bəng in Mapeo). But here the Yeli gloss is more informative than its Mapeo counterpart.

The shea and ironwood trees are treated as a pair. The two look very similar: both resist firing but tend to be stunted; both produce kernels, but these are larger in the shea tree; both have elongated leaves. However, Yeli Chamba note some differences. The leaf of the ironwood tree turns a vivid red, that of the shea tree does not; but the stem of a shea tree branch exudes a white sap when it is snapped. So, the ironwood tree is associated with redness and the shea tree with whiteness. The same contrast can be stated in gender terms: the ironwood tree is male and the shea tree female. This identification is used in the naming rites for boys and girls (in Chapter 5). However, the motivation for the use of shea leaves in snake bite cults is distinct: if the leaves are stripped from the branch of the shea tree, the bare twig resembles a snake. The use of the ironwood leaf in leprosy cults is linked to colour: its redness is reminiscent of the condition of the leper's skin. A second leaf found in the leprosy cult (nyɛdna, which I cannot identify) is from a bush that produces small dark leaves on a bright red stalk. Again, colour is the motivating element.

Like members of the counterpart Mapeo cult, Yeli Chamba explain the name of the leprosy cult by reference to the texture of elephants' skin, which resembles that of lepers, and by observing that the grease of elephants' flesh is like the excessive greasiness thought to be a symptom of leprosy. Goats, considered to have greasy meat, form no part of the entrance payments or reparations to the cult for the same reason.

The name for the epilepsy cult, la gbira, is presumed to be derived in part from the word for fire (la). I did not find an informant who could explain the second part of the name. Fire relates to the symptom quintessential of this condition for Chamba: those who lose bodily control fall into fires and burn themselves. Mapeo informants consider their la gənsɛn cult to be of Leko origin.

Yeli cults concerned with sexual and marital matters also resemble their Mapeo counterparts. The cult which catches the children of adulterous women, called vɔm dagan, is considered to be of Daka origin. Dagan is explained to derive from the Daka verb dag, to cleanse. As in Mapeo, the cult is associated with the leaf of the savanna ebony (kina or kisina, called gɛsi in Mapeo). The Mapeo impotence cult, jup nu or female cult, is in Yeli called trunk (as in tree trunk) cult, vɔm nyia. The exoteric rules and paraphernalia of the cult are identical to those in Mapeo.

Close resemblances are apparent among cults which fall into none of the three categories. Nɔga, the cult of stomach pains, exists in two distinct forms: female nɔga and owl nɔga (nɔga ken and nɔga disa), just as in Mapeo. Its leaf is called gban tudna, taken from a bush with sticky pods (probably Bauhinia reticulata) and believed to be able to cause the symptoms of the cult if eaten. Among the cult apparatus of *nɔga*, as in Mapeo, there is a pierced gourd to symbolise the pains inflicted on the victim's stomach. Two differences between the Yeli and Mapeo versions need, however, to be remarked.

First, as I have noted, Yeli Chamba link *nɔga* to the idea of menstruation. The onset of the affliction is said by Yeli informants to be slow and gradually marked by distension of the stomach and yellowing of the eyes. Eventually, the victim begins to pass dark-coloured urine. The description seems to suggest that the aetiology is restricted to a range of symptoms similar to those we would associate with hepatitis. The curative ritual, also practised in Mapeo, involves the removal of a beer pot from between the legs of the afflicted person. In some other contexts (for instance *jup ya* in Mapeo), pots represent women, more precisely women's open and interior space. Pot removal, which puzzled Mapeo informants, can be motivated via the Yeli link between *nɔga* affliction and menstruation, as antidote to an ambiguous feminisation. The affliction caused by *nɔga* has ambiguous features of pregnancy, because of belly distension (stomach and womb are covered by a single term), as well as menstruation, because of darkened urine.

A second difference concerns the choice of *nɔga* leaves. The leaf in the Yeli *nɔga* cult is believed to be capable of inducing *nɔga* symptoms if ingested. Mapeo choice is for the ironwood leaf. Yeli informants find this clearly inappropriate, since ironwood and shea leaves are held in contrastive relations none of which seems apt to express any link with the *nɔga* cult. From the Mapeo perspective, the choice is merely conventional; relations between the qualities of leaves and the characteristics of the cults in which they serve are recognised in few cases.

Identical tree products are used in the 'same' cults in Mapeo and Yeli under certain circumstances only. In a few cases, a single symbolic logic is shared. Thus, *langa*, known under the same name in both places, affects eyesight, and both explicitly represent the eye by the pod of the silk cotton tree during cult rituals. *Yaguman*, known in Yeli as *səra*, like the Mapeo version is associated with pointed leaves because swellings caused by the cult have to be lanced to withdraw pus. Identical leaves are sometimes used in the 'same' cults in both places, but for different reasons. In these cases, Mapeo cults use what, in Yeli terms, are appropriate leaves, but do so for conventional reasons; thus, shea leaves are used in Mapeo snake bite cults, but apparently without the rationales that explain this in Yeli. In the majority of cases, Mapeo associations between cults and leaves can be brought under no encompassing set of rules. As in the case of *nɔga*, from a Yeli perspective, Mapeo Chamba would be running too many cults with too few leaves. Yeli cults are at once less numerous and use a greater variety of leaves. To put this all another way: Yeli informants consistently anticipate a symbolic logic in their cult rituals; Mapeo Chamba happily accept appropriateness when it exists but they also accept that arbitrary attachment of a conventional vehicle may reflect no authority except that of past practices.

Like their Mapeo counterparts, Yeli *vɔm* are entered by payment, and an initiate is serially introduced to different elements of the cult practice and apparatus as he makes further payments. An account which Dura gave me of 'seeing' *vɔm dagan* is comparable to counterpart stages in Mapeo, although his account is more formalised than any I was given in Mapeo.

dup vɔm koa	cutting the head off the *vɔm* chicken
na na'a gba'a pɛnga	mounting big mother's back
lɔ vo yila	burying the goat's head
pi vɔm wu	entering the *vɔm* hut
pa nen ganu	taking in hand the medicine
pu gbasa	taking the baton

The initiate begins by offering a chicken to the cult, when he sees the leaves on which the cult is made. Next, he is allowed to blow the huge gourd horn (big mother) which is the distinctive instrument of the cult's performance. The evocation of mature female capacity by this enormous gourd instrument recalls the symbolism of a gigantic beer jar (five pot) in the Mapeo version of the cult (discussed in Chapter 3). Subsequent donation is of a goat. The head of the goat is not actually buried, but the cord with which it was strangled is kept in the *vɔm* hut. The next stage, entering the *vɔm* hut where the cult apparatus is kept, is self explanatory.

At the penultimate stage of initiation, the neophyte witnesses manufacture of the medicine used in the cult. As in Mapeo, most cults are associated with one of two medicines, classed as male or female (*gan ken*, female medicine; *gan van*, male medicine). Most commonly these are daubed on the temples, shoulders, back, chest and knees of a patient. In some cases a more specialised remedy is required: lancing in the cults associated with bodily lumps, an eye wash of 'male medicine' for those caught by *langa*. Medicines may be inhaled by those suffering from respiratory complaints. The final stage of initiation, taking the cult's staff in hand, is open to few individuals. But in order that there be a successor to the ownership of the cult, someone other than the current owner ought to attain this stage of induction. The staff features in the distinctive dance performed during the funeral wakes of cult members (discussed in Chapter 3).

The similarities between Yeli and Mapeo cults, looked at as collections of individual institutions, far outweigh their differences, which is what we would anticipate of communities so closely related—geographically, historically and politically. Yeli cult practitioners' knowledge has apparently been codified to an extent greater than that of their Mapeo counterparts. And further exploration confirms that leaf and colour symbolisms are better integrated in the

Yeli versions of the cults (Chapter 8). A few more of the cult names may be comprehensible in Chamba Leko than in Chamba Daka, although traffic in cults from Daka to Leko is also undeniable. But the differences between the two places concern individual cults less than the overall significance of regulation through cults as an element of ritual practice.

OTHER AVENUES TO THE DEAD

Mapeo rituals enlist the agency of the dead predominantly by means of cults. Graveside rituals are performed in Mapeo for the immediately deceased, and shrines are maintained to contain small pots which receive offerings of beer and chicken blood. But these channels to the underworld are of slight importance in comparison to the proliferation and particularity of cults.

In Yeli, *vɔm* is only one element of a ritual practice that also gives weight to direct propitiation of the dead. This difference crucially reflects the difference between notional hierarchy, in Yeli, and its absence, in Mapeo. In the chiefdom the activities of different officials are distinguished as specialised contributions to communal well-being in a way that is impossible in Mapeo. A corollary of this is that the dead are also differentiated, and the royal dead become a particular focus of ritual interest. In Chapter 6, where I describe the annual round of rituals concerned with the growth of staple crops, this distinction becomes very clear. Stages of the growth and maturation of the guinea corn crop are enabled by rituals that call on the assistance of both the royal dead and the priestly cults. Responsibility gradually shifts from former to latter as the crop matures. Graveyard rituals performed for the collective forebears of the royal matriclan during the growth of the crop are practically revealed to be complementary to the control exercised by indigenous patriclan priests over its harvest.

The apparent similarity of cults in Yeli and Mapeo belies their different significances as parts of divergent organisations of communal well-being. The next four chapters deal separately with the human life cycle, the annual cycle of cultivation, human relations with the wild and the properties, both general and particular, of forms of life. Each chapter deals simultaneously with the different ways these areas of human concern are experienced in Mapeo and Yeli.

5

THE HUMAN SPAN

THE COMPANY OF DEATH

Rituals that mark an individual's passage through the stages of life are at once public and intensely personal. Anthropologists have made a notable contribution to the study of the public aspects of these events: they have demonstrated how the stages of such ritual events are demarcated; they have shown how rituals at distinct phases of the life cycle—birth, initiation, death—are cross referenced; in terms of these characteristics, they have discovered similarities in the ways life cycle events are commemorated in societies that are unrelated historically. These efforts allow me to take for granted similarities between rituals in Mapeo and Yeli in order to concentrate on the differences.

Older Chamba men recount different versions of the good life that accord with their particular tastes, but if constant features were to be sought in these accounts, and abstracted from reactions to adversities, many of them would relate to ideals and norms which concern the human span. Ideally, children should be born normally, and relinquishing the world of the dead develop into normal young adults who undergo initiation with fortitude. Their farming, fishing and hunting activities should flourish and, living at peace with their clanspeople and co-residents, they should bear many children. The children and parents should endure illness and poverty, discharge their social obligations, increase their wisdom and die full of years and held in general respect. Parents should die before their children or sisters' children, and the efforts of these latter should assure that their deaths are celebrated and their memories cherished. To a great extent we know that this is how a good life should be, not because the ideals are always explicit, but because departures from the ideal pose problems of both a practical and intellectual nature that require explanation and action. Modern developments complicate these ideals because a parent's life may no longer be the model for the life of her or his child (Chapter 9).

Writing about a nearby people, Nigel Barley has emphasised how other
Dowayo rituals become comprehensible only when they are related to the
pre-eminent value of circumcision (Barley, 1983). Chamba also circumcise,
but the operation is not as drastic as its Dowayo counterpart, and the event is
less crucial to attempts at cultural accounting. This difference may relate to
two others. Chamba find gender difference less problematic than Dowayo:
whereas Dowayo are described as building gender difference through ritual,
Chamba seem to accept it as a fundamental, pre-cultural, property of the
world. Chamba emphasise rather the common problems of men and women:
sickness, poverty and wretchedness (all covered by the term *bu*; close in sense
to the French *misère*) and death. If Chamba rituals are to have a dominant
concern, and their explanations and practices a recurrent source, we would
have to say that all this occurs under the sign of death. The worlds of the living,
above ground, and the dead below are parallel planes of existence and cyclically
related. The life cycle involves a prolonged attempt to exert control over this
relation which becomes particularly fraught at death. Death must be co-opted
and its instrumentality put at the service of men's attempts to master their
lives. Death, rather than circumcision, is the critical condition.

Death begs questions which are unanswerable in a definite sense.
Traditional conceptions of an afterlife or the underworld are vague or contra-
dictory. Typical Chamba attitudes towards these ideas, at least as expressed to
me, seem sceptical and resigned. To know for certain about death one would
have to die. Once dead, knowledge of that state cannot be transmitted. Seers,
who are supposed to know more, say little. There is a conventional wisdom but
it is not treated as definitive. Because death is a dominant image in life, crucial
to Chamba notions of person and of ritual efficacy, a particular slant is
imparted to knowledge, or the possibility of knowing with great certainty.
Over and above disparities of knowledge between individuals, death intro-
duces a principled limitation to knowledge as such. About death, as an elderly
informant told me, the children of men know nothing.

FROM BIRTH TO ADULTHOOD

Living things reproduce, grow and die. Chamba accounts of the human
fashion of doing these things closely resemble accounts of the way animals,
plants or other living things do them. One could not be argued to be a model for
any of the others; but the human fashion is, in different respects, both like and
unlike the way in which all living things are momentarily going through the
same cycle. Processes of growth and decay potentially stand as mutual metaphors; this is clearly so for the growth of guinea corn and of children (Chapter
6).

The 'children of men', the reader may recall, are composite. Skull, head,
resemblance, incarnation, spirit and identity are characteristics of patrimony;
substance, flesh, blood are maternal qualities. Breath (*gɔngsi*, Mapeo;

gɔnsɛra, Yeli) is God given. Identity, or personality, is also related to reincarnation, and God may have a role in putting the underworld being into a baby. Quite how the melding of these qualities occurs is admitted to be unclear. Several processes are simultaneously at work. Men donate their seed; women retain blood. Seed is related to bone through whiteness, but so is milk which nourishes the newborn child. God, moreover, is responsible for all life. Titlɛsime's wife Kɛlu recounted an idiosyncratic version in which the sun and moon, respectively male and female, sleep together on nights when the moon cannot be seen. Since moon or month may also be a euphemism for menstruation and the words for God and the sun are the same, this might be a feminist marginalisation of the male procreative role. But I was insufficiently quick witted to have thought of this when the story was told me. The dead also exercise volition, since it is believed that *wurumbu* may choose reincarnation into a distant section of the patriclan if their closer relations have angered them. From this contested surfeit of agencies—men and women, blood, seed and milk, God and the dead—a child is born. Women and men 'bear' (*ngwan*, Mapeo; *lɛb*, Yeli) children. The idiom 'to bear' is subsequently subjected to what is recognised as extension from this primary reference (Chapter 2).

The analogy between human, animal and vegetable propagation is close. Animals, especially large animals, are identified with their substance or meat. Animality is close to the matrilateral side of human nature. Animals additionally must have breath, since they move, and they may have enduring identities after death. Mapeo informants suggest that there are animal *wurumbu*, as well as seeds belonging to the *wurumbu*; should a person find guinea corn or a chicken straying from the underworld this origin will become apparent in spectacular fecundity. However, it is unclear whether underworld crops are distinct types or linked to above world counterparts in the way that humans relate to *wurumbu*. The conclusion of some informants—that all animals have *wurum* counterparts—while consistent with some aspects of Chamba thought, is treated as a foible by most people.

Plants do not move and therefore lack breath, but they do live, grow and die. Many plants, especially fruit bearing trees, are described as female. The term 'child' is used for the fruits and seeds of plants. Plants are unlike animals in that their regeneration does not rely upon the union of male and female. The term for child might be translated in its more general sense of small; this, however, would ignore the capacity of the seed (unlike a small pot) for growth. In the case of the plant par excellence, it seems safer to speak of human and guinea corn growth as mutual metaphors without judging which is exemplary.

Processes of pregnancy and birth are described in different sensual registers: colour, moisture, and temperature. The hot sexual act provides for the conjunction of white male seed and red maternal blood. The pregnant woman reddens and fattens, her blood is retained to nourish the developing child in the damp, dark warmth of her 'belly'. Female processes occur in the world of immediate sense impressions, common to living things that move, and can be described in sensual terms. The masculine contribution of personality and identity may only be inferred. Its mysterious process, under the agencies of God and the dead, eludes statement in visualisable terms. The goal of these processes is a 'red child' (*mi ji re*), or newborn infant as we would say.

The death of a woman during pregnancy or parturition is the inauspicious outcome of the infringement of cult regulations or, worse, of witchcraft. Autopsy must be carried out and, in the case of a boy child or developed male foetus, circumcision performed to enable the forebear to achieve a subsequent incarnation. The animal nature of a breech birth requires thorough rites of cleansing (Chapter 2). Other physical deformity might be attributed to a variety of cults, but would not entail the death of the baby. Twins are specially named but no especial attitudes of fear or celebration are entertained towards them.

At naming, the babies are introduced to the number associations and tasks fitting to men and women. The naming ceremony, performed under the control of the patrikin, involves the sacrifice of a small fowl and the offering of beer upon the ground to the dead. Names may be drawn from the patrimony or refer to the circumstances of the parents. Commonly, a name is both that of a forebear and immediately appropriate. Should the baby's wailing demonstrate the name to be inappropriate it may be changed on the advice of an elderly grandfather or paternal aunt. Completion of the naming rite is demonstrated by sticking a bunch of leaves into the compound fencing: ironwood leaves for a boy or shea leaves for a girl. In the past, tiny replicas of a bow and arrow or a hoe were given to male and female children respectively. The simple actions— the giving of the sacrifice, the offering of beer—were repeated three times for a boy and four for a girl.

Normality is monitored a second time when children cut their milk teeth. Like breech births, those who 'held back' their lower teeth were considered harbingers of animal danger (Chapter 2). An English-speaking friend aptly caught the nature of this anomaly when he said that such children were too 'headstrong', for the odd dentition is seen not in terms of an abnormal haste in producing upper teeth but a wilful holding back, or sticking, of the lower teeth. In spite of links which suggest themselves to an outsider, associations with other practices involving teeth (women's tooth evulsion or relic taking at death) are specifically disowned by Chamba with whom I have discussed the matter.

Already a division of labours with reference to the child is apparent: matrikin monitor both the developmental crises which share overtones of animality (breech birth and anomalous dentition), patrikin oversee the ceremony of naming and the choice of name. Naming fixes personal identity (previously the child only shared in the name applicable to all patriclan members) and prefigures the acquisition of human language. Patrikin thus manage a transition between *wurum* and human, as they will also manage the transition to adulthood at initiation. Their brief is to disarm the possible refusal of the incarnated forebear to remain in human form, to forestall the possibility that it will choose to 'return' to the subterranean plane of existence. For their part, the matrikin assure that the child's excessive animal vitality is not such a threat to its fellows that the interests of the living are best served by its death. Together, matrikin and patrikin hold the ring during the tussle between the wild, the dead and the incipiently human.

Thus far, I have felt able to let the Mapeo account also cover Yeli Chamba. Some differences will emerge when we explore the analogy between reproduction of people and of guinea corn in the two places. But the divergences that concern me here occur in the later life crisis rituals: circumcision and death. In both Chamba places circumcision transforms boys into men by means of a ritual separation from the body, reminiscent in this respect of skull taking. Circumcision is carried out under the auspices of the patriclan, but the achievement of partition can be argued to operate on both the patrilaterally and matrilaterally derived aspects of the person.

Women's initiation through tooth evulsion was the prerogative of clans of Leko origin: although generally practised in Yeli, it formed part of the patrimonial culture only of those Mapeo clans of Leko origin. Marriage, rather than initiation, marked women's admission to adulthood. Adult males must be made though circumcision, but girls achieve adulthood as their bodies develop. Thus, regardless of age, boys enter young adulthood after circumcision, when they are termed *gapsi* and not child. The verb *gapsan*, meaning to divide, is related to this notion of male youth by some informants, despite tonal differences between the terms. Young women are distinguished as pre-pubescent (*sɛm*), unmarried (*mi birum*, literally naked because women adopted a lower garment of leaves at marriage) and wives (*ngwu*).

Once adult, Chamba are expected to fulfil their roles in the networks of sociality. For a man, establishment of a separate compound or a separate entrance to a compound shared with his father is especially significant. For women, the birth of children brings a definite change in status. Accession to office may again alter the relation between women or men and *wurumbu* in a dramatic fashion. In maturity, communication is resumed between the living and dead: men and women join *jup* or *jɛm* and take responsibility for managing the deaths of their close relatives. Changing social status proceeds apace with physical changes. Mature men become 'great men' (*nɛ wari*): in a metaphorical sense, because they see *jup*, but also more literally because the ideal elder in his full vigour imposes with his bulk and bearing. Women fill into mature motherhood.

To become aged (*ngwɔri*) is to tighten and to dry out, as a drum skin tautens after soaking. Old women may now be called *wɔ*, a term evocative of the verb to age. Old men may be called *danga*, and the suffix for child or small (*mi*) may be added to form compounds: old woman child, old man child. In the end is the beginning: old men, like children once more, discover that the *wurumbu* shave their heads, so that the hair no longer grows over all the dome of the skull. Their baldness is patterned. 'The head ashens' (*ti tɔman*, Daka) as hair turns white. The matrilateral fleshy component of men and women is subject to attrition as the blood dries. Old women become like men. All of this: drying, tightening, the whitening of the head, the dropping away of flesh foreshadows the inevitable and terminal transformation when the person will resume the existence of the dead. The memorial that will remain of their late human incarnation will be the skull, its hard stone substitutes and the round terracotta beer pots which receive offerings to the dead. And all of these are under the charge of the patriclan.

CIRCUMCISION

Because I have not witnessed a major circumcision ceremony in either Yeli or Mapeo, my description is based on oral accounts. Doubtless, the actual ceremony has vagaries that are lost in its recollection; since my predominant interest is in Chamba accounts of their rituals, the loss is not as serious as it might otherwise be. I do draw upon parts of two ceremonies I have seen in plains hamlets that issued from the Mapeo hill retreat, but one of these concerned a blacksmith clan and had atypical features. Mapeo and Yeli informants make different senses from the common ordeal of circumcision. In Mapeo, the boys undergoing initiation to manhood are the focus of the event; in Yeli, a second centre of interest is created by the demonstration of the different contributions that Yeli officials are capable of making to communal welfare.

Yeli

Bouba recalled a story told to him by the elders when he was circumcised.
    A leper who had lost his fingers had difficulty getting out his penis to have sexual intercourse, so he had his prepuce cut off. He found that sex was good with no prepuce and so others copied him. This is how circumcision started.

Bouba had trouble making much of this story and thought it probably no more than a just so story (*susuwa*, Leko). After all, no one would marry a leper or have sexual intercourse with him. Perhaps the story only deflected from the real purpose, for circumcision was a trial of endurance which tested the ripeness of boys' hearts for manhood. None the less we could remark some aptness in the tale.

Auspicious and inauspicious types of bodily partibility are contrasted: amputation of fingers, because of sickness, prefigures amputation of the foreskin, by cutting. Despite his inappropriateness as a model lover, the success the leper achieves in modifying his decayed condition persuades others to copy him. The 'redness' of the leper's body, and the 'heat' of his illness, may also find echoes in circumcision ritual. Whatever the case, I heard no other story in Yeli purporting to describe the origin of circumcision.

The circumcision operation takes place during March or April, the hottest part of late dry season, when the farms have been prepared to receive guinea corn seed once the first rain falls. 'Traditionally', the 'boys' would not have been considered strong enough to be circumcised before they were twenty years old. Now they are younger, 'real circumcision' with all its attendant rigours, elders will tell you, has not taken place for a generation. Modern medicines make the wounds heal quicker so the youths do not stay long in the bush camps. Some things, however, do not change. Women do not see the operation, nor do they know whether the boys have been brave, because the drums and their own singing drown any cries. Bouba recalled how the women sing as if they were men to encourage their sons:

Nyama we pa ri, wɔ—ba, wɔ
The sun shines on high, oh—father, oh

Nɛng van, mə lang bum—pɛri ya
Person man, I make war—overcomes me

(The sun shines above, oh father; as a man I must make war, even if I am overcome)

The song expresses a sentiment common to Yeli and Mapeo: circumcision is a test of manhood akin to war. Pain must be endured in order for youths truly to become men. However, the Yeli ritual has senses unknown to women who do not witness circumcision. Dura described the operation.

Surgery was entrusted to the most skilled cutter; his role was merely technical. The knife was called *kɔ wɛra*, chicken knife, in order to mislead women. Behind the surgeon came two priests (*ngwanbira*), each carrying one of two knives esoterically called *vad-tə-tə*. (*Vad* is the term for skull; *tə-tə* is said to mean mosquito larva.) When not in use, the knives, contained within an elongated gourd (*pɔb*) are hung, like mosquito larvae, from the roof poles of the priests' hut. They are suspended because it is dangerous to step over them. Two types of knife are distinguished: old man's skull and old woman's skull (*vad van dɔa; vad kɛn dɔa*). The former resembles an ordinary knife but has a metal handle; the latter is an iron point. The male knife is touched to the circumcised penis; the female knife is inserted into the penis to draw blood from a nick. The flow of blood enables a man to impregnate women. The old woman's skull knife is also used in the women's tooth evulsion ceremony, when an incision made in the upper gums provokes the fertility enhancing blood flow.

The likelihood of surgical hitches in the circumcision operation seems not to worry commentators, however the risk of fertility being misplaced is mentioned frequently. Should the cut foreskin fall upon the ground, it must be lifted with the *lama*, the sickle shaped tool of the priest, or else the youth will never engender children. His father must kill a goat on the spot. Lifting the foreskin with the *lama* and killing the goat respectively releases the hold of the dead and recompenses them for heating the ground with the blood of circumcision. This latter exegesis reminds us that the Yeli chief also is threatened by the heat of circumcision blood, and water is splashed upon the blood in the attempt to protect his life.

One of the last pieces of information Dura told me before I left Yeli concerned the use to which foreskins were put. His manner suggested that the knowledge he would impart offered the solution to many questions I had posed. The foreskins are hung up to become dry. Once dried, and barring the grave misfortune of their being eaten by wild animals, they are ground and mixed with the caolin powder carried in a small medicine horn around each priest's neck. This powder is used to mark a red line down the centre of the forehead of men attending rituals of cults owned by the priests. Applied in this way it strengthens the wearer.

After the circumcision operation, boys remain in the bush camp for about three months, throughout the first half of the wet season, waiting for their wounds to heal. The coolness of the weather and other measures, like tying leaf bandages, assist the healing process. The boys avoid contact with women because, as a number of informants prosaically expressed the problem, their penises would bleed if they became erect. They wear only leaves, but of no special kind. Food is simply left for them to eat, and no salt is added to their relish. If they asked for salt their soup would be watered. The relish contains no meat and is eaten from broken pots. Should a youth die, his food is retained to be given to his mother when his mates return. She will simply be told that he has been eaten by wild animals.

It is a time of hardship but one when the boys see great things: they learn to play *lera* flutes, their fathers pay for them to see the earliest stages of some of the *vɔm* cults, and the mask (*lang gbadna*) removes its wooden head in their presence for the first time. Grown men insist that as children they had no notion that there was a man inside the mask. Men visit the boys in the bush (but only if they have not had intercourse on the previous night) to give them instruction. Once the boys also hunted rats which they caught in large numbers to give to the priests (as described to Frobenius in 1911) but more recently they have given them gifts of guinea corn, for rats are less numerous than they were.

Eventually it is time for the boys to return to the village. Their parents must brew enormous quantities of beer. Informants recalled that their fathers were unable to sleep on the night of their return because of constant demands for beer. The boys' heads are shaved and their bodies covered in a red ochre of caolin and oil (*kasa*). They exchange their leaves for the cloth kilt that was the dress of adult Chamba men. The priests are clothed with the leaves of the shea tree (kəla) which they wear for three days. The chief, who has played no part in the circumcision rites, receives them clad in male dress. As the boys are led back by the priests, they are followed by the mask of the royal matriclan. *Susuwa*, tricksters, run ahead of the boys; they demonstrate to onlookers by cutting at their left forefingers with the forefinger of their right hands. If a youth stood immobile like a stone during circumcision, the tricksters throw a stone at his mother's feet. The women break into song and ululate.

Ya vaksa da le'a ba ri
Horse bad departs throws father

Bum na, wɔ, wɔ wɔ, ya wa be?
War in, oh, oh oh, horse child has?

(The bad horse departs having bucked its father; there is war here; has the horse a child?)

The main problem in interpreting this song, according to Bouba, is knowing what the horse refers to. If the horse is the circumcision cult, then the circumcision wound is like that which might result from being thrown by a horse. The horse (i.e. the circumcision cult) departs leaving the wounded boy; does it leave in search of its own child? In another sense, the circumcised boy himself could be the bad horse, for the boy has thrown off his father by becoming adult. To sing of the presence of war recalls the song at the time of the operation, in which circumcision was likened to war, because both depend upon men's fortitude. The horse is the animal of war. Women's songs emphasise the links between violent masculine pursuits and circumcision. Another song is considered to originate from the neighbouring community of Jampeu.

Val ga 'an nɔn bɛ, nɔ gaba
Death thing fearful is, fear circumcision

Death is to be feared but a boy should not fear circumcision. Three days after their return, the boys wash off the red dye of the cult (*vɔm kasa*), and their marginal condition is ended. Before considering the symbolism of boys' circumcision, it helps to compare its explicit counterpart among women's ceremonies.

For tooth evulsion (*nəgəl gɔ'nbia*), the women are divided into two groups. The women of the chief (i.e. the patriclans of the chief and his assistants, and the royal matriclan) congregate by the chief's compound, while the women of the *vɔm* people (*vɔmbira*: the patriclans of the priests) assemble at Dura's compound. The women's heads are shaved and their bodies reddened with ochre (*kasa*). Chiefly women are dressed in the leaves of the locust bean tree (*ləm*), which is associated with rain (Chapter 7); women of *vɔm* are dressed in *gima* leaves, a luxuriant tree, apparently a ficus, considered remarkable for retaining its foliage thoughout dry season. *Gima* evokes lushness nourished from the earth, and thus the role of priestly ritual in assuring plenty from the land they own; it contrasts with locust bean leaves evocative of the chief's control over rain.

Girls' two upper teeth are twisted out and their gums nicked with the female of the skull knives. They then exchange their leaves for those of a plant called *wa gɔ nyia*, child evulsed trunk. This is a leafy plant with small white flowers that grow close to its stem. Informants motivate its choice in terms of whiteness, which connotes fertility and nourishment, by association with guinea corn flour and milk. In common with youths returning from circumcision, girls remain in their special condition for three days before the red colouring is washed off. Then they reward the *vɔm* priests with one or two measures of guinea corn and with beer with which to 'wash the knives' before they are returned to their container.

Circumcision and tooth evulsion are under the charge of the priests; in neither ceremony does the chief assume an important role. Consistent with this, initiation rites are organised under the auspices of patriclanship and not matriclanship. Priests are the masters of partibility, and patriclanship is the cultural domain within which bodily partibility occurs. The paradigmatic separation is that between body and skull after death, when the skull is taken to the patriclan skull shrine. In different respects, removal of the foreskin to uncover the glans penis is analogous to the removal of facial skin to reveal the skull, and to the separation of skull from body. Evidence for the first resemblance might be taken from outside the circumcision ceremony. In Chamba sculpture the heads of (most male and some female) anthropomorphic figures are surmounted by protrusions in the shape of the tip of the circumcised penis. Head and penis head are recognised analogies. However, the foreskin, and not the penis, resembles the skull in its detachability from the body. Thus, it is no accident that the knives used to endorse the surgical operation of circumcision are called skull knives. Incorporation of the ground dried foreskin into powder applied to the head underlines identification between the two.

The ambience of the ceremonies is pervaded by qualities of redness, heat and the provoked flow of hot, red, blood. Circumcision occurs during the hottest time of year, and in the heat of the day. Youths, at their return from circumcision camp, and girls throughout their ceremony, are coated in red ochre. Blood is made to flow not only from a youth's circumcision wound, but from the orifice of his penis. By analogy, girls bleed from the mouth. Male and female informants are both clear that girls' initiation is to be understood as counterpart to the male ceremony. Detachment from the penis and detachment from the head are presented as analogous. Here, it may be useful to interpose the stylistic device, especially typical of Chamba Leko sculpture, in which the penis type protrusion of the male anthropomorphic figure has a counterpart in a bowl shaped addition to the female head. Small beer pots, identified with skulls in some contexts, can also be envisaged as the interior space ('belly') of a woman. Open and closed ovoid objects are vehicles of shifting perception: as skulls, as bellies, as glans penis.

The play of masculine and feminine qualities can now be summarised. During the circumcision operation the singing women identify themselves with the masculinity of the patriclan, especially expressed through blood shedding in war. But at the same time, and out of their sight, youths are feminised by being made to bleed from the orifice of their primary sexual organ in order to impregnate women successfully. Returning youths are clad in the garb of men, but the priests who perform the feminising operation adopt a dress of shea butter leaves, the female leaf. But women's fertility is not the technical achievement of the priest; no one suggests that tooth evulsion makes women able to bear children. Tooth evulsion operates upon their femininity to impose masculine qualities of patriclanship: partibility and provoked blood-shed. The instrument used on them is controlled by the priests, who also insert it into the penis.

The story of the leper who inaugurated circumcision, modifying a body that was hot (from illness) and red (from skin disease), and compensating so successfully for the detachment of his fingers that he became sexually desir-able, may be a just so tale, but it is thematically pointed. Yeli initiation ceremonies orchestrate properties of, especially, patriclan culture to play on a scale of reference from the individual body to the political community.

Mapeo

Large-scale circumcision ceremonies were held in Mapeo at intervals of about eight to ten years, although hamlets in the plain might choose to perform their ceremonies independently of the main village. My fieldwork did not coincide with a major Mapeo ceremony. As in Yeli, these are said to be attenuated in comparison with those of twenty years ago. I witnessed stages of circumcision ceremonies in two satellite hamlets of Mapeo and collected recollections of ceremonies; however, my most complete source is an account written by a missionary to Mapeo during the early 1940s (Cullen MS). Father Cullen collected his notes when circumcision was a critical and large scale undertak-ing, so that his report contains observations and accounts contemporary with events that my informants have to recall at many years remove. However, Cullen's notes are consistent with accounts to which I have listened in suggest-ing that Mapeo Chamba describe circumcision as an extended and elaborate sequence of events designed to test the manhood of youths. The wider sym-bolic allusions exploited in Yeli appear to be absent.

Cullen distinguishes four phases of the ceremony.

1. A month of beating which commences after the harvest is completed in the dry season.

2. Another month of beating accompanied by dancing, but with no drums.

3. Another month of dancing with drums: during the first two weeks the boys dance in the village and are given gifts of money; during the second two weeks they visit their relatives further away to dance.

4. This period ends with the circumcision ceremony, after which the boys spend three months in the bush until their wounds heal.

The circumcision ceremony and the return from the bush occur at roughly the same periods as the corresponding phases in Yeli. However, greater emphasis is given to the training prior to circumcision which begins once the elders resolve that the physical development of the uncircumcised youths requires a ceremony, rather than because of precise calculation of the years intervening since the last ceremony. A youth's mentor (called *nen* in both Yeli and Mapeo) is chosen by his father from the previous set of youths to be circumcised. He will be responsible for seeing the boy safely through his ordeal. Although the guardian's role is found in Yeli and Mapeo, it receives much greater emphasis in Mapeo, probably because the hazing of youths is a more pronounced feature also. The *nen* cuts a crooked stick to give to the boy in his charge (called *tɔma* like the chiefly insignium). Switches are also cut to be used for beating the boys. When the new moon appears, the boys are brought out before dawn to stand in a line outside the town. As the *nenbu* sit around a fire warming themselves against the cold of the harmattan, the boys stand stiffly in a line with their sticks—held in the right hand—crooked behind their necks. The left hand grasps the right wrist across the chest, eyes are shut and head thrown back. This is the posture to be adopted during the cutting operation. The boys must remain immobile; if they move, shiver or open their eyes they are subject to beating and reprimand by the *nen*. When the sun rises, the villagers come out to witness proceedings and the *nenbu*,

> march up and down behind the boys and around prodding and poking and jerking them like pigs at a fair. If a boy winces or draws back they flatten him with a shove and a load of abuse. The people stand around enjoying it. Then [some of the] neni's take some switches [and] others cold water in calabashes, which they have left especially outside all the night. They march behind the boys splashing water on their backs and abusing them. If a boy winces, two or three neni's join to leather him and all the people join with abuse. (Cullen MS)

The boys are then made to run and, since they have been standing for four hours, some of them fall and are hauled up by the *nenbu*. They leave for their *nen*'s compound where they work for him until late afternoon when they are again subjected to this training. Men to whom I talked claimed that beatings were also administered with the 'tail' of the masked figure (*nam gbalang*). So it continues for a month. During this period the boys are secretly given the first of a number of medicines to drink. This one is called *gɔn yilang bɛ*, the thief's medicine, because of the secrecy in which it is drunk.

When the new moon of the second month appears the boys are assembled and given another medicine (*gən wari*, big medicine) to drink. This medicine is an unpleasant tasting white mass, the source of which is kept secret. Some say it is a drug and makes you feel very distant. That night a big dance takes place with dancing but no drumming. The hardening of the boys continues, but they are slapped with the *nen*'s open palm rather than beaten with switches. They continue to stand outside in the early morning and to work for their guardians all day. But if they are not too tired they later put on metal dancing anklets (*sug*, usually worn by women) and dance all night accompanied by a small drum. At this time they visit many places where goats are slaughtered for them. Each night they proceed to a fresh site.

With the third new moon, the boys are assembled to drink another medicine in unfermented beer (*sim 'agan*). (Cullen calls this the big medicine (*gən wari*); my informants referred to it as *wagan* and believed the medicine of the previous month was *gən wari*.) That night a demonstration circumcision ceremony is held. The boys form a circle, standing in circumcision posture each with his *nen* behind him. A torch of grass is lit and held under the boy's nose by the master of the *jup* (*jup tu*). The *nen* advises him when to exhale through the nose so as not to inhale the smoke and cough, which would result in a beating. After this, the *jup tu* sets up a refrain on his flute and followed by drummers, the boys and their *nenbu*, and the women and girls, they leave the village to arrive at a place in the near bush. The women and girls then return to the village. The boys are advised by their *nenbu* to do as they are told and show no fear. The first boy is called into the circle of elders and is told to stand to attention with his stick. The *jup tu* squats in front of him and his *nen* stands behind. The crowd chants, 'Stand as if you were dead'. The boy's cloth is pulled aside and, as the crowd chants 'Give it to him', he slowly raises his left hand which has been covering his penis until he clasps his right wrist. The *jup tu* takes the foreskin between finger and thumb and draws it in and out while the crowd chants 'They are showing you'. Next the operator approaches the boy with what Cullen describes as pliers. The crowd chants 'He is coming', as he catches the foreskin and squeezes. Occasionally, the operator draws blood but the *nen* should remonstrate with him against making the boy afraid of the real operation. If the boy winces, the crowd turns away, but if he shows fortitude they cry out shrilly clapping their hands against their mouths. A further all night dance then takes place. After this, there is no further physical testing and the boys are given new clothes: by 1941 northern Nigerian gowns (*riga* in Hausa) and some coins. In the period described by Cullen, these coins were kobos (halfpennies) with holes in the centre which could be attached to the sticks (*tɔma*) with leather thongs. Some men still retain these *tɔma* with their coins still attached as souvenirs. During the second two weeks of the third month, the boys visit their relatives and are given coins, chickens and a goat by their maternal uncle. Beer brewed for drinking during this time is called *gap sim*, the beer of youths.

Just before the new moon appears for the fourth month of the ceremony the boys are gathered and one is chosen to be circumcised first; he is known as *mi banan*, a compound of child and another term apparently without etymology. This must be a brave boy since his fortitude is to be an example to the rest. The boys are told to prepare their beer, for when this has been decanted and fermented it will be time for circumcision. They are then dressed in the traditional short dancing kilts, with front and back panels of alternate blue and white strips, which are the prerogative of uncircumcised males (*'isi bɔrobɛ*). They borrow the beads worn by their mothers around their waists (and which normally hold the bunches of leaves worn front and back by married women), and these they drape over their shoulders and across their chests. A basket-work hat with ear flaps (*bələng*) is crowned with a bunch of long feathers from any large bird. Boys with wealthy kin may borrow various prestige items from matriclan, patriclan or father's matriclan members: a *tɔma* in metal, a brass knife with small heads on the hilt (*yak nɛ*, knife man), brass rattles to attach behind their dancing kilts (*nyan bələng*, horse hat; *nyan təksa*, horse snail, a smaller version of the former).

Their guardians (*nenbu*) lead out the boys by their crooked sticks (*tɔma*) in the early evening, and a dance begins which will last throughout the night. From this time the boys are forbidden to talk to girls who belong to patriclans other than their own (i.e. who are marriageable). Next morning, circumcision takes place.

Elaborate steps are taken to test the bravery which has been instilled. The boy's face is covered with a white paste of flour and beer (*bɔg*), which sets hard, and his feet are encased to the ankles in earth. A Mapeo saying associates the paste with finality, 'Once the *bɔg* is on, nothing can be changed', circumcision must follow. A grimace or shuffling would immediately be made apparent in the cracking of the earth or paste. For those who fear circumcision a special insult is reserved, *barumsa*; the term is locally explained in terms of the verb *bad*, to tie onto the back and *sa*, bird. The youth who runs from initiation, flies away from circumcision, is like a child, who ought to be carried on his mother's back. Fear at this moment of truth is never forgotten: an otherwise respected man in late middle-age (since dead) could offer no retort to this taunt thrown in his face forty years after the event.

In Mapeo, *jup* is said to circumcise the boys. Patriclans are conventionally grouped according to the circumcision cults they follow into alliances that are specific to circumcision. As in Yeli, the actual operation is carried out by anyone recognised to be skilful, but a knife associated with the circumcision cult must have been touched to the foreskin of the first boy to be circumcised and, according to some, this knife actually makes a small wound. The only circumcision ceremony I have seen involved boys from a clan of Chambaised Vere blacksmiths, and informants explained to me that it departed from Chamba practice in some ways, most notably timing since the circumcision was performed in late wet season. The boys stood stock still in their circumcision posture; they had been instructed not to move and after the operation to enquire whether the cutting had yet been carried out, for they felt no pain. The successful conclusion of each operation was marked by ululation of the women standing apart from the scene of the ordeal. In Mapeo, as in Yeli foreskins must be prevented from touching the ground on pain of the boy being unable to 'bear' children. Should the foreskin not be caught in a leaf, the boy's father would have to sacrifice a goat on the spot. Foreskins are hung to dry in the *jup* hut and will be ground to powder and incorporated into the ingredients of the red ochre (*kut*) used in the cults. As in Yeli, this is hidden knowledge.

After their operations, boys must remain for two to three months in bush camps. For a nominal payment, a head of corn or an arrow, the boys are shown the earliest stage, usually the leaves, of some *jup*. They may, for instance, see cults such as *ngwan ji* and *jup lum* (the snake bite cults), *jup dagan* and *jup ya* (both concerned with control over women), *la gɔnsɛn*, *kɔngla* and *gina* (cults of bad deaths), but they do not see cults like *nɔga* (causing stomach distension), or *karbang* and *jup nu*, which are the prerogative of older men. The boys also begin their initiation into the cults of their patriclans (*jarɔ*, at no cost, *bɔntɔng*, for a chicken and *yaguman*, for an arrow and a head of corn). Titlɛsime emphasised to me that the boys do not really see much; they are made to crouch or lie face down with their hands over their face. Their eyes are uncovered for a few seconds only, and mild beatings are administered to instil fear. Torches of burning grass may be shaken over their backs three times (the male number) and the embers extinguished by the guardians with the palms of their hands. The most important knowledge that must be instilled at this time is that nothing learned or seen may ever be revealed to women.

Boys of some clans choose new names from those proposed by their elders, and some men are known henceforth by the names they received at circumcision. Others of these names are rapidly forgotten. In retrospect, like most men put through comradely suffering, they recall the period in the circumcision camp as one of the most adventurous and happy periods of their lives.

In 1977, I twice witnessed returns from circumcision camps to the plains hamlets during late May. Mapeo elders were contemplating holding a circumcision ceremony in 1978 or 1979, but the inhabitants of the plains, grown impatient, had held their own ceremony beforehand. By general consent, the timing of the returns was two or more months earlier than it would have been in the past, when the boys returned late in the rainy season. The boys were younger than initiates a generation earlier. At Tim Kpi, some half a dozen boys wearing grass skirts and calabashes on their heads were met by men who gave them food and beer. It was not clear whether all the boys had surgically undergone circumcision, or simply had received a small nick to endorse an operation carried out at the dispensary soon after birth. On their return from circumcision, the fathers of these boys might have been dressed in the man's

costume of a blue and white narrow loomed cotton kilt (*'isi sɔran*), but in 1977
the boys were kitted out in pan northern Nigerian gowns, with plastic shoes,
sunglasses, umbrellas, caps and towelling turbans; one wore a portable radio
on his shoulder. Boys were carried shoulder high or wheeled on bicycles along
the track to the village. There they were welcomed by the women and a speech
was made to say that strangers had arrived and should be welcomed with food
and drink. At Kojoli Jabe, the return was similar. Although there was no
singing, Titlɛsime told me that the flutes were intoning *mɛm yɛn nyenan*, the
circumcised children are entering. At this point the *jup* is said to leave the
children (*jup vɛt mɛmbu*), and the circumcision knives belonging to the patriclan are put away. The father of each of the boys gives three (the male number)
pots of beer to the cult master, or *jup tu*, for the cult to leave his son. The boys
dance to their own compounds where they are given cloths and other presents.
Some feign not to recognise their mothers. Just as in Yeli, this is the moment a
mother would learn that her son had died in the bush because the elders
returned the food she had prepared for him throughout his period of absence
and told her that the youth had been eaten by an animal.

Tooth evulsion for women was never carried out by all Mapeo clans; it was
considered a Chamba Leko trait and its practice was restricted to clans claiming an origin from the east. Like Yeli Chamba, Mapeo Chamba tooth evulsion
has a significance in women's development similar to men's circumcision, and
they likewise use the same knife for both operations. Pragmatically, informants insisted that the tooth removal allowed medicines to be given to a woman
during childbirth even if her mouth was clamped shut. Neither men nor
women could be persuaded to find a further significance, and all disowned any
connection with beliefs and practices which we might guess to belong to the
same set of ideas (such as the fear of 'upper tooth cutters', or the removal of
teeth as a relic after death). Clans which did not perform tooth evulsion
substituted no other ceremony for it. Such clans as performed the ceremony
were forced by the Fulani administrators during the 1920s, presumably on
colonial prompting, to restrict the operation to insertion of the circumcision
knife to open slightly the gap between the front teeth. Now even this custom
has died out, and young Chamba men and women claim to find tooth evulsion
unattractive.

In formal terms, Yeli and Mapeo ceremonies of male and female adulthood
are quite similar. However, interpretation of them is at some variance. In both
places, circumcision is held by priests under the auspices of patriclan organisation. However, in Mapeo the event is seen as an ordeal of manhood and
assimilated under the general rubric of *jup*. The Mapeo rituals do not manufacture male fertility, though they risk its loss. Youths undergoing circumcision might be married and fathers. Two features of institutional organisation
truncate the interpretation of the Mapeo rite: thoroughgoing contrast with the
women's ritual is precluded because many clans do not perform the women's

ceremony; a motivating analogy with the organisation of the political community is not available because of the absence of chiefship. The associations that remain intact are those proper to patriclan culture, to the distinction between village and bush, and to the contrast between childhood and adult initiation to *jup*. Otherwise, in its emphasis upon circumcision as a test of masculinity, the Mapeo interpretation tallies with the exoteric impression gained of Yeli circumcision by female observers there.

RITUALS OF DEATH

The parsimony with which Chamba specify forms of being in their lifeworld invests the relations between the living and the dead with overwhelming significance. Chamba are dogmatic that the moment of death is one of instantaneous transition. The verb of transformation, or shape changing, is used with this implication (*bit*, Mapeo; *bid*, Yeli). The human life cycle may consist of a gradual transformation from the predominance of characteristics of the dead to the predominance of the human—and back, but the cycle ends with a punctuation point. Chamba observances at death have no effect on the condition of the deceased. Circumcision makes the man, but mourning does not make the dead. Commemorations of death are performed for the living: to demonstrate the status of the late person and his or her kin, deflect misfortune or plead for blessings.

In Yeli and Mapeo the mix of these motives differs. Mapeo informants stress the status aspects of funeral, and especially of the wake as the major mourning for the deceased. The dead share this interest in their status, since the attention of the living is imagined to deflect the anger they would feel were their passage not properly marked. Yeli accounts additionally represent the dead as a source of fertility and power. This is most clearly demonstrated in the collective commemoration held annually for the royal forebears and recent dead.

Mapeo: death and the performance of society

Chamba in the modern administrative centre of Ganye advised me how frequent were deaths in Mapeo. In part they supposed this was because of the prevalence of witchcraft in Mapeo (a product of the 'traditional' character of the place), in part they generalised from the fact that returning travellers always reported funeral celebrations in Mapeo. Although my first visit to Mapeo was timed to coincide with the major annual harvest festival, I witnessed a burial and wake in the same few days. Longer acquaintance has only reinforced the recollection of Mapeo as a place where a funeral ceremony of some sort is usually to be found somewhere. During dry season there is a wake most weeks, and ceremonies may run end-to-end in different locations. Wakes, moreover, are only one of half a dozen types of funerary performance. Through these events, death is made to seem pervasive in Mapeo daily life.

The visibility of funeral performance is enhanced by a number of factors, among them the relatively large population of Mapeo village and its attached hamlets, the relatively late date of the establishment of Muslim or Catholic influences in Mapeo (which meant that older people dying in the mid-1970s tended to have been traditionalists), and the relatively elaborate sequence of mourning events (relatively, in each case, referring to a comparison with other Chamba communities of Nigeria). Mapeo Chamba interpret their own concern as attention to a Chamba tradition which has fallen away in other places. But there are reasons not to concur wholly in this judgement. Absence of hierarchy and proliferation of funeral observances may be related aspects of Mapeo organisation.

Another Mapeo superficiality might detain us briefly. I had difficulties understanding the complicated structuring of sociality into spheres of matri-clanship, patriclanship and privileged abuse described in Chapter 2. With exemplary forebearance, Mapeo Chamba informants tried to untangle my confusions in a revealing way: 'When I am dead . . .' the explanation would start, 'so and so will take my goats, so and so will bring so many pots of beer, the X will bring their cult dance and the Y their flute band . . .' and so on. It seems as if the nice calculus of mutual obligation and right supposed to inform mundane behaviour helpfully becomes visible in actions following death. Ritual seems to mirror life. But pursuing these relationships, I learnt that many of them are virtually devoid of other specific obligation. It is easier to argue that a relationship such as joking between clans derives its daily signifi-cance from the services partners provide for one another at their funerals, than *vice versa*. Likewise, affinal relations, once the immediate dues of marriage are discharged, are most specifically defined by potential funeral obligations. Where everyday relations are more important, towards close kin, special age mate friends, and hamlet co-residents, there is still a funerary counterpart in specific and defined service. Co-membership of men's cults, a pre-eminent form of masculine sociability, similarly entails specific funeral services. All this means that Mapeo Chamba funerals are complex, protracted and rule governed events—not only for visiting anthropologists but in Chamba eyes also. Because of this, observances at death are experienced as events that actualise a social structure of rights and obligations, values and norms. This is not because African notions of person prefigure later self-conscious ideas of office in western thought (Fortes 1987: 89), but because some African notions are themselves officelike in conception.

Mapeo Chamba funerals invoke virtually every significant type of relation-ship that exists between people singly or as members of categories. Moreover, they do this in highly circumscribed and rule-governed contexts. During these events everyone knows what they should be doing. As a consequence, people often acquit themselves well; Mapeo Chamba do funerals well together, and given the character of Mapeo Chamba society this is no mean feat. Funerals are exemplary enactments of sociality.

It is, therefore, not accidental that Mapeo Chamba find funerals instructive about their culture. As soon as people grasped my interests as an ethnographer, they were persuaded of the absolute necessity for my attendance at every funeral performance. By being there, and behaving appropriately while there, the quality of Mapeo life would effortlessly become apparent to me. I believe Mapeo Chamba made this assumption because they experienced its truth.

Funeral services demand a degree of co-operation between members of different clans which is without parallel. More unusually, the ceremonies involve the different religious communities of Mapeo: the traditionalists, Muslims and Christians. This is possible because the terms of the celebration are defined by the religion of the deceased (typically traditionalist during the mid-1970s). The curtailed funeral distributions on the deaths of small children are devoid of great importance in the traditional scheme. I have witnessed Christian sons request prayers at the gravesides of their fathers without changing the Chamba character of the funeral wake. Funerals are one of the few remaining events in which Mapeo Chamba are able to act collectively with the sense of their territorial and dialectal identity and across the grain of the emergent religious differences. This circumstance may not persist when they have to commemorate the deaths of Muslims and Christians more frequently.

By claiming funeral ceremonies to be exemplary performances of sociality I do not deny that they are competitive affairs subject, as are other public events, to judgements about scale and success. But stressing this motivation alone fails to explain the scale of co-operation. Wakes are less the last expression of relations that have been important to a person during life, than they are occasions for the performance of an inventory of social roles—whether these were significant during the life commemorated or not. This is the precedence between affairs of the life and the death that Mapeo elders drew when they responded to my queries about relations between the living in terms of mutual obligations at death.

Chamba broadly-based clanship systems do not seem to foster a high degree of interest in the fate or desires of individual dead. The dead are most dangerous in the years immediately following their burial, when curses they may have made during life have to be deflected by offerings on their tombs. At this stage, they are still addressed as mother, father, maternal uncle and paternal aunt. Other than this the dead, as forebears, do not figure largely in Chamba explanations of misfortune. Genealogies are not recalled to name the distant dead, and relics of the dead tend to be aggregated rather than distinguished. Chamba beliefs stress the transformation that occurs at death, and the translation of the dead to the underworld. In the chiefdoms, dead chiefs and priests exert more persistent influence over the living. But Mapeo achieved no accepted hierarchy; so no clan is able to convince others of the special significance of its dead. Mapeo is the least 'ancestral' variant of a not very 'ancestral' Chamba culture.

Mapeo funeral observances are held in a sequence which varies little for the culturally differentiated Mapeo patriclans. Some patriclans do not perform some of the stages, and this is taken as further evidence for their cultural distinctiveness. But the sequence is sufficiently similar for informants to reason most of the time that different clans are simply doing the same thing in their own ways. The rider, in their ways, is important because the exact manner in which each stage is performed is described as highly variable and considered to be characteristic of the distinctive patriclan culture involved. Most funeral observances may either be held as separate occasions or run end to end as a single extended event. Three characteristics of Chamba (and most traditional African) funerals deserve passing mention.

Full mourning occurs only for 'deaths'; the demise of children, especially before they are able to speak, but traditionally before initiation, is termed 'return' rather than death. A small distribution of beer marks the occasion, which is particularly dolorous. Even this remembrance was previously denied to breech births. Elaborate wakes, conducted in almost festive mood, are reserved for the aged dead, who became senile. In these cases, the breath of life ran its course to exhaustion; death was not caused by the hand of man (witchcraft) nor by the hand of *jup* but by God (*Su*), or rather, the finity of God-given breath.

Funerals are not conducted for bad deaths: caused by bodily decay or the loss of bodily control that results in burning. Known witches, who were clubbed to death with staves, were reportedly thrown unceremoniously into the bush. Full funeral celebrations are held only for adults who do not die badly; and the scale of remembrance is greatest when life ran its full course.

Attendance at funerals (most particularly wakes) is obligatory for kin, clanspeople, affines, co-residents, joking partners, fellow cult members, age mates and friends. But it is an obligation which appears voluntary: presence excites no comment, only the absence of those who ought to attend is considered to be motivated and becomes a subject of local interest.

Wakes, like all Chamba gatherings not influenced by some variant of world religion, are fuelled by beer. Pots of beer must be provided to satisfy specific obligations to classes of mourner and to offer hospitality to the large number of people drawn to the occasion. Beer and meat are virtually synonymous with sociability. However, beer drinking and meat eating at funerals are controlled, connoting a regulated sociability. Excessive beer drinking, associated with the highest form of being well together, occurs during the harvest festivals and at *jup* meetings rather than at wakes. Beer drinking is more prominent at the annual, collective commemorations for patriclan dead. But these events are envisaged as critical to the prestige of the sponsoring clan (members of which do most of the drinking).

Funerals, and especially wakes, consist, in summary, of the performance of obligations following approved deaths and under the sign of controlled sociability. They have numerous stages.

Burial (*we nin*) takes place on the day of death. The corpse is wrapped in cloths donated by the children of the deceased, his or her father's matriclan and members of other matriclans united by common clanship. Some older people store at least a single cloth as a contribution to their own burial shroud. A length of narrow, local cloth is retained by traditionalists to tie their shrouds. (I knew older Chamba who regularly included these items in the small parcel of possessions they carried when they stayed in their farms.) The bundled corpse is further encased in a mat and carried to the patriclan graveyard to be interred in a shaft and niche grave. For the owners of patriclan cults, esoteric activities are performed once the mourners leave the graveside. The wrappers, or some of them depending upon clan custom, are removed for reuse before the grave shaft is sealed with a flat stone or inverted large pot. During wet season further ceremony will be deferred, but in dry season burial is immediately followed by 'crying (not weeping) the death' (*we kpan*) or 'death water' (*we 'og*, where water refers to clear beer). Although the corpse has been interred by this stage, the connotations of the term 'wake' best describe the secondary ceremony after burial.

The wake is a three or four day and night event (following conventional African connections between numbers and gender) involving dances and gifts. It is to this, largest scale personal event, that my suggestion of an exemplary performance of society applies. Despite its scale and expense, Chamba informants are clear that the wake has no bearing on the fate of the deceased or the capacity of the living to communicate with him or her. Nor is the wake the occasion for the redistribution of the deceased's goods or statuses among inheritors, nor for the propitiation of the dead person, nor for detecting the cause of death. These activities have separate names and, although they may be performed during the period of the wake, they may equally take place on another occasion. None of them is an instrinsic part of 'crying the death' or performing the 'death water'.

Numerous performances, which I shall only enumerate here, make the complex of observances at death highly protracted. *Pɛn giran*, the contagious or dangerous thing, is a highly secretive exoneration from witchcraft performed by representatives of the matriclans related to the deceased. Each representative drinks 'thick beer' from a single large calabash before two of those attending wash their hands in the lees allowing the beer to drip onto the ground. Offering the beer to the under ground dead will result in the automatic sickness of anyone who caused the death by witchcraft. A further exoneration called *sori pɛn*, forked twig thing (because a relic, usually nail paring, of the dead is held in a three pronged stick—like the support of a household pot) is part of the funerary observances of some but not all clans.

Lera players in Sə ji mum hamlet, Mapeo.

Additionally, there should be a ceremony for the redistribution of the deceased's property (bɔn 'ən, 'climbing the granary') at which further distributions of beer are made. Later, the death will be recalled during the annual ceremony held by the patriclan for its collective dead (we sim, death beer; described in Chapter 3). 'Skull taking' (tɛn wuri) for aggregation to the patriclan skull shrine occurs two to three years after death. This is a relatively private act carried out by his children (for a male deceased) or her brother's children (for a female). Further collective ceremonies are held as much as ten years apart to make offerings to the small beer jars of the patriclan or matriclan dead. More irregularly a commemoration is held for the dead members of some, though not all, cults (jup kpa wari, 'the cult cries the big man'). In their entirety, Mapeo observances after death are protracted and complex, and would appear more complicated if I described the differing ways that patriclans performed the 'same' events according to their lights. All the acts that appear to Chamba to be instrumental occur outside the wake. Yet when Mapeo Chamba talk about the funeral it is to the wake that they refer. 'Crying the dead' is expressive rather than instrumental in the Chamba scheme of distinguishing such things.

Exactly what occurs during the wake depends upon the clanship affiliations, gender, and career of the deceased. At the wake of an elderly male traditionalist, the following elements would certainly be present. The wake begins when the bamboo lera flutes play in the entrance hut to the 'death compound' (we ya). A man's compound is likely also to be his 'death compound'; a senior male of the hamlet provides the 'death compound' for outmarried women or for men who established their homes away from their clan's hamlet. Not all clans possess lera bands, this is an item of the cultural differentiation of patriclans, but those who lack this musical resource can call upon their joking partners, kpɔmbu, or hamlet co-residents, ya isa tu bu, those of the compound entrance, to supply the flute band for them. Clans which lack lera usually have bands of gourd horns which they are able to bring to funerals. A further resource, the masked dancer nam gbalang, also forms an element of this mutual support between co-operating patriclans. Wakes for elderly women are similar to those for men but last four days; the performances of the men's contagious cults are substituted by the women's cult of jɛm consisting of songs accompanied by the clanking of small hoes that are women's cult instruments.

Until about ten p.m. the lera flutes continue to play in the entrance hut of the death compound. The men's music accompanies the women's dancing and singing. Many lera songs concern death, and performers say that they recall their own losses even as they mourn the individual who has died. They cry not only for the immediately deceased but especially, so they tell me, for their own mothers and fathers, brothers and sisters, whose memories are recalled by the words and tunes of the lera songs. After lera has stopped playing, a succession of the men's cults to which the individual belonged will arrive to perform in front of the compound or to lead singing from within a mat enclosure which has been prepared for the occasion. The women present at the wake avert their faces so as not to witness the cult performances, especially those of the disease-causing cults. Late at night the women retire to sleep in the entrance hut where they will also pass the following two nights.

The following day, the wake resumes early when the 'beer of waking the death sleepers', *sim jimsi we lam tu bu*, is brought. Further cults perform during the morning, and their members are rewarded with stipulated amounts of beer, or, in some cases, the payment of a goat. Not all cult groups to which the deceased might have belonged will be able to attend the compound of death, this depends upon the individual cult charters, but if he has been at all active there will be cults to represent his patriclan, matriclan, father's and possibly grandfather's matriclan. Other performances may be brought by joking partners or clans united by common clanship. Each patriclan has its particular set of relations of co-operation in this division of labour. The afternoon's activities differ. The patrikin of the dead person perform dances which dramatise his ability as a farmer or hunter, or some office owned by the clan. Joking partners may pose as transvestites or fools during these dances. At some stage of the afternoon's proceedings, one or more of the masked figures enters to dance outside the death compound. Each of these performances has to be paid for by the principals of the wake (notably children, sisters' sons and 'children of the matriclan'). A further general and formal distribution of beer is made by the deceased's close patrikin to representatives of the patriclan, matriclan, father's matriclan, mother's patriclan and paternal grandfather's matriclan. The man's sons must make a donation to their father's age mates, which should include a goat. A goat or cow should be slaughtered to feed the mourners, and a further animal killed so that close relatives of the dead man can take something away with them.

The matriclan of the deceased also have obligations. Apart from their share in the general responsibility to supply beer to all those attending the ceremony, they must give a goat to the matriclan joking partners and brew beer to give to the attending matriclan cults. In the case of one of the major patriclan cults (*bɔntɔng*), the matrikin must give a goat to the patrikin in order for the cult to perform. If the deceased was a woman, then the past affines with whom she stayed for a period of years would be expected to contribute beer in recognition of her farming services even if she bore no children during the marriage.

The women spend a further night in the entrance hut of the compound of death. They are rewarded the following morning with a goat, the 'goat to raise up the old women' *vin jimsi wɔbu*, so called because they would not leave until receiving it. With this payment the wake comes to an end. My terse description is not supposed to do justice to the zest of the event, but to emphasise the scale of co-operation required and the precise calculus of obligation set in motion.

Why should an exemplary performance of sociality take place during events following death? The efficacy of all instrumental Chamba ritual is attributable, in some part, to the power of the dead. Might the prominence of wakes be related to this? *Jup*, the most powerful of Mapeo instrumentalities, attend a man's wake to demonstrate that he was not 'for nothing', a man of no substance. There is symmetry in the presence at death of the institution that causes deaths and remains effective only because of relics of death and the power of the dead. However, wakes are explicitly not instrumental. Proper commemoration averts the wrath of the recent dead, but makes no appeal to the underworld dead collectively.

The scale of co-operation and the mood of solidarity typical of wakes argue for a different interpretation closer to the terms of Chamba exegeses. Death is described by Chamba as a transformation and experienced by the living in terms of estrangement or defamiliarisation. Unlike cultures that are 'ancestral' in tone, Chamba notions privilege a hiatus between living and dead. The underworld is an unknown country. In the face of the transposition and transmutation of the dead, funeral wakes assert the values of sociality and of the living. Speaking of their feelings during funerals, Chamba stress their memories of the deceased person and, time and time again, the more general reflections on those they have loved and who have died which are prompted in them by the familiar songs and tunes of the *lera* music. In the stress upon large-scale and precisely calculated mutual obligation to a common purpose, an idealisation of social life in the face of common mortality can be discerned. Given that so many misfortunes are attributable to social tensions and the failure to observe mutual rights, co-operation may offer intimation of a harmonious living that would transcend death. Without this undertone wakes could not be the exuberant and sometimes optimistic recollections of life they are.

Yeli: hierarchy and exemplary death

Mapeo wakes dramatise the sociality given a person by virtue of clanship, time and place of birth, as well as what that individual made of his or her endowment in life. In the end, the quality of life and the manner of death determine the scale and mood of the event. In this sense, Mapeo wakes are egalitarian. The annual commemorative ceremonies of Mapeo patriclans are also egalitarian. They differ from one another by virtue of the variety of patriclan cultures, but they support no hierarchy because the patriclans admit no mutual ranking. The Yeli image of community, in terms of a hierarchical, interdependent, differentiation of parts encourages a different perspective in which exemplary deaths and exemplary bodies have pertinence for the entire community.

The royal matrikin, and pre-eminently the Yeli chief, preserve the cool centre of the community from which health, fertility, accord, rain and well-being emanate. Priestly patriclans control the heat and sickness of *vɔm* cults. Through his assistants the chief orchestrates the efforts of his community simultaneously to ensure the welfare of their village and to domesticate those forces (rain, locust and smallpox) upon which the pre-eminence of Yeli depends. Death of the practitioners of these arts instigates crisis involving the localisation and transmission of their powers. The problem is posed differently for the chief and the priest. Since the chief is pre-eminently passive, a resource in himself, the drama of succession requires that the late chief be placed among the dead and a successor chosen to embody his position. As more active agents, the priests' successors must master the techniques and aptitudes of their predecessors. The distinction resonates with the imagery which associates the chief with his body (and indeed the royal matriclan with their common physical substance) and the priest with his skull, the seat of identity, knowledge and personality. Distinct problems of death and succession in the two cases are entailed by the dissimilar ways that continuity is conceptualised.

In strictly formal terms the annual commemoration of royal deaths in Yeli is a counterpart to the commemorative ceremonies of the Mapeo patriclans, also held annually (Chapter 3). Contrasting these two events would involve setting the image of differentiation and co-operation in Yeli against the antagonistic order of exclusive patriclans in Mapeo. However, because of their similar scale, involving entire communities, and by virtue of the shared sense participants evince that they instantiate collective life, Mapeo wakes and Yeli royal commemorative ceremonies make a more enlightening comparison.

I twice witnessed a series of rituals that are supposed to be carried out every other year in Yeli (in 1977 and 1984, postponement due to a bad harvest had breached the biennial rule). In its essentials, *val batna* (death beer) is not a complex event. Its apparent objective is to assimilate deceased members of the royal matriclan, *gad kuna*, to the collective dead of the clan. Proceedings are financed by the children of the dead who should donate at least one goat, a cockerel, a basket of guinea corn for beer making and a bunch of guinea corn heads. In addition to this, they pay the blacksmith's wife a small sum to make the miniature beer pot (*vad nyin wa*, skull pot child/small) which will be added to the royal shrine at the end of the ceremony. The design of the pot indicates the gender, state and status of the corpse it represents. Round pots represent women, pots with flattened bases are for men, while chief's pots are built onto bases which make them taller than those of other people's. A single knob represents a navel and multiple, small extrusions may be added to any of these designs if death was caused by smallpox. The addition of new pots to the clan collection also serves as the opportunity for sacrifices to be offered to the dead collectively. This outline is obscured in performance, at least to the outsider, by the fact that three distinct and self-contained events, with rather similar names, are performed sequentially and together referred to as *val batna*. Properly, these three rites are: *val batna*, death beer, *vag batna*, stone beer, where the reference is to the stone hunting shrine of the clan, and *vad batna*, skull beer, during which new pots are added to the royal clan's pot shrine.

In 1984, people began arriving to witness or take part in the performances on the evening of Sunday 15th July. Many had crossed the border from Nigeria, for the main direction of exodus from Yeli has been westwards, where several villages have been established just inside the Nigerian frontier. Since the chief's compound cannot be used as the 'compound of death', the majority of the visitors lodged in the compound of the next oldest member of *gad kun* whose home became the focus of performances during the next day. Throughout the night, women sang to the accompaniment of the small hoe blades they clanged together. Their songs were heard but not witnessed by men, since in Yeli, unlike Mapeo, singing *vɔm kɛn* (women's *vɔm*, equivalent to *jɛm*) is hidden. This *vɔm kɛn* belonged to the royal matriclan, and marked the deaths of three women among the four *gad kun* who died during the preceding year. The man's death was signalled by Dura, the chief priest, blowing on an animal horn (*ya gasa*) during the night. The notes of the horn were said to be tonal counterparts of *la val val*, the flame flickers, which also puns the term *val*, death. Bouba volunteered that the only other occasion he knew the horn to be blown was in the event of attack, then it would sound *la tɔru*, there is fire here, and every man would recognise a call to arms. Earlier in the afternoon, the stones (*vaga*) of the chiefly clan's hunting shrine had been coloured and put into order (discussed in Chapter 7), and a chicken killed by cutting off its head (*dub vaga*, decapitating stone). The chicken had run headlessly about, a propitious omen for the clan's hunting.

On the following day, performance resumed in mid-morning when the blacksmith chief (*gad lama*) led drummers and gong players accompanying a dance to celebrate chiefship. A cloth print of a lion was hung over the fencing of the death compound, for want of a genuine lion or leopard skin, and women dancers wielded the spears of chiefship. The first dance was called man's dance (*nab van*) and the second woman's dance (*nab kɛn*). At different times, three masks (*lang gbadna*) belonging to the Yeli matriclans danced singly or in combination. The royal mask danced slowly and alone, an indication—I was told—of its great age; the mask seemed tetchy lashing out at crops as well as dancers. Bouba noted that it had a 'bad head', slightly misshapen in the mouth with short horns. Pregnant women should avoid sight of it in case their children were born with ungainly heads. The mask's gong-beating chaperon, the elder of the royal clan whose home served as the 'death compound', had to harangue it into dancing at all, and it periodically tried to sit on the drum and altogether arrest proceedings. By early afternoon, the *lera* flutes of the chief were brought out by their custodians led by Gban Ti, a son of the chief but acting in this context as a patriclan appointee. In turn this performance gave way to the *sɔsa* pipes of Jɛngnɛbba patriclan, instruments made of simple calabash tubes. Jɛngnɛbba and Gbantinɛbba performed because some of

Persuading the royal mask to dance.

the royal dead were members of their patriclans. At dusk, *lera* recommenced and the mask of the royal matriclan emerged a last time to drive away onlookers allowing the dressed log (*val wadkea*, dry corpse) to be rushed out of the death compound and away towards the hill where it was thrown into the bush.

In some respects, *val batna*, death beer, is a counterpart to the Mapeo wake or death 'water' (*we 'og*). Apart from the relatively compressed nature of the event, and its simultaneous remembrance of more than a single death, the absence of men's *vɔm* is the most notable difference. *Vɔm* is specifically excluded from the funeral rites of the royal matriclan; this is a question of incompatibility between the heat of *vɔm* and the coolness desired for royal rites.

For several reasons, events the following day started slowly. It rained in the early morning, which kept people under shelter, and about two hundred visitors to the small hamlet had to be fed before events could resume. In addition, the official (Da Dena) responsible for making offerings to the skulls (*pɔb vara*) no longer lived nearby; although his duties had been taken over by Dura, it was necessary for him to attend to oversee performance and taste the beer that had been prepared in his name for taking to the shrine. Eventually he arrived, drank a pot of beer with Dura and Bouba and declared that it was of fitting quality. Another pot was taken for an observance called 'kicking the calabash over' (*magɔ tan*). At burial, the calabashes of a deceased woman have a little oil put in them and are left inverted at her graveside. During death beer, the calabashes are turned right side up again and have no further significance.

By midday, visitors who had come only to see the dancing and drink beer left Yeli, and the real business of skull beer (*vad batna*) began. Amidst a clattering of gongs the main officiants made their way out of the village, past the site of the older Yeli village and up the hill towards the graveyard. On the way up is a place where the chief's assistants (*gbana, kuna* and their patrikin) stop to look for the *vad*, small spider (the same term as skull), of the royal matrikin. They brush around a stone looking for a small, light-coloured spider. Red spiders they reject as 'joking partners', but once the light-coloured spider is found the women ululate, hand gongs are beaten and *gbana* picks it up on a head of guinea corn and runs to the pot shrine. The spider is deposited from the head of guinea corn among the pots and *gbana* then calls the head priest, Dura, who emerges from the stone behind which he has concealed himself during this time. The actors are now in place to make the offerings (*pɔbnbia*).

From the front the layout looks like this: beyond some large black boulders is the royal graveyard, and male members of the royal matriclan, along with the chief's sons, his assistant (*kuna*) and the priests Dura and Da Dena are installed in a small grotto. Below them is the large collection of small pots which has accumulated over the years on the death of royal matrikin. To the right and slightly below the pots are the Yeli men and to the left and further below are the

Part of the collection of skull pots for the Yeli royal matriclan. All have been spattered with ochre and corn paste, and the new pots (detail in bottom picture) are stopped with locust bean leaves and heads of guinea corn.

Yeli women, who for this occasion have to wear the old women's garb of leaves tucked into their waist bands at the front and back. Ideally, they should also untress their hair, but their reluctance to comply forced the chief (in 1984, although not in 1977) to issue a general amnesty on hair tressing. Some younger women have also added undergarments to the leaf dress, a modesty that had apparently not been of concern in 1977. The anthropologist, as well as some Christian members of the village estranged from traditional practices, witness the ritual from further off facing the shrine.

First the women are asperged with water. In this context, the water is called dew, *misa*, the most cooling type of water and a euphemism for rain. The analogy with rainfall is also evoked by the spraying of water from the small leaves of a sprig from the locust bean tree (*lɔm*)—customarily used this way both in Yeli and Mapeo. Cooling protects women from the consequences of being in a place normally forbidden to them. Next the four new pots are brushed with burned feathers plucked from the wings of a white cockerel to 'remove the blacksmith's feet'; the feathers are thrown away. The throat of the cockerel is cut, and its blood drips onto the four pots. Beer is poured and drunk by the officiants; a little beer is put into the pots and some of the lees turned onto the ground in front of the pots. Brilliant white corn paste (*kɛn kum suma*), removed from the brewing beer after its first boiling, is spattered over new and old pots alike. Then a goat is sacrificed by Dura who punctures its windpipe with the circumcision knife that he wears around his neck on ceremonial occasions. To some onlookers it appears that the goat is simply laid upon its side and expires as Dura places his hands on it. After this, both men and women are daubed with the corn paste on their foreheads and stomachs. There is a special treatment for a woman failing to conceive: Da Dena uses two fingers to trace lines in corn paste to either side of her belly and daubs paste on her upturned palms which the woman must clench in order to carry fertility from the hillside back to the village. The pots are spattered with red ochre of kaolin mixed with shea butter oil (*kasa*) and finally stopped with bunches of locust bean leaves. The chicken is cooked and eaten and some of its insides left before the pots. The goat is butchered and its horns left by the pots. The meat, taken by the officiants to the village, is cooked and eaten there. The chief, meanwhile, supplies beer to a gathering of the population behind his compound.

On the final day, the main officiants, along with the *vɔm* priests (said to attend only to show their general approval), visited the chief to share beer. Because of his age, the chief had remained within his compound throughout. Dura and one of the chief's son had returned to the hill during the morning, whether to drink the beer left in the small pots or to turn it onto the ground was not clear. Previously, goats brought to Yeli had to be cooked and eaten there. Now, with the dispersal of the community, the children of the dead were expected to give the head, a foreleg and a backleg of the animal to their hosts but were then permitted to return to cook and distribute the remainder of the meat in their own communities, where they had also prepared beer. Like so many traditional Chamba events, these are admitted to be not quite what they were.

I never witnessed the burial of a Yeli priest, so my account is entirely reliant on report, but the significance of royal death ritual becomes clearer by contrast with this other exemplary death. The priest is said to be 'buried by vɔm': his burial is carried out by vɔm experts, the general populace is kept from the graveside during the final moments of burial, and vɔm horns play during his funeral wake. His successor is supposed to place a long gourd (pɔb) over the head of his predecessor and then cut through the neck. The operation elicits both distaste and fear. Skulls are 'taken' only after the flesh has rotted; shedding of the late priest's hot blood to take his skull is fraught with danger. The skull must be cleaned and preserved with red kaolin paste—as skulls always are. Only after this may the priest adopt the style of hairdressing distinctive to his office and be considered to have replaced his predecessor. Ideally, the late priest will have instructed his successor in the performance of ritual and ensured that he has 'seen' the cult apparatus under the guidance of an instructor who may safely reveal it. Once the choice of a successor to priesthood is clear (in Yeli as in Mapeo), he is believed to strengthen his powers by killing close kin, particularly his own children. The entire community depends upon acquisition by the priest of the ability to deal actively with the dangers that vɔm pose to the living.

Rituals for chiefly and priestly dead contrast point for point: lera in the royal ritual contrasts with vɔm for the priests, vɔm is specifically excluded from the royal rituals in which its practitioners, from 'indigenous' patriclans, have no role. Contrast between the impartibility of royal bodies and the extreme separation inscribed on the body of the priest has previously been remarked, but the point can be developed. The major sacrifice at the royal pot shrine is made without animal bloodshed—by puncturing the windpipe of a goat. Severance of the priest's head involves abnormal human bloodshed. Moreover, the priest's severed head is contained in a gourd as are the knives (called skull) that are used in circumcision. Gourd containers and instruments pervade priestly vɔm, but pottery vessels, including the 'skull pots', are associated with chiefship in several ways. The redness of blood is the dominant colour of the priests' death ritual but not of royal deaths. These are coloured white: the colour of guinea corn flour and of the lees from beer brewing—the medium through which the royal dead bestow fertility. This colour contrast is co-ordinate with a thermal distinction: the royal dead must be cool, participants in their ritual are sprayed with dew, hot vɔm are excluded from the event which is held during the period of the heaviest rains, after guinea corn has been planted. Priestly rituals involve the heat of cults, of illness, and of the letting of human blood.

CIRCUMCISION AND DEATH

Informants in Yeli and Mapeo may on occasion find circumcision akin to a kind of death. But the equation is never made the other way around: death is not a kind of circumcision. Any analogy between the two life crises has to be seen from the perspective of death which is vital to Chamba conceptions of the empowering of ritual. But the analogy does not have exactly the same significance in the two cases. The interpretation of Mapeo rituals of circumcision and death is truncated by the institutional framework within which they are organised. The differentiation of patriclan cultures in Mapeo argues for their historical distinction and incommensurability. No wider organisation is able to encompass these differences in a shared design unless we count the transient performance of sociality during wakes. The suggestiveness of the associations Yeli Chamba recognise to invest priestship and chiefship means that the actions of these officials can bring into play the very qualities of the life world: its shapes, shades, temperatures and so on. The antithetical characteristics of the officials permit the experience of a synthesis of worldly properties through ritual.

Within the lexical series—death, skull, relic, corpse, the dead, spider—that occurs in both Chamba languages, Yeli Chamba consistently favour 'skull' not only when Mapeo Chamba would use it, but also in contexts when they would use the term for the dead, or when they would not use any term from the series. Thus, circumcision knives in Yeli are named by compounds of skull; small beer pots to commemorate the dead, that would be dead pots in Mapeo, are skull pots in Yeli; the ritual called death beer in Mapeo corresponds to one called skull beer in Yeli. Skull is a more prominent idea in Yeli and more explicitly analogous to foreskin as a detachable part of the body. Although the identification between these body parts can be applied to Mapeo practices (such as the inclusion of ground prepuce in ochre applied to the forehead) it is difficult to argue that there is even an implicit sense in which the skull/foreskin analogy is recognised there. The Yeli exegesis can be transferred to Mapeo only as a logical entailment of other practices.

The analogy between circumcision and skull-taking also helps to understand why in Yeli circumcision is believed to coincide with the death of chiefs. Informants explicitly made this link through the idea of hot bloodshed menacing the chief's coolness and making him unacceptable to the cold beings of the underworld. But my impression was that they found the explanation unsatisfactory as a statement of the relations felt to be at stake. Circumcision, like skull-taking, involves the partibility of bodies, and matriclan chiefship relies upon the opposite image: the retention of royal substance, in order for the chief to be able to embody the welfare of his people. Yeli chiefship is predicated upon the denial of skull-taking that allows the royal matrikin to localise their substance in a matriclan graveyard. Circumcision and chiefship are logically antagonistic in terms of Yeli ideas. Mapeo egalitarianism, it hardly needs adding, generates no comparable tension between ideas.

6

THE ANNUAL ROUND

GUINEA CORN: CAPACITIES FOR PRODUCTION,
CIRCUITS OF CONSUMPTION

Chamba villagers describe themselves, before anything else, as farmers. Like other African farmers they express strong preference for one staple food, dismissing others as mere hunger breakers; for Chamba this food is guinea corn. To ask whether a person has eaten something is to ask whether she or he has eaten guinea corn. Despite having put away an apparently hearty meal of rice, yam or maize, an older Chamba would feel free to respond, in aggrieved tone, that there had been nothing to eat that day. As if this were not emotional load enough for one crop to bear, recall that guinea corn is not just *the* food but the means to make *the* drink, beer. Conviviality without beer, in the traditional scheme of things, is a contradiction in terms; beer is the root of Chamba celebration (death beer, death water, skull beer, beer farming . . .), as holy is the root of our holidays. In this respect, as in others, change is afoot. Muslims ought not to drink and some Christians either do not drink or do not drink the local brew. Traditionalists loudly protest the increasing scale of local commercialisation of beer brewing; though it is difficult to guess the period to which their nostalgia for beer as gift applies. As food, however, guinea corn remains unassailed.

Changes concurrent with increased monetisation of the Chamba economy have probably altered the sexual division of labour required to produce the livelihood of families. A consequence of this has been a loosening, more discernible in some concerns than others, of the older associations between gender and activities. Whether entirely accurately or not, older informants talk of a period before the introduction of groundnuts when farming tasks were definitely divided. Men cultivated guinea corn and women cultivated bambara groundnuts; although this did not imply that they did so alone. The two crops were often interplanted, or women might have additional plots of bambara nuts—sometimes on abandoned guinea corn farms. The heavy task of bringing land into cultivation was predominantly done by men. Men and women carried out the chore of weeding together, although women might work alone on their personal plots. Work parties rewarded with beer and food, and organised on a roughly rotational basis (so that the same people worked the farms of all co-workers in turn), were called to carry out the main, repetitive task of weeding either two or three times during the growth of the corn. On the last occasion, the lower leaves would be stripped from the guinea corn plants. Areas within and immediately adjoining the compound were intensively culti-vated to produce a wide range of plants, fruits and useful products: okra, taro, cocoyam, sweet potato, maize, sesame, rope plants, pepper, sorrel, pumpkin, calabashes and various other soup leaves. Other plantstuffs were gathered from the bush by women, in the case of soup ingredients, shea butter kernels, etc., and by men in the case of building and thatching materials and some less accessible fruits, like locust beans.

The division of labour in production mirrored distinctions in ownership, preparation and consumption. Men owned the guinea corn crop stored in their granaries, women owned the bambara groundnuts and most of the soup ingredients. All food was processed and cooked by women. In Yeli, I was told that beer preparation was once a wholly male affair after the germinating grain had been ground by the women. The same seems not to have applied in Mapeo.

The first major change in these arrangements is said to have involved the popularisation of groundnuts and their commercialisation during the colonial period. Groundnuts were assimilated to women's crops, and are still widely seen as such. However, once they became a major source of income men took up groundnut cultivation, which required that men's and women's groundnut fields were to be distinguished. Beer also became subject to sale: a practice condemned by some older men, who argue beer to be something properly gifted to others and received freely (but who nonetheless enjoy the regular availability of refreshment and profit from supplying corn to their wives). The preparation of beer for sale became a women's monopoly. Women may also sell a proportion of the beer they make for their husbands. The rough norm seems to be for a husband to anticipate his wife will produce a little more than one pot of beer to every two standard measures of corn, so that she can retain any extra pots. This can, and frequently does, lead to argument about the diluted strength of the beer, the number of pots of beer that should be available and so forth. One effect of brewing for the market has been, according to people's recollections, to increase the proportion of beer that reaches its consumers via women rather than men. It seems likely that the absolute amount of guinea corn used for beer making has also increased. In the past, the distribution of beer by women was largely restricted to ceremonial occasions, such as their women's cults or else particular events such as the harvest rituals. The prolifer-ation of men's cults meant that much beer was consumed by men in places from which women had to be absent. Previously, the distribution of beer to lubricate the wheels of sociability was predominantly a male role more than a female role, and among women occupied older rather than young women.

Except in rituals from which women are absent, men do not generally cook food and never prepare flour. The three stones of the cooking hearth, and the grinding stones for making flour, are virtual symbols of women's roles. The upshot of this division of labour was that guinea corn in the form of food was predominantly associated with female effort, while guinea corn in the form of liquid was usually distributed by men. The staple crop thus entered two different circuits for consumption. A third option was for guinea corn to be sold. The practice of exchanging guinea corn with pastoralists is certainly two centuries old, and levies of guinea corn were exacted from producers as payments to cults, as periodic offerings from Mapeo to Yeli, and during the nineteenth and early twentieth centuries by different Fulani adminstrative regimes.

The range of relationships sustained through guinea corn in the forms of food and beer differed. Food was predominantly prepared in order to feed the co-resident members of a compound. In polygynous or extended compounds, women might take turns to cook food. A wider distribution could occur at festivals or to feed workers collaborating in farm labour parties. Beer, on the other hand, was normally consumed by a wider range of people and in many more places. The sight of beer pots being headloaded from one place to another around the village to discharge social obligations is part of the daily scene. The obligations these passing pots represent are largely, but not solely, the affair of men. Men used guinea corn as a token of value in their public lives while women were, and are, more concerned with guinea corn as a value within the domestic sphere. Competition between spheres of use may cause conflict; women's brewing of beer for cash, and the suspicion that they divert domestic resources to this end, are denounced as antitheses of traditional order by some men.

While judgements of the quality of food are quite frequently voiced, and some women are known habitually to leave more lumps in their fufu than others, interest in food preparation does not begin to match the nicety of the judgements made of beer. As well as a specialised vocabulary of beer preparation, there is a general distinction between two types of beer, thin and thick (*sim 'og* and *sim 'im* in Mapeo; *batn wəla* and *batn nyingsa* in Yeli), and one of the types is sometimes specified as appropriate to a particular ritual offering. Special terms also distinguish beer that has not finished the process of fermentation from that which is ready to drink and that which is a day past its best. An etiquette of drinking informs even the most informal occasion. Beer is an elastic form of gift: able to be given to several people in different ways simultaneously. Unless bought by collective subscription, beer is always given to a particular person who then shares it with those present. The 'head of the beer', the first calabash from the pot, is usually given to an elderly or respected person. The metaphor also turns up in a curious injunction, since the chief of Yeli is expressly debarred from taking the first or last calabash of the beer. Refusing the head or bottom, he takes only the body. The filled beer pot becomes analogous to a person.

Despite the relatively equitable partition of agricultural tasks, 'farming' is pre-eminently associated with women. A number of pieces of evidence point this way. If we look at the verb to farm we find that it is closely related to the word for hoe (both are *ban*). Farming is the process of cultivating the land with a hoe, rather than for instance slashing at undergrowth with an axe or machete, excavating with an iron-shod digging stick, or even cutting the corn at harvest and plucking the heads of grains or fruit. The hoe is related to a particular type of agricultural work, a repetitive turning of the soil to remove weeds or break the hardening surface of the land. The hoe is pre-eminently a symbol of women. This applies particularly to an all metal hoe, with the head in the same plane as the handle, that Chamba claim to have been their traditional agricultural tool before the introduction of the wooden handled hoes they now use in which the blade is hafted so as to point back towards the user. Pairs of miniature, traditional, metal hoes are clanged together as a repetitive, percussive accompaniment to songs performed in women's cults. A large version of this hoe is the insignium of leaders of the women's cults. Worn hoes may be used to represent female characteristics (for instance in the impotence cult of *jup nu*, Chapter 3).

Because men and women both hoe, the strong association between one sex and that implement does not simply reflect practice but takes account of the motivations between other instruments and their users. Women's association with the hoe contrasts with men's relation to the instruments of hunting and war; men not women shed the blood of other creatures. Support for this level of exegesis can be found, in the manufacture of miniature hoes for girls and miniature bows and arrows for boys during their naming ceremonies. Within agricultural activities, the farming work of women with hoes contrasts with the cutting work of men done with sickles at harvest. Men take possession of the crop and all the labour it represents by cutting—in the same way as the patriclan takes possession of boys by circumcision and of the dead by skull separation.

This glossing of the distinction is writ large in official insignia. The women's cult leaders carry large metal hoes; their male counterpart priests have sickles with zig zag points that represent lightning. What then of the chief? Like women, the chief does not shed the blood of sacrificial animals. His insignium is the curved stick (*tɔma*) specifically explained as a tool for beating his subjects without drawing their blood. The reader may recall from my descriptions of circumcision in the previous chapter that replicas of the *tɔma* are carried by circumcision candidates. At least in Yeli, this suggests identification between the bodies of the boys undergoing circumcision and the chief (who problematically seemed to have little part in the ceremony that endangered him). In parallel fashion, we shall see how the Yeli chief gradually cedes his responsibility for the growing guinea corn to his priests, who are masters of cutting and separation. A contrast between gender-related tasks in Mapeo is in Yeli put to the service of defining the roles of political and religious hierarchy in the reproduction of the community.

THE STAGES OF GROWTH: YELI

Human growth and the growth of guinea corn are analogous in Yeli Chamba descriptions: both begin with a sowing of seed (*wu kanu*, to sow). In women, this sowing is followed by the cessation of menstruation (*sɔ da-u ya*, moon (month, menstruation) leaves there). Retention of blood, otherwise lost at menstruation, is the first sign of pregnancy; a child is not yet formed, but blood is accumulating to make this formation possible. According to Yeli informants, whether men or women, every month women become redder and fatter as they build up blood in their bodies, and then blacker and thinner as this blood leaves them. The early stages of pregnancy are therefore discernible as a reddening of the woman, especially of her stomach (it is called red belly, *bagal yɛla*). The analogy with guinea corn is close. Tiny shoots from the seed are 'white', but as they break through the ground they become 'red' (*yɛd di yɛla*, guinea corn sprouts red). The appearance of these shoots marks the time for breaking the 'guinea corn seed container' (*yɛd lum pɔba*), as I describe below.

As the guinea corn grows in the moist, cool atmosphere of early wet season, it turns darker (*dinga*, black or dark). And it grows until it 'hides the chicken's shoes' (*yɛd dɔ' ko dun-taba*). This is the proper time for the annual mourning rites (*val batna*, death beer) of the royal matriclan, that I described in the last chapter. It is also the time for 'hill beer' (*kɔl batna*), that I describe shortly.

The appearance of swelling—in the guinea corn or in the pregnant woman—is described in the same terms: *yɛd pa' bagal*, *kin pa' bagal*, the guinea corn or woman finds (*pa'* or *bɔb*) belly. This is the signal for *kay batna*, when the spirits of smallpox are called from the bush.

The end of the term of pregnancy is described in various ways: *bagal dɔ ya*, the belly ages, or *sɔ dɔng ya*, the months are sufficient, or *ngwu ya*, it is ripe. Now the child will come out, *wa pi ya*. In guinea corn also fullness precedes the children's (*yɛb* plural of *wa*) coming out, *yɛb pi ya*. This is the time of the cult performance called *vɔm ninga*.

As the corn becomes heavy its 'children' (seeds) hang down their heads, *yɛb bak yil ya*. The 'guinea corn children' are said to fear the cult that has played (*nɔ vɔm*). This is also the uncircumcised month, *sɔ za*, because the true nature of the guinea corn is not yet known—just as the true character of a boy cannot be known before he has undergone the test of circumcision. The time corresponds to that when *vɔm za'ana*, the circumcision *vɔm*, would perform if a circumcision ceremony was to be held during the year. From hereon no drum may be beaten, nor any loud noise made, until the harvest cults commence.

The ripening of the guinea corn (*ngwu ya*) corresponds in human development to the ripeness of the child's heart for circumcision. It is time to see the truth of the matter. Cutting the 'heads of corn' and circumcision of boys are tests that reveal true character. In other respects, harvest is like skull-taking, a removal of heads. The corn stalks will dry out and die, eventually (if they are not taken for some domestic purpose) they will be burned and become ashes. The corn is stored in the large mud-walled granaries, the largest of which are as tall or taller than huts in Chamba compounds.

Growth of the crop may more generally be divided into two phases. The first, from sowing to the appearance of the seeds, is likened to the period from conception to birth in humans. The second continues the analogy from birth until circumcision, following one set of associations, or from birth to skull-taking, following another. This division corresponds to another. During the first phase the growing plant requires coolness and moisture for it to darken and grow; during the second it lightens, dries out and assumes the determinate colour of its type. Humans also undergo transition from a damp, childlike state, to a drier, hotter condition. In old age they tighten and become less moist until the head becomes 'ashen' and finally, at death, flesh disappears. The transition between the moist and cool stage of development and the hotter and drier stage also witnesses a changing focus of responsibility for the developing crop.

Four major observances occur during the first phase; all are under the control of the chief of Yeli, who is responsible for providing the means to carry them out but not for performing them himself. The first of these closes the planting season; the second concerns memorial of the royal dead, which we have seen to be the occasion of a women's fertility ritual (Chapter 5); the third observance is an offering to the royal ancestors; and the fourth a gathering together of spirits, ultimately under the control of the chief, which are the means of his control over smallpox. I shall initially describe the first and third of these events. I have seen neither of them which are performed alone by the chief's priest, Dura. I am reliant on him for descriptions.

Yɛd lum pɔb

Yɛd lum pɔb literally means guinea corn seed gourd container (*yɛd*, guinea corn; *lum*, seed; *pɔb*, a cylindrical gourd container). Performance of this ritual coincides with the appearance of fruits on a tree called *zama zama* (possibly, *Entada sudanica Schweinfurthii*). The significance of this association could be explained only as conventional. The fruit and leaves of the tree are inedible for humans, but some of the fruits are taken by Dura when he performs his ritual which suggests that there is something more to this than I could find out. The chief contributes guinea corn and red bambara groundnuts for the ritual. Bambara groundnuts were the women's crop before the introduction of groundnuts (in Leko they are called *wad Samba*, Chamba groundnuts). The twinned offerings of seeds and nuts represent the fruits that men and women possess at the end of their labours. The crops are contrasted in terms both of gender and colour: guinea corn is the small white seed of men, bambara groundnut the larger red nut of women.

The priest leaves alone for the hill behind Yeli village, where he breaks the *pɔb* or gourd container. Returning he gives some seeds to members of his patriclan, who plant them in their farms. After this, the time for planting is said to be closed. We have previously encountered this type of gourd in two contexts: as container of the priest's head at skull-taking and as container of the circumcision knives, also known as skulls. Depending upon context, the *pɔb* is capable of evoking either belly or skull, or indeed both. Context would suggest belly/womb as the more likely of the two images here. Performance of this action precipitates the descent of the royal mask, *lang gbadna*, 'into the river'. In fact, the apparatus is stored in a cave, but it cannot dance from this time until after the harvest, when the chief gives Dura guinea corn to bring it back. In some respects, the mask is pre-eminently a representation of the wild, so it is fitting that it is banished from the season of cultivated growth—just as, we may recall, animality in children is banished from the village.

Kɔl batna

'Hill beer', *kɔl batna*, is performed alone by Dura on behalf of the chief. As he described it to me, it involves his going to a cave on the hill where the spears of past chiefs are kept. (*Tɔ sɔm*, yes spears—compare *tɔ mɛmbu*, statues supposed to respond to their owners' demands with 'yes, I shall do such and such'—the term is in Daka, recalling the Daka origins of the chiefship.) Each chief of Yeli has one of these spears, and should he bury it, smallpox would break out in the community. The chief of Yeli showed me his spear, a short metal lance with a pair of iron clappers suspended to either side of its point. Should he die, having buried the spear in a place unknown to his priests, there would be no way of halting the smallpox epidemic. Dura takes red and white paste (*kasa* and *kɛna*) to put on the spears and also on the iron knives of past chiefs, as well as onto a brass knife, with an ornate hilt, that is normally kept there. The lees of a pot of beer (*batn nyingsa*) are spread before the objects. These actions are interpreted by Dura as a straightforward offering to the past chiefs.

Kɔl batna inaugurates a period of abstention called *giri nyam*, which becomes particularly severe after *vɔm ning*. Loud noises are prohibited since they attract illnesses which roam about. The guinea corn is also vulnerable: mutton should not be eaten because sheep are cool, soft animals which die easily when sickness comes, and the guinea corn might do the same. Male farmers should not have sexual intercourse before going to the fields (an

injunction which does not seem to apply to women), and metal bowls should
not be taken into the fields. Once kɔl batna has been performed, the royal
funeral celebrations and fertility ritual takes place (described in Chapter 5).
For this period, the injunctions against drumming are relaxed. A final event
during this phase of the development of the corn assembles the spirits of
smallpox.

Kay batna

Kay batna is another composite of the term for beer, but efforts to gloss kay
tended to be circular: kay batna was named after the place in which it took place
(kay zɔng), but then the place was also said to be named after the event. The
central feature of this place is a small thatched hut without walls. The supports
of the roof are made of ironwood (sana). Each support is in three sections: a
standing forked stick supports the roof, and this upright is itself maintained
standing by two other forked sticks wedged against it, giving it a tripod base.
The uprights are set onto, rather than into, the ground. If the hut should be
blown down, a sacrifice of a sheep (or, if that was unavailable, a goat and some
sheep's dung) would be necessary to cool the spot before the hut could be
re-erected. Failure to do this would risk smallpox being loosed on the land.

Inside the hut are numerous small stones to represent smallpox (bəgələg).
The entire assemblage was given into the custody of Dura and his Sama
patriclansmen by the royal matriclan at a time shortly after the new arrivals had
shown both desire and aptitude for the responsibility by spoiling chiefly rituals
from which they were excluded. Even before this, the stones had been brought
to Yeli from Sugu, its twinned chiefdom to the west.

Kay batna occurs three or four days after the full moon of the month called
sɔ dinga, the black month. Traditionally, this is the hungry month which
explains its epithet: 'black' or 'dark'. Mapeo informants, asked about this
ritual, which precedes their own harvest celebration, claim that a donation of
guinea corn would once have been sent by all the places that recognised the
control of Yeli over smallpox. No work could be done during the two days
when the spirits of smallpox (kɔna mɛmbu in Daka) congregated. Mapeo
villagers would simply stay at home and drink beer.

Various specific donations are required within Yeli. The chief provides at
least two baskets of guinea corn to make beer. In 1984, one of these baskets was
of maize, but the beer made from this non-traditional crop was unacceptable as
an offering and could be used only for entertainment. 1983 had seen an
exceptionally poor harvest, otherwise the contribution would have been more
substantial and have consisted entirely of guinea corn. The oldest woman of
the royal matriclan, who is given the honorific title of mal kena, paternal aunt
woman, donated shea butter. Few women go through the laborious process of
making this traditional cooking oil now that groundnut oil is a convenient
substitute. The chief of smiths provided three pipe bowls and should have

The *kay* hut.

given two new mats. In the event one of these was made, during the ritual, by someone else. *Kuna*, the chief's assistant, was responsible for finding a large garden egg, and a pumpkin (in both cases the variety specified was that considered traditional to Chamba: *daksi Sama*, Chamba pumpkin, and *pɔd bira*, white garden egg). He borrowed the pumpkin, having none himself. He forgot the tobacco he was required to bring, and this oversight also had to be made good. Dura, the officiating priest, supplied the makings of the red and white dyes (kaolin and lees from beer mash), as well as brewing the beer and bringing along a chicken. The chief, in addition to grain for beer, provided a calabash of guinea corn, some salt, and arranged for cooking the staple meal to accompany pumpkin soup on the day after the main rite. Eventually, all these specific items were assembled to be used during a sequence of events that lasted (in the observer's time scale) from a Friday evening until the following Monday.

On the first evening, Dura brought two pots of beer to show to the chief. One of these was to be drunk by the Sama clansmen on their way to the hill; the other was given to the woman who had supplied shea butter. She invited the chief and others to share this with her at a small distribution held behind the chief's compound. The first full day of the event is said to belong to the Sama patriclan. Other than these clansmen, only a few specific officials may be present: the chief, if he wishes (the age of the incumbent in 1984 meant that he was not present at most events outside the village), the chief of smiths, the chief's assistant (*kuna*), and the priests (*ngwan*). In the early morning, Dura collected chiefly regalia from the chief's compound; the items he took were those he also carried for 'hill beer': the bent truncheon, insignium of chiefship (*vunɛd tɔma*), the chief's spear (*vunɛd dinga*), and a bronze handled knife. Additionally, he carried a spear and the insignium (*lama*) of his own office. Other priests possess *lama* in the shape of sickles; a different pattern of *lama*, uniquely associated with priests of the Sama patriclan, including Dura, is of entirely wooden construction, with an elbow terminating in parallel wooden plates reminiscent of the mouth of the Chamba mask.

Approaching the *kay* hut, the Sama clansmen threw dry earth ahead to warn of their arrival and paused to 'wash' themselves by rubbing red ochre onto their foreheads, arms and feet. Into this dye had been mixed cuttings from a succulent of male medicine (*gan van*) that grew by the edge of the site. Knives were left outside the precinct of the hut. The area around the hut had become overgrown since it was cleared the previous year. Initially, they uprooted the grass around the hut by hand; as they worked away from the hut itself, the men were given 'hoes' in the form of potsherds to assist their work. Later, these were carefully collected. The workers paused periodically to refresh themselves with small quantities of beer; heavy drinking was forbidden. The site gradually emerged from the undergrowth. The hut was enclosed in a small precinct entered between two standing stones. Small stones, like those in the hut itself, were embedded in the ground between the entrance stones and the hut. A pot, to the right of the hut for an observer facing it, was filled with water periodically to 'cool' the workers with spray from a sprig of locust bean leaves. Once 'clearing the place' was complete, the event could begin in earnest.

The two spears, the insignia of priestship and of chiefship, and the bronze knife, as well as stones inside the hut and littering the approaches to it, were sprinkled with red ochre (*kasa*), white paste (*kɛn kum suma*), and blood from a chicken's mouth. Tobacco, salt, guinea corn and the clay pipes were placed among the stones. Beer lees were reversed on the ground, and water poured over the backs of Dura's hands placed palm down upon the lees in order to make the ground 'heavy' and 'wet'. All this was performed wordlessly.

Silence was broken when Dura recited the names, as far as he could recall them, of his predecessor priests. *Kuna*, the chief's assistant, recited names of past chiefs but could remember very few of them. Dura then demanded a sheep of *kuna*, but the latter responded that it had not been a prosperous year, so he could offer only a pumpkin. Pieces of pumpkin, then garden egg, and then pumpkin again were skewered on grass stalks and laid before the hut entrance. Other skewers were later stuck into the roofs of the huts that the chief and Dura kept for their ceremonial apparatuses (in this context called *vunɛd wula*, huts of the dead or forebears). Pumpkin was a conventional 'cold' substitute for a sheep at *kay batna*. Before this action, the chief and Dura, but no-one else, had been tabooed from eating the new pumpkin (but not garden egg); now the prohibition lapsed. This completed the 'begging' (*pɔbnbia*).

The third phase of action was 'calling the dead/forebears'. Throughout the event, the chief of smiths and the Yeli chief (deputised by *kuna* on this occasion) sat together on one of the mats brought by the former. Dura used a second mat, that should also have been brought by the smith, to replace that left to cover stones in the small hut the previous year. The old mat was discarded into the adjacent bush. Upon the new mat were placed an antelope horn, *gasa*, and a special set of *lera* flutes (*led gidna*, the contagious or prohibited flutes) belonging to the chief. The antelope horn was blown three times softly and three times more forcefully to 'call the *vunɛpbira* and also to call to the guinea corn to ripen'. Dura then addressed the dead telling them to come to eat and drink, but not to stop on the path, nor to work for anyone else. If they subsequently left, then they would take a son and daughter from anyone for whom they worked. He emphasised that food, drink and fire were waiting for them in Yeli.

The speech was designed to attract the agencies responsible for smallpox and retain them in the *kay* place, 'working' only at the behest of the chief of Yeli. After this address had been made, there was some more drinking before the participants returned to Yeli in the evening to report to the chief that all had gone according to plan. During their return, the Sama clansmen emphasised that they were permitted to steal 'whatever they wanted' from the farms through which they passed. In fact, they took only small quantities of ground-nuts, but made a great show of eating them. Had there been sufficient beer to dance that year, then the Sama would have stayed at the *kay* place late into the night.

The following day, food was prepared early; the meal consisted of the guinea corn staple, ground with its husk and without winnowing, and pumpkin soup. In alternate years, but not on the occasion I was present, there is said to be a big dance accompanied by *lera*. Men must remove all clothing from their upper body and dance crouching on their haunches. Dura, leading the dance, would have held a calabash full of guinea corn seeds, Chamba bambara groundnuts, cow peas (*kora*) and *sulwa*, which I cannot identify. This calabash of seeds is substituted for the seeds left the previous year in the chief's regalia hut. The old seeds are simply turned out. Sama patriclansmen, but no others, would have returned to the hillside site and danced three times during the night. Dura should have gone to the hillside on the third day (Monday) also, to light the fire and blow the horn a third time. I fancy he did not bother to do so in 1984.

Local opinion is clear about the objective of the sequence of actions. Spirits responsible for illness, particularly smallpox, roam in the bush and are especially dangerous around harvest. By offering foods associated with the Chamba past, they are persuaded to come to the small hut outside the village and to remain there. Close proximity to these *vunɛpbira* invites danger to participants in the event who take a variety of precautions (leaving metal objects outside the precinct, remaining sober, clapping, strengthening with medicines, cooling with spray . . .).

As part of a sequence of actions performed during the growth of guinea corn, *kay* beer has additional significance. Growth of the guinea corn proceeds apace with a shift in concern from the *vunɛpbira* under their guise of royal forebears towards their aspect as malevolent spirits of disorder. In terms of organis-ational effort, the chief, his matriclan and his forebears, who were the prota-ganists of rituals insuring the germination and early growth of the corn, are displaced by the priest and his clansmen, who take responsibility for the later stages of growth until harvest. This change is obscured by the fact that the head priest, Dura, is a major actor throughout. In an attempt to clarify the situation for me he explained that sometimes he 'works' for the chief, and the chief's matrikin, and sometimes he 'works' for himself and his own clansmen as a priest. During the early rituals of the year (breaking the seed container, 'hill beer', royal 'death beer'), he works as priest to the chief; during the later rituals, involving the harvest *vɔm*, he works as priest to his patriclan; *kay batna* gave Dura pause to think. On that occasion, he concluded, he was working a bit for both. The 'black month' represents, therefore, a turning point in concerns. *Kay batna* occurs at full moon, but the end of the month/moon finds preparation well in hand for the performance of harvest *vɔm*.

Vɔm ning

The harvest *vɔm* belongs to the 'indigenous' patriclans of Yeli: to the Nyεmnεbba patriclan, the original owners of the land, and to the smiths, Sema. The performance that I witnessed in 1984 had been amended, like other communal events, to accommodate the facts that not all those who should have been present still lived in Yeli, and that the 1983 harvest had been so poor as to preclude general beer brewing. The gathering took place just outside Gbandiu, one of the three Yeli hamlets in Cameroon. A hut in the *vɔm* clearing (*vɔm zɔng*), with matting rather than mud walls, acted as 'container' for various of the *vɔm* instruments and paraphernalia. Large inverted beer brewing pots, no longer fit to serve their original purpose, concealed other cult apparatus, and numerous medicine plants grew on the edges of the clearing.

Members of the sponsoring Nyεmnεbba patriclan, including their priest (*ngwan*), had come from the Yeli hamlet on the Nigerian side of the border to attend. Additionally present were representatives of Sama, Dura's patriclan, and Jεnga (equivalent to Yambu in Daka). In mid-afternoon, when Bouba and I arrived on the scene, gourd horns were stacked to the side of the dancing area after having been repaired. A tuned set selected for use was embellished with a criss-cross design in guinea corn paste. Moves were afoot to decorate the horns with porcupine quills, but ominous clouds gathering overhead persuaded officiants to skip this adornment and continue in haste. The largest of the horns, called 'mother' of *vɔm ning*, was decorated with the horn of a witch-duiker, *gbo'a* (see Chapter 7), stuck upright onto the top surface of its final section.

The performance had a number of stages. Initially, three pots of beer were brought, of which the first, a thin beer, was to welcome those attending. Some beer from the second pot of thick beer (*batn nyingsa*) was poured onto the ground to 'make it heavy'; the remainder was poured into a clay bowl (*dəga*) and divided among those initiated into the cult. A third pot was used for general drinking. Two small pots filled with beer were stuffed with the leaves of the shea butter tree (the feminine associations of which are discussed in Chapter 8). Beer was daubed onto the *vɔm* horns with the leaves, and finally the leaves were run up the horn stems and flourished in the air. This action was said to encourage the guinea corn to grow tall. Along with the leaves, participants held sprigs of a small plant called *sigəna*, used to represent the guinea corn. Next, the participants assembled all the equipment for use in the dance: the horns, sack rattles, metal rattles, a bow puller and the sickles (*lama*) belonging to the different priests. A member of Sama patriclan circled the stack of equipment making small holes with the point of an antelope horn, he was followed by a Nyεmnεbba priest who planted the *sigəna*. After circling the drums, they shuffled towards the equipment, repeating the entire procedure twice until they had performed the actions three times in all. Finally, all the *vɔm* equipment was knocked over (*vɔm sudnbia*).

Three priests (Dura and two *ngwanbira*) then took their spears and standing behind the drums threw the *sigəna* to each side. Each recited the names of his predecessors and the names of past chiefs, in so far as they could remember them. Every priest wore a small stoppered horn on a neck thong, from which he contributed a small amount of *kasa*, red kaolin powder, for one of their number to mix ochre. A red line was marked down the centre of the forehead of each initiated member. Some male medicine was next cut and divided in two. One part was impaled on the sickle of the presiding priest, the rest was put into a calabash and mixed with water. Non-initiates had to look away as Dura apparently spat some of the mixture over the horns.

The dance that then began was led by the chief of smiths carrying the sickle of the cult, who was followed by Dura playing the largest of the horns and then the other horn players. They circled the precinct three times before leaving along the path towards the hamlet. When the procession returned shortly, Dura had shea butter leaves draped around his neck, and a leaf (*vɔm gila*) had been placed over his horn. The metal rattles were replaced in the *vɔm* hut. The dancers circled the enclosure three further times, this time leaving Dura alone speaking into the horn. 'The women ask; the men ask, has *ngwan* Silba [the owner of the cult, but absent] carried out *vɔm ninga*? Why do they ask so much? It depends on me? What has it to do with you?'. Dura replaced the large horn by the side of the *vɔm* hut, and as he did so swayed from side to side in order, he later said, to avoid back ache which was one of the symptoms associated with the horn. After this a general dance was begun on the instruments. In years when the preceding harvest had been better the women would attend to dance, but in 1984 they could not be invited. Later, *vɔm ning* gave way to *vɔm ding*, black *vɔm*, belonging to Jɛngnɛbba patriclan, and played with a similar set of tuned gourd horns.

The following day the chief was collected by Dura to be escorted to drink some beer with the *vɔm* officiants and express his approval of their actions. *Vɔm ding*, that is to say the players and their horns, then left the *vɔm* enclosure and, avoiding the chief's compound, arrived at Dura's home. There, the officiants were given a pot of beer and food. Later, they came to the chief's compound, where they were given a further pot of thin beer and another of thick beer to 'moisten the earth'. They also received seven lumps of guinea corn food to eat with a soup of dried meat. Eventually, they departed back to the Nigerian side of the border, where the custodian of the cult now lives.

A number of themes are evident to participants in this event. Making the cult is believed to encourage the growth of guinea corn. The weed, *sigən*, 'planted' during the *vɔm* ritual is inedible and occasions severe nuisance on farms: it produces prodigious numbers of seeds and its leaves cause itching which makes the task of uprooting it unpleasant. But, according to Dura, planting *sigən* expresses the hope that guinea corn will be as abundant as the weed. No-one could explain why the seed had to be planted with a horn, rather than a hoe. There might be resonance of image in sowing a non-domesticated plant with an instrument from the wild. Perhaps an association is suggested between the fertility of the wild—which need not be encouraged through ritual—and the fecundity desired of cultivation.

Other aspects of the event are explicable by its status as a *vɔm* observance which shares features with other *vɔm* (whether they concern the growth of guinea corn or not): the siting, covertness and use of gourd horns are such characteristics. Other features include the threefold (male) repetition of actions during the event because of the company of the dead, as well as the drinking of medicine and marking their foreheads with ochre by participants to fortify themselves against the hazards of such proximity to the dead.

The amount of paraphernalia involved is the result, informants say, of the number of cults participating: large metal rattles are from *vɔm van*, the 'male cult' concerned with snake bite; use of shea butter leaves is partly to be explained by their association with snake bite cults. Gourd horns derive from *vɔm dagan*, the cleansing cult. The numerous sickles and spears are from the apparatus of a variety of cults. *Vɔm ning* thus orchestrates offerings made to several cults via representative pieces of apparatus. In *jup kupsa* (the Mapeo variant) by contrast, the harvest dance is separate from the offerings to disease-causing cults.

At *vɔm ning* the chief's responsibility for the harvest ends and this task is assumed by priests, especially those owners of the earth whose occupancy predates immigration of the royal clan. From hereon, the chief is required only to endorse and support their actions. A variety of changing conceptions coincide and reinforce one another: the guinea corn no longer requires heavy rain as it did earlier, from hereon it will ripen in dew and heat. The chief's *lera* flutes, which cool and bring rain, must be replaced by the gourd horns of the 'hot' *vɔm*. Simultaneously, the guinea corn is losing its 'dark' colour and assuming shades of maturity; 'birth' is complete and the corn is undergoing the dessicating process that will last until cutting. The ambience fostered by the chief and his royal matriclan forebears is gradually displaced by the clan culture of the indigenous patriclans represented by their *vɔm*. Human growth and the growth of the staple crop are made mutual metaphors in Yeli thanks to analogies drawn between maternity, matriclanship, and the chief and paternity, patriclanship and the priest in the development of both.

THE ELABORATED HARVEST DANCE: MAPEO

The growth cycle of guinea corn is the same in Mapeo and Yeli; the two places are only a few miles apart. Most of the terms used to describe this process in the Mapeo dialect of Chamba Daka are close counterparts of the descriptive terms used in the Yeli dialect of Chamba Leko: the corn sprouts from a seed, the growing plant becomes pregnant (*sam pu*) and the children 'come out'. Beyond this point, matters diverge.

In Yeli, the development of the growing guinea corn plant is reflected in its colour changes. Thanks to a colour triad of the type classic in African colour symbolism, changes in plant colour can be described in terms also applicable to the human body: light, dark and red. The analogies cannot hold in Mapeo because Chamba Daka has a fourth colour term, covering green/yellow, that has the effect of establishing different colour contrasts for vegetable matter and human bodies (Chapter 8). This subversion of the close resemblance between human and guinea corn development may be one reason that Mapeo Chamba do not explicitly describe the two processes as analogic. There is no Mapeo counterpart to the division of labour between the chief's matriclan and the priests' patriclans in Yeli. Priestly officials in Mapeo preside over the later maturity of the crop as it ripens in the heat before cutting, but the earlier growth in the damp, cool and heavy earth has no obvious champion such as the chief of Yeli. This absence from Mapeo is part of a pattern of differences.

No Mapeo clan is able to encourage conception (of seeds, animals and women) as the royal matriclan, by virtue of its royal forebears, can for all who live in Yeli. In the rough and ready egalitarianism of Mapeo, skull or pot shrines are significant only to Chamba whose forebears are commemorated there. Positive encouragement for the early growth of the guinea corn is so slight that Mapeo observances suggest only avoidance of impediment. The early part of the wet season is virtually devoid of performances. Yambu patriclans hold their 'death beer' at this time, but this clan commemoration is unrelated to growth of the guinea corn. The oldest men of the community meet to perform the impotence cult (*jup nu*); and the feminine associations of both the cult and the time may explain why this is the appropriate moment for their single annual meeting. However, this cult also is overtly unconcerned with farming.

On the face of it, the sequence of Yeli performances concerned with the early growth of guinea corn is simply absent from Mapeo. However, while this is so in one sense, two provisos must be entered. Control over rainfall in Mapeo is an attribute of the power of the chief of Yeli. The absence of early wet season ritual, seen from this perspective, recognises a relative powerlessness. Secondly, the Yeli chief's fertilising power was constructed to the detriment of women who otherwise control impregnation and early development, of both children and guinea corn, through their bodies and their farm labours. In the absence of chiefship, women's power over conception and growth is undeniable.

The ceremonies of late farming season, by contrast, are more elaborated in Mapeo than in Yeli. The pre-eminence of *jup*, and competition between clans in terms of cults, provoked an escalation in the scale of activity around harvest time. Because *jup* are associated with taboos (*giran*), an idea that partly explains and validates their efficacy (Chapters 2 and 3), and since guinea corn is taboo to virtually all cults, harvest time is the occasion for a protracted series of ceremonies designed to render the new crop safe to eat for the community in general and more particularly for members of cult groupings who would otherwise be 'caught' by their cults.

Mapeo harvest ceremonies last four months. The major public celebrations take place in successive months, roughly between late September or early October and early January. *Jup nyɛm* inaugurates the series at harvest and renders the corn safe for consumption. The following month is that of the largest celebration, *jup kupsa*. Celebrations during the two succeeding months have virtually lost the public character claimed for them in earlier times. *Jup nyɛm gɔgan* and *jup kupsa gɔgan*, as their names suggest, are described as later stages of the two earlier performances.

Most of the terms have etymologies. The initial element of the names of the rituals events, *jup*, is the generic term for cult. *Gɔgan*, the suffix for the later stages, means grinding, which is logical since these events come after the beginning of harvest. *Nyɛm* and *kupsa* are more problematic. Mapeo informants commonly gloss *nyɛm* as home: the cult permits the crop to be brought home, or else calls the guinea corn home. However, the terms have different tones. Yeli commentators explain *jup nyɛm* as evidence of the derivative nature of the Mapeo rituals which were copied from those owned by their own Nyɛmnebba priests. This gloss is unknown in Mapeo. The many Mapeo villagers whom I have asked claim not to know any etymology for the term *kupsa*; some note that the celebration is named for the month in which it occurs, others that the month was called after the dance. Neither argument illuminates the sense of the term. A majority of Mapeo commentators believes *kupsa* to be a Leko word and predicted that I would find its sense in Yeli. No one in Yeli could enlighten me, but this presumption—that the unknown would be known in Yeli—is a Mapeo habit of mind as I have noted earlier.

There are several reasons for the density of events surrounding the four harvest festivals. Each performance consists of a series of dances held under the auspices of different clans and in different hamlets on successive nights. Disagreement over the rightful ownership of each dance is pervasive, and gains importance from more general dispute over precedence within the community. A second cause of complexity is that concealed *jup* rituals are conventionally timed to coincide with each public performance of a dancing *jup*. While the dances take place within the hamlets, and are attended by virtually all Mapeo Chamba, other rituals are conducted in the cult places at the foot of the hill. With so many things happening at once, the ethnographer is at a loss where best to be. After witnessing events in whole or in part three times (1976, 1977, 1984), my account remains partial.

Jup nyɛm

Jup nyɛm has a good case to support claims to its pre-eminence among Mapeo cults although, as we have seen, the terms in which Mapeo Chamba set up this argument render it impervious to resolution. Everyone agrees that the first stage of *jup nyεm* (called *sankin*) now belongs to Gbanmεmbu patriclan (children of *gban*). It is also agreed that Gbanmεmbu are of Yeli origin, and that they took responsibility for entertaining officials sent from Yeli to collect the tribute that Mapeo Chamba once paid there. The levy of corn and chickens was made by the chief of Gbanmεmbu in whose custody were the smallpox spirits (*kɔna*) which underwrote such authority as he possessed on behalf of the major centre which controlled this misfortune. *Sankin* is sometimes called the '*jup* of the earth/land' (*jup sɔran*), meaning that whoever owns *sankin* exercises a right over all the Mapeo land. Beyond this, consensus breaks down.

Gbanmεmbu's claim to pre-eminence within Mapeo is susceptible to different glosses. One of them, which reads the past in patriclan terms, asserts that Gbanmεmbu arrived from Yeli and inaugurated the harvest cult which demonstrates their ownership over the land. The other, which reads the past in terms of matriclanship, agrees that the Gbanmεmbu arrived from Yeli, but claims that the cult belonged to the matriclan of *nε kusum bε kun* (people of the hill matriclan) who were the indigenous ritual specialists for chiefs of *gang van ji kun* (chiefs of the red rock matriclan). This selectively echoes some Yeli accounts that 'chief of the red rock matriclan' (*gad bɔng yεl kun*) was displaced by the incoming chiefs' matriclan (*gang kun*). It is difficult to guess the circumstances in which such accounts first crystallised. Proponents of the matriclan view of history would bring their account up to date with the claim that the harvest festival became a possession of the Gbanmεmbu patriclan only when the administrative chiefship of Mapeo was assumed by members of the *dɔng kun* matriclan in highly confused circumstances during the early colonial period. Gbanmεmbu thus became chiefmakers to the *dɔng kun* matriclan.

Different interpretations of the ownership of *sankin* are related to differing conceptions of legitimate chiefship. According to the patriclan account, Gbanmεmbu are chiefs because they are both immigrants and masters of the major cult. Effectively this is a model of priestly leadership. The version which appeals to the earlier presence of two matriclans relies on a more conventional Chamba account of the separation of powers: indigenous peoples control the *jup* of the land while immigrants are chiefs. This is, in some respects, similar to the Yeli model. A third model proposes that the chiefs are matriclan immigrants but the priests are drawn from a patriclan which, although originally composed of Yeli immigrants, has been established in Mapeo longer than the chiefs—a modified version of the division of powers. Mapeo Chamba dispute not just ownership of the right to commence the harvest celebration, but also the significance of that contested right.

Practically speaking, the administrative system determines that chiefship will remain with *dɔng kun* for the foreseeable future and that the traditionalists will have little say in who holds the office; the last two chiefs have been Muslims anyway. However, the disputes remain crucial to traditionalists and

The harvest gourd horn band in Mapeo (1977).

figured prominently in their accounts to me of what was demonstrated by the dances. In 1977, when I was able to follow events most fully, there was a further complication. Although the *jup nyem* cycle was supposed to be inaugurated in Mapeo, in fact the first dance took place in a small hamlet about five miles away from the village (called Sam 'Og on the River Kila). The sponsors were from a clan of one-time blacksmiths (Dengbu) who had migrated from Mapeo into the plain. For their part, they claimed that their *jup* (*jamka*) had a traditional right to start the sequence since they were smiths. Mapeo Chamba interpreted their pre-emption as evidence for the disrespectful nature of blacksmiths—even blacksmiths who had abandoned their profession—and did their best to ignore them. None the less, that the ritual occurred when it did suggests yet a further model of pre-eminence within the community. Mapeo clans may be able to perform their harvest festivals together, but this ability implies no agreement about the significance of what they do other than a general recognition that disagreements were epiphenomena of the struggles for pre-eminence among clans.

The inception of the ritual cycle in Mapeo is very stark compared to the density of the action I described from Yeli. During the day, elders of Gbanmembu patriclan gather in the compound of the cult owner to hold discussions about the organisation of the event. They pay particular attention to the likely sufficiency of beer, which has been brewed from a guinea corn levy of two measuring bowls from each adult clansman. The beer has to quench the thirsts of all who come to play the horns or drums; should it run out they will simply stop playing and 'spoil' the cult. The horns, rattles and drums are brought out and repaired if necessary. As a token of their agreement, the elders then share a pot of beer. The dedication is brief. The players, most but not all of whom are members of the owning patriclan, gather just before dusk in a clearing behind the clan's main hamlet. The owner of the cult takes the largest gourd horn, called the mother (*nya*) of the cult, and intones into it, apparently in Chamba Leko. This language is little understood in Mapeo, especially when distorted through the gourd horn. As explained to me the message is addressed to the guinea corn, asking it to come home (though this explanation probably derives from the gloss of *nyem*, in *jup nyem*, as home) and requesting that nothing bad occur. I suspect that listeners impute the message rather than understand it word for word. Once this invocation is made, the dance begins.

Seven gourd horns are accompanied on a pair of sack rattles, wielded by the players of the two largest horns, and by three drummers. The players move into the matting enclosure (*jup kuna*, cult container) designed to conceal them from view and, as they do so, dancers assemble in the cleared area in front of the enclosure. The band sets up a furious melody of booming, shuffling, crashing and drumming which continues from dusk until the following morning. For their part, the dancers execute a repetitive dance: three steps in and out, and then three steps sideways slowly revolving in concentric circles. Both dancers and players pause frequently for the refreshment which the host hamlet must provide for them. The refrains of the horns are said to be traditional, but new words are added to them each year which pick upon faults committed in the period leading up to the dance: theft, adultery, meanness or some irritating character trait. Around midnight most of the dancers return home to sleep and the orchestra plays on alone until daybreak.

On the second day of the festival, *sankin* resumes playing in the enclosure during early evening. Then the hand drum is raised high above the matting fence to signal the end of the dance, and the women disperse quickly to avoid seeing the horns leave the enclosure. A quick supper is taken, and the dance recommences at a second site where dedication has already taken place. Three dances began simultaneously on the second night in 1977. They belonged to the priests of Mapeo, *ngwanbu*, drawn from patriclans which claim an easterly, Leko, origin. Two of the *jup* are said properly to belong to the patriclans, the third belongs to the elephant matriclan but is effectively in the possession of the patriclan. Only one of the three priests is presently resident in Mapeo village, the other two live in hamlets outside Mapeo where their patriclans migrated when the hill refuge dispersed. But each returns to his forebears' hamlet to begin the *jup nyεm* dance, which then transfers to the modern hamlet.

On the third evening, the dance moves to the hamlet of Natup under the auspices of the Yangur patriclan. This stage of the dance, called blacksmith's wife (*kpe ngwu*) for reasons no one could explain, once belonged to a slave of the bushcow clan. When he died it was agreed that the cult should pass to his patrikin, Yangur. I always suspected there was something more to this trans- action, but was unable to elicit further information. On the fourth night a final stage of the cult is held in Sə ji mum. This dance is called *wɔng ngwu*, Wɔng woman, and is said to belong to a clan of blacksmiths of Vere origin who live in the plain. They gave the cult to a son of an out-marrying woman so that it could perform in Mapeo. Again, I was unable to learn more about the circumstances of the transference.

In addition to the stages of *jup nyεm* which 'dance', informants told me of four stages which no longer danced. One of these, *nya jun* (*nya*, mother; *jun*, possibly groundnut paste), came into the possession of Dəngbu patriclan when the *dəng kun* line of its previous, matriclan, owner died out. It is said that the cult used to cure barrenness in women (compare Yeli above). A small amount of beer is still brewed for it. A further three stages of the cult are supposed to have been seized from erstwhile matriclan owners following witchcraft allega- tions or injuries. Little detail could be gained about these subversions. Only one other stage of the cult is performed outside Mapeo, and this apparently belongs to a matriclan in the plains hamlet of Bɔsi van.

Leaving aside detail now, let me recap the situation in 1977: the earliest dance, held by blacksmiths outside Mapeo, was marginalised by Mapeo informants; the right to inaugurate the harvest celebration in Mapeo was involved in disputes over chiefship which rendered its ownership open to at least three glosses; the three stages *jup* of the second day performed competitively, and one of them properly belonged to a matriclan; the performance of the third day had been transferred from matriclan to patriclan ownership under circumstances that were unclear; the performance of the fourth day belonged to a blacksmith clan that has donated it to a daughter's son. Four defunct stages had been taken out of matriclan ownership by patriclans. What appeared on the surface as a joyous festival of dancing, drinking and singing— and indeed it was this—was also the subject of competing claims of labyrinthine complexity. For what it is worth, my interpretation is that a few of the more populous patriclans of the community have been able to annex stages of the harvest festival, often at the expense of matriclans, and move them into their own hamlets. Most of the more important Mapeo hamlets are, thus, able to host a stage of the dance. Whatever process accounts for the present situation, the contrast with Yeli is clear. One reason Yeli exegesists can relate performances to the qualities of both the world they affect and the officials encharged with carrying them out, is that the institutional contexts of performance and interpretation can be imagined as stable. This condition did not obtain in Mapeo; in fact, ground and figure were reversed in that performance was interpreted as ground to discern the figure of organisation rather than vice versa. *Jup nyɛm* was interpreted as a display of the state of institutional conflict in Mapeo.

Guinea corn is taboo (*giran*) to the majority of Mapeo *jup*. When I accompanied Titlɛsime to the hillside in the daytime during the 1977 dances, apparatuses of numerous *jup* had been taken out to receive offerings before consumption of the new corn. At the meetings I visited, members gathered to 'repair' (*nɛgsi*, literally to make sufficient) cults concerned with bad deaths (*kɔngla, tɔlɔng, la gɔnsɔn*), snake bites (*sun sun, ngwan ji*), swollen stomachs (*nɔga*), sight defects (*langa*), bodily swellings (*yaguman*), as well as the women's cult (*jɛm*). With few exceptions, no particular rationale determines whether beer is brewed for cults during *jup nyɛm* or its successor *jup kupsa*.

Jup kupsa

The second cycle of dances in Mapeo carries far greater importance in the eyes of younger members of the community than does *jup nyɛm*. There are more stages of the dance, more beer is brewed and more people attend from outside Mapeo. For Chamba outside Mapeo, *jup kupsa* is *the* Mapeo festival. However, for the elders *jup kupsa* is less important, a celebration rather than an instrumental ritual. *Jup kupsa* is said to promote peace and agreement within the community, and it is considered wrong for any member of the community to be absent from it. A younger informant offered that if *jup nyɛm* is like Christmas then *jup kupsa* is like New Year.

The ownership of *jup kupsa* is not subject to the same degree of dispute as *jup nyɛm*. Although ownerships are known, and the owner of each dance may be called cult chief (*jup gang*, or the Fulfulde *ba laru*), most hamlets of the Mapeo culture and dialect area hold a stage of the dance. *Jup kupsa* is irrelevant to disputes over chiefship or the ownership of the land.

The cycle is inaugurated by the priests (*ngwanbu*) of the Jangbu and Sanbu patriclans of Mapeo and Tisayeli. To speakers of Mapeo dialect of Chamba Daka, *Jang* also means Chamba Leko, so that the ownership of the cult by these patriclans marks its eastern origin. The calabash horn bands may also be referred to as *jup Jang*. The stages of *jup kupsa* are very numerous; below I summarise only those performed in Mapeo.

	Owner	*Clan*	*Place*
Day One	*ngwan* Jambumi	Jangbu	Jang bum
	ngwan Tisayɛli	Sanbu	Tisayeli
Day Two	*jup gang*	kɔm kun	Na tup
Day Three	*jup gang*	kɔngla kun	Sabon Lai
	jup gang	jam kun	Da Lira

After three days of performances in Mapeo the *jup* 'goes' to the next village, Lengdo, and thence into the bush (i.e. the villages of the plain). At the end of each performance, which is identical to the *jup nyɛm* dance, a mound of earth is heaped behind the dancing place around which is attached a rope, like that used to bind heads of guinea corn into sheaves. This action is called 'tying the *jup*'s guinea corn' (*tang jup yiri*). It shows that the cult has agreed (*dəng*) to the harvest commencing.

Just as *jup nyɛm*, *jup kupsa* is the occasion for various other esoteric *jup* to be given the new guinea corn. In 1977, I saw the repair of various cults: the residue of stomach distension cults not repaired at *jup nyɛm* (*nɔga*), snake bite cults (*ngwɔm* and *jup lum*) and more of the women's cults (*jɛm*). However, the cult definitively associated with this time is *jup ya* (leaf cult). This *jup*, concerned with marriage and with sexual misdemeanours (Chapter 3), increased in popularity during colonial times and currently belongs to several matriclans and patriclans. Its expanding ownership may correlate with attempts by administrative agencies, both colonial and independent, to regularise Chamba marriage practices (Fardon, forthcoming a).

According to Chamba norm, wives were returned to their patrikin on their husband's death. Usually they would remarry, even if aged; occasionally they chose to remain with their sons. However, if the husband was an initiate of *jup ya*, each of his wives would have to donate a goat to the cult before remarrying or resuming sexual relations. The cult is said to have become a regular adjunct to *jup kupsa* during the thirties and forties. Male informants correlate its popularity with the increasing monetisation of brideprice, and with the burgeoning cash income that women were generating from their groundnut crops, and from the preparation of beer for sale.

Commenting on the *jup ya* rituals of the harvest festival, informants are most likely to draw attention to the preparation of a huge communal meal of yam (*gɔ*). This meal may be shared by initiates and non-initiates alike, but the latter have to leave without any thanks, 'like dogs'. In the past, but not that I have witnessed, Mapeo Chamba remember pots which overflowed with cooked yams and were sufficient to feed all comers. *Jup ya* rites are held simultaneously with *jup kupsa* by clans in a conventionally accepted order.

The distribution of cooked yam, another smaller cooked tuber called *sakum*, and fried melon seeds (*sina*), is considered the most remarkable aspect of the 'repair' of the women's *jɛm* cults. Like *jup ya*, *jɛm* is associated with the harvest time. Also like *jup ya*, beer brewed by women for their cults is said not to be *giran*, and it is through brewing beer for *jɛm* that older women contribute to the abundance of refreshment available during *jup kupsa*.

Despite the prominence of the cooking and consumption of yams and melon seeds during the celebration of *jup ya* and *jɛm*, despite the clear association between these two cults and the harvest celebration, and despite the sexual themes common to the two cults, no informant could explain the timing or character of the rituals other than in terms of convention. That the analyst could think of several reasons is irrelevant given that local exegesis offers no purchase on their possible relevance.

The final stages of the harvest festival

The final two stages of the harvest festival, the 'grinding' (*gɔgan*) versions of *jup nyɛm* and *jup kupsa*, can be passed over briefly. Seen as repetitions of the earlier cycles, performed by the same owning clans, they are nowadays observed in desultory fashion or not at all. The inaugurating clans, at least, take out the apparatus to play, but there is no general dance or beer brewing. In the past, it is said that dances took place on the model, if not scale, of the earlier events. None the less, the final rituals logically complete a series of performances. At *jup nyɛm*, supplies of the old guinea corn were exhausted in beer brewing and the new crop was called home. *Jup kupsa* celebrated the harvest by drinking the beer of the new guinea corn and culminated with the guinea corn standing in a pile, represented by a mound of earth behind the musicians' enclosure. The last two stages completed the domesticating theme by grinding the guinea corn. When the cycle of celebrations draws to its close by January, the harvest activities are virtually complete and the dry season is two or three months old. The guinea corn will have been returned to the village and stored in the granaries. Ritual interests are turning towards commemoration of funeral wakes for a backlog of deaths that could not be mourned during the farming season, but may receive their due attention now that grain is plentiful and farming activities have ceased to press heavily on the time available to cultivators.

7

THE ANIMATE WILD

In nineteenth century Mapeo and Yeli, the distinctions between village and bush or grassland (*po* in Daka and *fɔg* in Leko are also generic terms for grasses) must have been neater than they now appear. The hamlets were on the hillside, the farms were at the foot of the hill, and the bush was the area beyond the farms which was imbued not only with the dangers of the wild but also with the menace of slave raiders. Nowadays, some of the hamlets have been moved to the sites of the old farms, others are out in the plains and the bush has become diffused in between these and the scattered farms. The demise both of slave raiding and most of the larger mammals has led to the bush being less full of danger and of possibility than once it was. But its symbolic associations have outlived this decline in its potential.

Village, farm and bush are not identical types of place. Chamba Daka say they are going to farm (*gɛri ban*), as they say they are going to any other bounded place—a market, a village or town—but in going to the bush they say *n gɛt na po*, 'I am going into the bush'. The locative *na* has the sense of 'among' (as in the hamlet name *na tup*, among the shea trees), or surrounded and enveloped by (when the term is used to indicate something put into a bag, or encased in a wrapping). The bush surrounds, envelops and contains the individual who ventures there. It is an environment one is 'in', rather than a place one is simply 'at'.

Western views of the nature/culture dichotomy are susceptible to interpretation in at least two ways: oppositionally, as establishing a division between two spheres, or hierarchically, when culture is envisaged to be built upon a natural substratum common to living things. Chamba notions are open to a comparable gloss. In some circumstances, the terms village and bush establish oppositional parameters. In others, the features common to living things are recognised to cross this boundary. All living things are gender differentiated and share properties like colour and number. Living things are propagated by gender related processes; all living things bear and have children. Entities possessing breath (gɔngsi) are able to move and have feelings. Moving entities which make noises communicate with one another. Sentient beings have characters, which are less mutable in animals than in human beings. Animals have no choice but to obey their intrinsic character; to the extent that humans are governed by animal natures, they become animal-like. Thus, witches are bad and animal-like, while animals which kill by indirect means are witches. All living things are involved in processes of death and regeneration. Thus, the 'children of men' derive some characteristics from the dead, others from the wild, and possess qualities proper to humanity. Other agencies, like cults and masks, may be understood to a greater or lesser extent as like people. To remark only an oppositional view of bush and village would remove most nuances from the contexts in which Chamba locate human agency.

The bush may be envisaged in terms of the presence of animal and vegetable species that do not occur in the village, or in terms of the absence of human plan and effort from its design. As a resource, the bush supplies wood for building and for cooking-fires, grass for thatching, mat-making and basketry, leaves and fruits for soups, game for meat, stones for grinding corn and a host of other materials to which human ingenuity may be applied. Cultivation and husbandry alone could not support life, so it would be misleading to make the bush seem a less mundane place than it normally is. Men and women make regular trips into the bush to provision their households.

It is the more distant bush, with its greater dangers, that is a male rather than female preserve. I do not think that women would ever pass the night in bush. Deep bush, especially during darkness, is a place where sudden danger occurs without warning. Since men are considered quicker to action than women, they are better equipped to react to emergency. This notion of the bush as a place of potential relates to the absence from it of human plan and corresponds to the idea that the bush is the realm of the fantastic. Shape-changing tends not to occur in the village, and extraordinary finds of sculptured stones, or strange plants with potential medicinal value may only take place in the bush. Some of these strange discoveries find their way into the apparatus of Chamba cults, the powers of which are thereby related to the bush.

The bush, then, harbours the potencies, positive and negative, of undomesticated fecundity. The productivity of the domesticated sphere of women, animals and plants can be encouraged, but the wild is less amenable. Human effort can only be assisted in finding what is already there. Hunters may avoid actions which are known to be dangerous—sexual intercourse before hunting, or hunting in company with one of the anomalous human types (Chapter 5)—and they may take further actions to obviate the dangerous consequences of killing particular animals, but no ritual is performed to make the bush 'bear'. The bush should be fecund by itself. Although most Chamba realise that in recent times the large mammals have disappeared, and the forest has

Masks at the Yeli royal death beer (1984).

diminished, they find difficulty in imagining that their own actions could have been responsible for this state. The related notions of the wild as vast, encompassing and self-reproducing suggest that the creatures of the wild have merely relocated, become more wary, or been locally hunted out.

THE CHAMBA MASK

The virtually pan Chamba mask seems an evident place to begin to explore Chamba representations of the wild. But the mask is not wildness unalloyed, rather we shall find it to be a third composite type of being. 'Children of men' are composites of the wild and the dead with a leaven of distinctly human sociality. Cults, I have argued, are envisaged as composite agents in which the power of the dead predominates. Masks complete these possibilities because they are composite creations in which the wild predominates.

On purely formal grounds, the mask figure is a gratifyingly distinctive image. Its looming bulk is made up of two elements: a huge wooden head and a costume of layers of fibre. Together, the head and dress entirely conceal the body of the creature's human personator. To look at the head first: its central element is a tall, hollow, hemispherical dome from which two thin, flat, parallel plates, about as wide as the dome, project forwards to represent a gaping mouth. Between the mouth plates, hidden from onlookers, is a small vision port and, behind the mouth, ears are carved as small semicircles open to the front. In some examples, a low ridge longitudinally bisects the cranial dome and joins the wedge-shaped nose that rises from the upper surface of the top mouth plate of all masks. Two curving horns, in the same horizontal plane as the mouth plates, project to the rear. Some masks have distinctive ornamentation, such as light-coloured elements (studs with conical heads, coins or cowries) to represent the eyes. The undyed fibre costume is attached in two layers—the first to holes around the base of the headpiece, the second tied around the dancer's waist. A further layer is sometimes, not always, suspended from the ankles to disguise the wearer's feet. A braided rope, the tail of the creature, may be worn down the back of the masked figure or else carried by an attendant who uses it as a whip to strike at bystanders. The overall effect of the fibre costume, at least for central Chamba masquerades, is to transform the limbs of the wearer into a single bulky body that flows and quivers during the dance.

The generic term for the mask varies in different Chamba communities. In Mapeo, it is called *nam gbalang*. The first element of the name is universally glossed as *nam*, an undomesticated animal, or 'thing of the bush'. The second part is problematic. In Mapeo, I was more than once told that *gbalang* referred to unruly or uncivilised behaviour. To help me, one informant explained that it was 'like a woman in your compound who does not know how to behave and is always breaking her pots'. But I never heard *gbalang* used in this sense. Indeed I only heard the term as part of the name of the mask or else used in explicit

The Yeli royal matriclan mask (1977).

analogy. On several occasions I overheard the joking taunt at the expense of fellow villagers (especially at men with large, round heads, freshly shaven) that they had a 'head like *nam gbalang*' (*ti ka nam gbalang ti*). The point to the joke does not involve appearance alone, since Chamba assume the shape of a person's head to be indicative of character—anyone who resembles *nam gbalang* in appearance might be expected also to copy its behaviour.

This link between the shape of its head and the character of the beast seems to explain how informants are able to gloss the term *gbalang* in terms of the creature's characteristic conduct. Several terms with assonant associations also refer to features of the head: *kpəlang*, bald; *gələng gələng*, hooked—like the mouth of the mask, or the beak of the hornbill, called *təng gələnsi*; *bələng*, hatless or dishevelled; *bələng*, the type of hat with earflaps surmounted with feathers worn by boys at circumcision; *tələng*, an antelope for some, for others a unicorn, identified by its long straight horn, the animal is credited with powers to kill its hunter by witchcraft and its horn has medicinal properties. The name of the mask connotes personal qualities via semi-homophonous associations among terms describing peculiar features of the head, or modifications to features of the head.

Pursuing this line of enquiry takes us back to associations I have noted previously. Facial resemblances are, according to dogma, transmitted through the father's side. That this is indeed dogma is demonstrated by the occasions on which informants, who have asserted this to be the case, have remarked that some of their children take after their father and others after their mother. Nevertheless, the dogma clearly belongs with other notions that Chamba interrelate: patriclanship, reincarnation, identity, personality, head and skull. A friend supported a well-known rumour, that a fellow clansman was the son of a man other than his father, by appealing to observable evidence, 'But look, his head is not like that of the X (the speaker's clan), it is a Y (allied clan) head'. The link between head shape and character permits both general and specific judgements about character. Thus, some patriclans are reputed to share particular characteristics, and some individuals have characters that can be read off from their heads. 'Look at that man who is always making disrespect (*nak sunglung*)', the tone of my commentator is jocular, 'his very head is a disrespect!'

Chamba Leko, including Yeli Chamba, have different generic terms for the mask. In Yeli dialect, the mask is *lang badna*. *Lang* is said to derive from the verb to frighten (also *lang*). *Badna* has no local etymology, but it is also the name of a different masked figure, less widely distributed, in which a pointed fibre helmet substitutes for the wooden head. This might suggest *badna* as a generic term for masks. The epithet frightening, used of a creature of the bush, evokes other animals which inspire fear. I discuss the stone shrines, to which Chamba hunters must add a flat stone each time they kill a dangerous animal, later in this chapter. For Yeli Chamba, the mask represents, among much else, the unruly, animal dangers of the bush.

Among Chamba Leko to the south of Yeli, the term for the mask differs again. There it is called *vad*, skull. Looking at the conformation of the mask head, it is not difficult to discern a cranial dome to which mouth and horns have been added as projections in a single plane. The conventions for depicting ears on the skull, open circles in bas relief, are those used in anthropomorphic sculptures. In this light, the mask head seems like a human skull with added animal characteristics: the dead and the wild have been aggregated. Yeli perceptions of the mask, albeit their term for it differs, also encompass this vision. Not only are Yeli Chamba aware of the terminological usage of their southern Chamba neighbours, but they call the fibre dress of the masquerade *vad yɛsa*, skull leaf, and explain this phrase in terms of the alternative name that southern Chamba give to the mask. Whether the same, specific recognition of a relic of the human dead at the centre of the mask head can be attributed to Mapeo Chamba is difficult to decide. No direct equivalence, of which I know, is drawn between the mask and the skull, but human and ancestral components in the mask composition are recognised as I shall demonstrate shortly.

In additon to its generic name, each mask has a personal name. For Chamba onlookers, every mask is distinctive: each belongs to a particular group of people (usually specified as a clan), has gender characteristics (in Yeli and Mapeo shown by colouring conventions), a particular style of execution (noticed in minor differences of shape and ornamentation) and individual characteristics (such as its dance, or the occasions on which it appears).

In most of Chambaland, including Mapeo and Yeli, masks are coloured red if they are male and black if female (for conventions elsewhere, see Fardon, forthcoming b). Either scheme of colouring may be embellished with a white central stripe. Chamba uses of the colour triad are highly contextual, but in the case of the masks both red and black are evocative of animal dangers: red is related to blood, especially the blood of the hunt, black to the dangers of the night and possibly to those hidden dangers which include the black animal avatars of witches. Since witchcraft is transmitted in the matriclan, it seems appropriate that the female and not male mask is dark coloured. Stones collected in hunting shrines to commemorate the deaths of dangerous animals are also colour coded to indicate the form of danger they posed to the hunter.

Individual mask names are always compounds of two terms. One element, usually the first, specifies the gender of the beast, and does so with terms that apply to humans rather than animals. Male masks are frequently 'chief' something; female masks may be called 'mother' or 'grandmother' followed by an individual name, or else have the term for woman suffixed to their individual names (for examples see Fardon, forthcoming b). The same convention is followed in at least one other instance: the names of individual stages of the harvest cult in Mapeo, many of which are prefixed or suffixed by female terms. The human analogy implied in this naming is clearly non-accidental, since gender suffixes for animals differ from those for humans in the female case. The supposition that mask naming evokes the human qualities of animals, and the animal qualities of humans, is reinforced by other explicitly human analogies of the mask.

In the art historical literature on this area, Chamba masks are usually described as 'bushcow' or 'buffalo' masks, and placed in a category of horizontal theriomorphic masks distributed more widely among Chamba and their neighbours. The designation has an element, but literally only an element, of local accuracy. Chamba informants make a particular identification not between the mask and the bushcow, but between the horns of both. I have heard the mouth of the mask likened to that of a crocodile. The ears and nose, both integral parts of the cranial dome, are said to be human, and resemble those of the columnar figures that Chamba sculptors make of humanlike subjects. However, it is upon the resemblance between the mask and the bushcow that informants most readily seize. Chamba informants also state, with reference to female masks, that they are representations of the founding ancestresses of the owning clan. To understand how they can at once be bushcows and ancestresses requires us to return to the subject of Chamba matriclanship.

Although there are numerous Chamba matriclans, the widely distributed bushcow clan constitutes a virtual grundnorm of matriclanship. Every Chamba knows the story of its origins and most investigators have come away with some version of this tale (e.g. Frobenius from his enquiries in 1911, Cullen from his researches in the early 1940s, Fardon in the late 1970s apparently independently). Tales similar to this one are to be found in quite distant parts of West Africa. The story tells how a hunter saw bushcows shed their skins to wash in a river. He hid the skin of a beautiful girl who was therefore unable to rejoin the herd. On consideration that he keep her origins secret, she agreed to become his wife and bore him a son and daughter. When he referred publicly to her animal origins while drunk, she and her son resumed bushcow form and impaled the garrulous husband on their horns. They returned to the bush, and the clanspeople trace descent from the loyal daughter who refused to help kill her father.

The basic plot line may be retold with more or less detail. A very similàr story, though without a *dénouement* in the death of the hunter, accounts for the origins of the elephant clan. However, of all the matriclan origin tales, which together are marginal members of the class of just so stories (*tit jɔn*, Daka; *susuwa*, Leko), the origin of the bushcow clan seems to say something most relevant to Chamba about the nature of matriclanship. Judging from the frequency of its repetition, this is the allegory that seems to ring true.

The story, and the mask, share affinities. The most striking of these is the role of transformation (marked by use of the verb *bit*, Daka, or *bid*, Leko). The bushcow ancestress sheds her skin to become human; conversely the masquerader assumes both his costume and beastly disguise. If the cranial dome puts the masquerade under the shadow of death, then we may note an evocation of that other, and most crucial, transformation—between the living and the dead. Women, we may recall, donate substance to their children, through blood and milk; women are fleshier creatures than men according to Chamba, and female figures are generally bulkier than their male counterparts in Chamba sculptures. The bushcow, a large animal, but not sufficiently malevolent to warrant adding a stone to the clan hunting shrine, is, like the elephant, 'just meat'. So it seems appropriate that the ancestress of the bushcow clan is generally seen as a sort of ur-matriclan ancestress, a paradigmatic case of which other cases are less adequate instances. As hunters, men attempt to dominate animality, but the story, and indeed the masquerade performance, suggest the fragility of their control. From the matrilateral perspective, humans share animal substance with the creatures of the wild. So it is no contradiction that the masquerade may simultaneously evoke images of the bushcow and the ancestress, since both are animal donors of substance.

However, the bushcow's horns are only one element of the mask. The gaping mouth evokes for some the jaws of a crocodile. In Yeli, the mask is said to return to the water during the height of the wet season when it does not dance. And in Mapeo, an informant of the Dəngbu patriclan explained that his clan's mask represented an ancestress captured from the water by the clan ancestors. Her dance mimicked the movement of so large a creature through the water—like a hippo surfacing for air. Since deep water is also one abode of the dead, this association might lead us back to the relation between the mask head and the skull.

The mask enters the village to dance on numerous occasions: notably at rites of passage such as chiefmaking, circumcision or the festivals of mourning and remembrance of the dead (Chapters 3 and 5). Since masks are usually stored outside the village, the appearance of the creature enacts a movement from the bush into the space occupied by the villagers. The dancer is robed on the margins of the hamlet, never within a compound or a hut.

The masked figure is accompanied by a custodian who leads it into the performing area while striking a small double hand gong. Occasionally he may speak to the creature to coax it into dancing or to warn it against unruly conduct. The creature's dance alternates between periods of immobility, standing or crouching with an almost imperceptible quivering, and a curving, swivelling, marching gait, redolent of swaggering pride. With the increasing tempo of the hand gong, the creature dips its wooden head and its fibre dress billows up behind. For some observers, this element of the dance is reminiscent of the buffalo as it lowers its head in the charge. Experienced masqueraders claim it to be the most difficult part of the performance to manage since the wooden head is liable to slip forward spoiling the controlled line of the movement and simultaneously removing the dancer's upper teeth.

Occasionally, one of the older women will dance with the mask, accompanying the gong beats with the rhythm of her iron leg rattles. Some masks, like that of the royal matriclan of Yeli, are said to be truculent and 'old'. They dance slowly and reluctantly. Others are frenetic and lash out at bystanders and crops in ill temper. Its dance finished, the mask is led out of the crowd by its custodian who continues to beat the iron gong.

The atmosphere of the dance is predominantly ludic. Spectators comment on the vigour of the dancer, and his control over the creature's movements. The best performances suggest regulation of a highly strung energy. A slight frisson of playful apprehension is apparent, and shrieking younger women run off when the creature approaches them. The relation between the custodian and the mask dramatises a grudging acceptance of man's dominance by the beast from the bush. But this authority is shown to be fragile; only under the close supervision of its custodian is the mask prevented from running amok. The drama of scantily sufficient masculine control appears to accentuate the female characteristics of the bulky animal and resonates with the relative independence from their husbands that Chamba women often enjoy.

The evident pleasure Chamba derive from the mask as an idea, and the suggestiveness to them of its performance, seem to rest on complex associations which may be intuited between a variety of otherwise diverse relations: between the living and the dead, male and female, the domesticated and the wild, and between the clans that own the different masks. A noteworthy absence in these associations is any reference to cultivation. The only explicit reference to guinea corn that I know in the context of the mask is an injunction, apparently uniquely concerned with the Yeli royal mask, against the masquerader eating guinea corn food immediately prior to dancing. Failure to observe this regulation is thought to menace the dancer with leprosy. No informant to whom I spoke could explain why this behaviour might provoke disease. Explicit avoidance of guinea corn might mark the creature's dance as a phenomenon of the wild: the conception of leprosy evoked in the ritual of *kay batna* (Chapter 6) suggests that the disease is caused by undomesticated forces of the bush that the chief of Yeli attempts to control. Alternatively, leprosy might seem an appropriate sanction because it is an affliction linked to excessive bodily grease and the mask represents, among other things, the idea of large, fleshy animality. In the absence of any indication from local exegesis such suggestions are speculative.

Other explicit avoidances relating to the mask are few. The masquerader needs to be a skilled performer but not of necessity a member of the owning clan. To the best of my knowledge, no prohibitions are placed on his sexual activities before dancing. It is considered bad for the body of the dancer to be visible during the dance, but again no specific misfortune results. In the case of

A Mapeo mask during a wake. The dancer's feet would not be visible in Yeli.

the Yeli royal mask, it is said that pregnant women avoid seeing its misshapen head for fear that the heads of their babies will turn out to resemble it.

The spectacle of the beast of the wild dancing among the village compounds, its animal features projecting from a human skull, is probably irreducible to its individual elements. Informants' statements about the performance pick on some or other aspect of this totality as their attention, or the ethnographer's prodding, directs them. But explicit exegesis is likely to be an impoverished version of the experience. The masquerade is a wholly non-verbalised performance: it works through rhythm, movement and vision. I can only indicate the contexts from which elements of the totality are brought into play; their conjunction has a latency in which different observers may discover more or less, and the same observer various things on different occasions.

To this outside observer, the Chamba mask seems so powerful an image because it is at once man-made anomaly and exemplar. When humanity, the dead and the wild are envisaged as spatially discrete forms of life—within, below and surrounding the village—the mask has the sense of a man-made anomaly that enters the village from the bush and combines the features of the dead and the wild. Under such interpretative conventions, the mask is the exemplary crosser of boundaries. However, in the light of the composite nature of the living, dead and wild, the mask is not anomalous but exemplary. It demonstrates visibly the disparate qualities that co-exist in all agencies of Chamba life: the dead, animals, cults and the Chamba themselves.

CREATURES OF THE WILD AND OF THE VILLAGE

Coming to creatures of the wild via the Chamba mask alerts us to the ambiguous potential of animals as images as well as counter-images of the human condition. In both Chamba languages a distinction is made between wild and domesticated animals, or, in closer translation, between 'things of the grassland' and 'things cared for' (in Daka *pɛn janan*, in Leko *'an zan zan*). The same idiom may be used to describe an attached, usually young, member of the compound: *nogin jan gun* (Daka), I fed and cared for him.

The generic term for domesticated animals is used rarely; they are usually enumerated as chickens, goats, sheep and so forth. Although a range of domestic animals is maintained, not all seem to figure greatly in Chamba imagination. Cows (*na* in Leko and Daka) are owned by few men, although a dim recollection is maintained that Chamba Leko once had herds of dwarf cattle like those kept by some of their neighbours. Horses (*nyan*, Daka; *ya*, Leko) are rarer yet, and usually recalled in the context of older warmongering actions. Some Chamba informants claim that the term once applied to local ponies rather than the Arab horses that are seen today. A few ducks, guinea fowl and very occasionally turkeys kept around the compounds have scant importance as domesticated species. Donkeys to carry burdens and the occasional domestic cat similarly excite little work in the imagination.

Sacrificial animals, whether offered at graves, shrines or cults, are of only three types: goats (*vin*, Daka; *vo*, Leko), chickens (*kpa*, Daka; *ko*, Leko) and sheep (*təmsi*, Daka; *bɛd*, Leko). Of the three, the chicken is a routine offering, goats are offered more occasionally and sheep killed infrequently. In itself, a chicken seems to be an unmarked sacrifice. On a few occasions a white cockerel is particularly called for, and this may motivate an otherwise neutral offering. More generally, offering a chicken gains significance from the manner in which the bird dies: by decapitation, having its throat cut or being beaten to death, so that its blood is retained. This logic, contrasting decapitation and the shedding of blood to death accompanied by the retention of blood, is homologous with that between the patriclan imperative to partibility (evident in circumcision and skull removal) and the matriclan imperative to the retention of substance.

Goats and sheep also may suffer sacrificial slaughter either by having their throats cut, by asphyxiation after a small incision has been made in the windpipe, or else by beating. One or more goats is a required part of the entrance payments to the overriding majority of Chamba cults; a sheep is required in a minority of cults. In Yeli, the sheep is particularly thought of as a chiefly sacrifice. Informants reason that the sheep, especially a black ram, is a cooling sacrifice. Unlike the goat, the sheep is considered to be cold. To complete the roster of important domestic animals, it is necessary to add to the three sacrificial animals only the dog (*ngwana*, Daka; *yagad*, Leko). Apart from acting as hunting companion and scavenger around the compound, the dog gives its name to one of the matriclans of Mapeo. Its hunting propensities, and the facts that it is neither sacrificed nor killed expressly for its meat, make the dog an ambiguous member of the class of domesticated animals. To the best of my knowledge, the sheep (elsewhere than in Mapeo or Yeli) is the only fully domesticated animal to have a matriclan named after it.

Chamba classification of animals of the bush ('things of the grass': *pɛn poran*, Daka; *'an fɔg bɛ*, Leko) tends to be particularising rather than generalising. Smaller creatures are more likely to belong to generic classes, but most large creatures seem, at least in lexical terms, to be one-offs. Since clear classes, with rules of inclusion and exclusion, are largely absent, few problems are posed by the classification of anomalous creatures. Resemblances between the animal lexicons of the two Chamba languages are striking given their very distant relationship.

Larger animals of the bush are called *nam* in Chamba Daka. Chamba Leko seems to lack a non-composite term for such creatures, which they may call 'bush meat'. Classification of mammals within this class is rarely lexically marked but depends rather on the recognition of clustering affinities. The names of larger animals are rarely compound forms or descriptive terms; the overwhelming majority cannot, therefore, be glossed. Broad classes of birds (*sa*, Daka; *nu*, Leko), fish (*wuk*, Daka; *dib*, Leko), and snakes (*ye*, Daka; *bisa*, Leko) are recognised, and members of these classes are likely to bear names that identify them through colour, sound, habit or by analogy. Generic classes become more numerous among the smallest creatures; thus there are classes of ants (*busum*), locusts and grasshoppers (*ga*), frogs (*koye*), snails (*təksa*) and so forth in Daka. Some members of these classes, but not all, are called after the generic term and distinguished by a suffix.

A number of clusters can be identified among the larger mammals. The antelopes, gazelles, bucks and duikers are the pre-eminent meat animals. Yeli and Mapeo terms for these animals are relatively similar, although the identification of English equivalents is suspect given the infrequency with which larger mammals are seen and the fact that those able to identify animals from pictures in handbooks are seldom experienced hunters themselves.

Daka	Leko	English
bɛrɛng	*sa bɛrɛng*	gazelle
bəy		bushbuck
	gbo'a	Grimm's duiker
kərum	*kərum*	reedbuck (bushbuck Yeli)
	kpən	reedbuck (Yeli)
mɛnjum	*mənjang*	sable antelope
	murub	water buck
nam ji	*nam da*	cob
sa	*sa*	oribi
sɔng	*sɔra*	roan antelope
tɔlɔng	*tɔlɔng*	unicorn/oryx?
ya wəran	*ya wurum*	(red) duiker

Despite its likely deficiencies, this list demonstrates both the convergence between Daka and Leko terms and their non-composite nature. Of the entire list, only *nam ji*, the red animal in Daka, is confidently glossed by informants as a composite of *nam* for wild animal. Even this etymology might be suspect given that *nam* occurs also in the Leko term.

Two of these deer-like ruminants receive special attention. *Tɔlɔng* is identified by informants with illustrations of the Beisa Oryx which, according to the Collins Field Guide, does not occur in Chambaland. None the less, when I was shown a three foot long straight horn with a twist at its base, that a friend bought from a trader as a *tɔlɔng* horn, it most nearly resembled that of an oryx. *Tɔlɔng* is considered by Chamba to be dangerously witchlike. The animal feigns death. But should the hunter see its eye blink, madness and death will break out among the members of his compound. On this account, *tɔlɔng* is the name given to epilepsy cults in both Mapeo and Yeli. Epilepsy, and madness to which it is closely linked as a condition involving loss of bodily control, are via these associations indexed, like witchcraft, to the wild.

Similar associations attach to *gbo'a*, Grimm's duiker, at least in Yeli. The Field Guide description of this animal, as nocturnal and solitary, corresponds closely to Yeli perceptions of its habits. Grimm's duiker is a witch (*dɔra*) that pretends death in order to kill its hunter. *Tɔlɔng*, along with *gbo'a* in Yeli, are members of a class of evil things (literally 'bad things': *pɛn vɛ*, Daka; *'an vaksa*, Leko). Although this class is fluid, most informants would also include in it the lion and leopard, as well as the bush pig and two birds with bizarre habits. These animals manifest most clearly a capacity for malicious intention to kill their hunter by means varying from subterfuge to what is described as witchcraft.

The leopard (*gbe*, Daka; *gɔ*, Leko) and the lion (*nyik*, Daka; *gba'al nyig*, Leko) are both associated with chiefship in Yeli. As well as 'bad', these powerful animals may be described as 'frightening things' (*pɛn koko*, Daka; *'an kosa*, Leko). Yeli classification additionally includes them in a class of biting animals (literally toothed things, *'an nɔgɔl bɛ*). In 1984, the Yeli chief still possessed an aged leopard-skin bag, but live leopards and lions existed in recollection rather than actuality. A modern cloth print of a lion substituted for the skin of the real thing during the annual royal death beer (Chapter 5).

The bush pig (*si* in both languages) is a more present threat. In Yeli, this animal is likened to the human anomaly of the upper teeth cutter, since it is believed to be born with its tusks already formed.

To the lion, leopard or bush pig is attributed a malicious intelligence that exists in lesser measure in other animals. The bushcow (*yɛt*, Daka; *zɛl*, Leko) possesses something of this malevolence, as, to a slight degree, does the elephant (*kɔngla*, Daka; *dɔn*, Leko). Both animals give their names to matriclans, and elephant additionally is the name of the leprosy cult in both Yeli and Mapeo.

The most humanlike of animals are the monkeys and baboons. A few Chamba refuse to eat them on account of their resemblance to people: a friend claimed to feel revulsion at the idea of stripping the flesh from the hand of a monkey; another said he had given up monkey flesh after he killed an infant monkey and saw tears running down its face. Baboons (*kpin*, Daka; *gbɔnga*, Leko) may seem less human than patas monkeys (*kɛm ji*, red monkey in Daka; *da'a*, Leko), vervet monkeys (*kɛm ke*, mad monkey in Daka), or colobus monkeys (*kɛm kasala*, Daka; *sala* or *sal pɛsi bɛ*, colobus among the creepers in Leko) but all pose a considerable threat to cultivators. When packs are sighted there is a general call to men to round up their dogs and grab staves to hunt them, for monkeys, like witches, are beaten to death without shedding their blood. In a Yeli story, the monkey accepts this fate. The animals have gathered at pig's request to bathe in a medicine that will make them immune to hunters' arrows. Monkey argues that man is justified in hunting him because he destroys crops. An argument with pig ensues, and monkey insults him on account of his ugly upper teeth. In the ensuing struggle the pot of medicine is upset and only *tɔlɔng*, the straight-horned antelope, succeeds in washing himself as the liquid flows away. *Tɔlɔng* acquires his sinister powers, but monkey is shown to sympathise with the human predicament.

Of numerous birds and snakes, I shall discuss only a few examples with prominent human associations. These must include three particularly ominous birds: the touraco (*sa lo*, Daka; *nu yɛla*, red bird, Leko), the nightjar (*tama*, Daka and Leko), and the owl (*disa*, Daka and Leko). The first two are often discussed together. The touraco is the only bird for which the hunter may claim a 'stone' (see below). Hunters describe the rarity of this bird and the difficulty of killing it, since it scampers around the tree shouting. The hunter must remember to shout out some nonsense syllables in the language of the bird (*pəgələ pət*, according to Daka informants); should the bird cry them first, the hunter will die. *Tama*, which also means butterfly in Daka, is like the shadow image of the touraco. The latter is highly visible but difficult to kill, the nightjar is seen only at evening and during the day is able to sit camouflaged upon its eggs even by the side of a well-used path. Usually, it is avoided rather than killed. In some stories the two birds are joined as male and female. A Yeli story relates how villagers pursued a pair of witches, one a man the other a woman. They surrounded the couple in the bush and lit a circle of fire to drive them out. From the midst of the smoke they saw the touraco and his wife the nightjar fly up to escape them. No sign of the witches was found within the fire.

This story is also told in Mapeo, as is another, which claims the touraco to be the transformation of a notable, unnamed, Chamba warrior who became a bird in order to escape Fulani pursuers. Various schemes are proposed to pair male and female among the birds. Outside the story told in the last paragraph, no credence seems to attach to the idea that touraco and nightjar are male and female. Daka informants identify the blue plantain eater as the male *salo* and the violet plantain eater as its mate. All nightjars are apparently considered female (*tama wɔ*, old woman nightjar) with the exception of the male of the standard wing nightjar, with prominent long standards, which is thought to be the male of the group as a whole (*tama langan*, perhaps surrounding, or long, nightjar).

Disa, meaning owl in both languages, behaves both as a generic term and as the name for larger types of owl. Yeli informants may specifically call the large owls, cult owls (*vɔm disa*). According to different informants, owls are either transformed witches or witches' familiars. Their hooting close by a compound may presage death, while their unblinking, large eyes and nocturnal habits confirm them as birds of ill omen.

Of many distinct snake types one has particular importance: the python is termed chief of the snakes in Daka (*ye gang*), or snake child in Leko (*bisa wa*). It lives in the underworld with the dead. The python is among the very few creatures for which the successful hunter can claim a 'stone'.

Van, a hunting shrine in Tisayeli hamlet, Mapeo. Male medicine plants grow by the side of the shrine. To the right are a pair of iron gongs and a gourd horn covered in genet skin.

'STONE': THE HUNTING SHRINE

The visitor to a Chamba village would be likely to notice collections of flat rocks stacked between pairs of narrow stone uprights. These hunting shrines are known simply as stone (*van*, Daka; *vag*, Leko). Usually they belong to patriclans, although the matriclan shrine of the Yeli royal clan constitutes, as so often, an exception to the rule.

The killer of a dangerous animal adds a stone, commemorating his kill, to the collection. To do so is at once prestigious and precautionary, since the ritual protects hunters from the dangerous consequences of killing. According to Mapeo accounts, a hunter must donate two pots of beer in order to place his stone, or else he will suffer from back ache. A cloth is tied around his left wrist as part of the ritual, although no explanation of this practice could be found. Yeli accounts suggest that no stone is placed for the killer of a woman, although a ritual must be carried out to prevent his going mad.

Periodically, rituals take place at stone shrines to assure the success of hunting. Then the individual stones are coloured to indicate the animals they commemorate. The rules for this differ in Mapeo and Yeli (and other variations occur elsewhere in Chambaland). The variety cautions us that overall design may be more important than precise detail.

Mapeo version
white stone: roan and sable antelope
red stone: bush pig, leopard, lion, bushcow, touraco, python
red round stone: man

Yeli version
red stone: python, touraco and man
black stone: bush pig

In Mapeo, large, but not especially dangerous, animals—ignored in Yeli—are accorded white stones. Horns of other antelopes, gazelles and buck may be hung by the shrine although no stone is placed for the kill. Dangerous animals are commemorated by black or red stones. Mapeo informants suggest that red stones are taken for all dangerous animals, with that of man being distinguished as a round stone, representing the skull. If round stones substitute for human skulls, then it might be suggested that flat stones represent the horizontal line of an animal's skull. In Yeli, red stones are placed only for human deaths and the humanlike deaths of pythons and touracos. In Yeli alone is the bush pig likened to the human anomaly of the upper teeth cutter. Black is appropriate to both the bush pig and the human anomaly. Leopard and lion are royal prerogatives in Yeli, and must be surrendered to the chief. Their deaths are not recorded in the clan shrines. The bush cow is said to be 'just meat'.

All the commemorative events that I have witnessed at hunting shrines have occurred at funerary ceremonies: either during the funeral wake for an individual, or during the collective 'death beer' held by a clan. An individual's hunting achievements are recalled during his wake. His 'stones' are brought from the clan's shrine, and successful hunters tauntingly offer them to men who have placed no stones so must refuse to grasp them for fear of back ache. For killers of elephant, albeit no stone is taken for this kill, a re-enactment of the hunt is staged in which a grass-covered man substitutes for the elephant. At the wake for a pig killer in Mapeo, a beer pot (in this context called 'bush pig pot') was taken to a crossroads at the edge of the village and smashed between two stones taken from the shrine for the purpose.

The collective death beer involves a more elaborate ceremony. The stones are coloured and arranged carefully. Between them are placed leaves from the ironwood tree. Although Mapeo informants described this practice as simply customary, Yeli commentators found it motivated via the red colour and masculine connotations of the leaf. Other apparatus may be lodged by the shrine: for instance, a buffalo hide war shield, or a calabash horn covered in genet skin on occasions I have witnessed. The climax of the event involves an augury for hunting during the year. A chicken is decapitated and thrown to the ground. If it runs headless around then the omens are good; should it fall 'like a stone' then something is amiss, and the clansmen must consult to discover whether disagreements between them are affecting the outcome of the ordeal. The test is then repeated, but should it fail again the consequences must be endured for the coming year.

ANIMAL IMAGES

When we make an inventory of them, it is apparent how pervasive are the animal images in Chamba representations of themselves and their cults. As a normal element of the person, animality relates to matrilateral relationship. Animals furnish the prototypical matriclan names, even if the majority of matriclans are not named after animals. Elephant and bushcow are ancestresses in both Mapeo and Yeli, dog is an ancestress in Mapeo but not Yeli; Mapeo has a clan which some gloss as 'bird children' clan (sa mɛm kun), while Yeli has a baboon clan (za gbɔngal kuna, gbɔnga, anubis baboon). (Outside Yeli or Mapeo we could find the ant clan, sheep clan, hare clan, and a clan named after a fish species.) When matriclans are not named after animals, their names are drawn from features of the wild: the sun, mist, and red rock clans; from characteristic attributes like gluttony (loves guinea corn clan), blindness (nyəd kun, Yeli), or being a blacksmith (kpe kun, Daka; lam kun, Yeli), or, in this context at least, being a Koma (kɔm kun in both places). These characteristics are associations of matriclanship rather than patriclanship.

All humanity has animal associations, but these associations predominate dangerously in the cases of breech births, upper teeth cutters, and witches.

Their animality must be controlled. In the first two cases, matrikin take responsibility for removing the excessively animal child from the community. Witchcraft is an excessive animality transmitted between matrikin. Human-like animals are the counterparts to animalistic humans. The monkey, the animal with most human characteristics, is killed in the same way as a witch. Owls, touracos and nightjars are witch birds because of their peculiar habits which suggest malevolent human-like intelligence. The bush pig, in Yeli, is an animal analogue of the upper teeth cutter.

Animal remains, animal representations and animal associations occur frequently in the apparatuses of Chamba cults. Many of these animal images draw only upon the most prominent characteristic of a creature: terracotta tortoises as lumps, dogs' skulls as biting, terracotta sheep as bandy legs . . . However, the identification of cults as things of the wild (as well as of the dead) is quite specific in, for instance, the notion that the throwing tool of the bəntəng cult was given by a lion, or the declaration to women whose sons have died during the time of the circumcision cult, that their deaths were caused by creatures of the bush. More generally, by virtue of their location outside the village and the more outrageous noises they cause to issue from their meetings, cults are pervasively associated with the bush and the animals that live there. The Chamba mask dramatises both the qualities of the wild and the idea of shape-changing that is so crucial to Chamba belief. Witches may become black baboons, or owls, or dark hybrid creatures which shoot fire from their anuses. Dangerous birds, like touraco and nightjar, may be metamorphosed witches or warriors. Cult objects may be donated by a shape-changing lion, and a matri-clan may be founded by a shape-changing bushcow or elephant. The ideas of concealment, and of things not being what they appear to be on the surface, correspond closely to Chamba conceptions of the cult as an institution whose very business is concealment.

THE DEATHS OF ANIMALS AND THE SHEDDING OF BLOOD

The treatment of the human body differs under matriclanship and patriclan-ship: 'one mother' relations are predicated on the retention of substance; 'one father' relations on partibility (skull-taking, circumcision, and for Leko clans tooth evulsion in women). The distinction coheres with that between the activities of men, who shed the blood of creatures other than themselves in hunting and war, and women, who retain their own blood to provide the substance of new children. Hunting, warfare and childbirth are all dangerous, but in ways considered the lot of men and women. The confusion of male and female proclivities in relation to blood threatens other dangers.

Women's monthly blood-shedding is potentially dangerous to the male activities of hunting and warfare. The pollution of menstruation is a provoca-tion to the dead risking their wrath or rendering the men's cults nugatory. Chamba are dogmatic that women never kill even domestic animals, and I have witnessed no exception to this rule. Men 'urinate their own blood' only when they have been 'caught' by the women's cult (*jɛm*) or by the stomach distension cult of *nɔga*. In both cases, I argued that we may interpret the affliction as feminisation. Explicitly, in the Yeli case, the distension of the stomach and darkened urine that are symptomatic of *nɔga* affliction are akin to pregnancy and menstruation. Both in Mapeo and Yeli, the curative ritual requires the removal of a beer pot (i.e. belly) from between the legs of representative women of the matriclan caught by the affliction.

A logic cognate with the gendered distinction between ways of shedding of human blood invests sacrificial offerings. Animals are killed whole (and retain their blood), or 'cut' (that is have their throats slit), or are decapitated. The maximum contrast in disposition of human bodies at death occurs in Yeli: the aggregation of royal bodies and body parts, to lie in their matriclan graveyard, is diametrically opposed by the removal of the priest's skull before his flesh has rotted.

Extreme partibility and mobility at the death of domestic animals occurs at the auguries of the hunting shrines when chickens are decapitated and, if the signs are propitious, run headlessly spraying their blood. The opposite extreme, blood retention and immobility, occurs in several contexts. At the annual funerary commemoration of the Yeli royal matrikin (Chapter 5), the sacrificial goat is killed by puncturing its windpipe. According to onlookers, the priest simply places his hands upon the animal and it dies. Sacrifices of chickens at the women's cults similarly require the victim to be immobile. In complete antithesis to the sacrifice at the hunting shrine, chickens given to the women's cult are placed upon the ground and the sacrificer's restraining hands are lifted three times to see whether the chicken flies off. Only an immobile fowl is suitable as offering. These contrasting styles in the deaths of animals coincide with the values that invest the human body under the imperatives of matriclanship and patriclanship. The pre-eminently masculine hunting rituals involve maximal partition, while events that fall under the exemplary matriclanship of the Yeli royal clan, and within the cult rituals of women, demand retention of blood and physical integrity.

Outside special performative contexts, according to the recollections of informants in Mapeo, the deaths of animals would once have corresponded to their status as domesticated ('fed and cared for') or wild ('things of the bush'). Cutting the throat and draining the blood of fowl and livestock is an innovation from Muslim practice; domesticated animals were once killed by beating and retained their blood. Wild animals, with the exception of monkeys which are human-like, were shot or speared. Seen in these terms, the beating to death of known witches treats them as akin to domestic rather than feral animals, while enemies slain in battle are akin to the animals of the hunt, and stones may be placed in the hunting shrine to commemorate killing them.

If domestic animals were killed entire, or if Chamba routinely think about the deaths of animals in the light of this belief, then we must be careful in deciding which form of ritual slaughter is specially marked. The bloodshed of hunting rituals, and the killing of animals in patriclan cults, might be the practices most strongly marked as antitheses of the normal treatment of domestic animals. The status of animals killed in matriclan cults remains ambiguous. There, the mouths of fowl are invariably cut, and the lower beak twisted in order for blood to drip over the cult apparatus. The beak is subsequently held closed, and the bird's death brought about by beating, usually on the neck. Sheep and goats, after being castrated if male, are also beaten to death with stones while their mouths are held shut. The perfectly round stones used to kill these animals are those with which women have ground guinea corn into flour. Worn too small by continued use, they are discarded by the women and taken to cult places by the men. Death is thus inflicted with blunt instruments fashioned by women, which can hardly fail to recall the blunt truncheons of chiefs, which punish without drawing blood.

In the important matriclan cult of *karbang*, the performance of the animal's death is not at an end after it has been beaten lifeless. The initiates are led around the cult precinct, eyes trained to the floor, in mimicry of hunters following the spoor of an animal. Coming upon the slain animal amidst whoops of triumph they proceed to slap it vigorously across the chest with their open palms. Symbolically, the creature which has already been multiply associated with the values of matriclan sociality is made to evoke wild animality.

The death of 'feral' animals in matriclan shrines neatly returns to the beginnings of this discussion of animality and the female associations of the Chamba mask from the bush. Animals, their habits, parts, habitats, and deaths are pervasively cross-referenced with humanity, its types and its qualities seen from a variety of perspectives. The hierarchical organisation of Yeli, with its apical summative contrast between matriclan and patriclan officials, whose qualities are differentiated point by point, allows informants there to detect a common pattern stretching from relations between men and women in the compound to the most extensive affairs of the chiefdom.

8

INANIMATE WILDERNESS, AND THE NATURE OF THINGS

Without breath a living entity is incapable of movement and of feeling, 'Does wretchedness grip a tree?' (*bu gut tim ɛ*? Chamba Daka proverb and personal name). To ignore someone's misery is to treat him like a thing incapable of feeling. Except to press this point about incomparability, the inanimate character of plants makes them poor vehicles for expression of human affairs by direct analogy. Animals share more obvious characteristics with human beings, and because of their habits contrast suggestively with the human condition.

The distinction between domesticated and wild is less neat in the case of trees and plants than for animal species. Crops are grown around the compound as well as in farms. Trees are left to bear useful products in the village as well as outside it. Some trees, like roneo palms, may be planted in the bush. Useful trees may be afforded a degree of protection when fields are burned. It is less clear than in the case of animals which plants are and which are not tended.

Guinea corn, the overwhelmingly significant source of food and beer, and red bambara groundnut, its cultivated counterpart in women's work (Chapter 6), have no obvious antitheses or analogies in the wild. Other cultivated staple crops are mere hunger breakers. A few useful fruits, like tamarind and locust bean, are chiefly prerogatives, and in this context are explained to have been planted by the dead rather than men. But it is difficult to argue analogy between the chief and these trees in the way that one can for the leopard or lion.

Rather than trees, plants or roots in their entirety, Chamba attention fixes upon usable attributes of these. Plants share their most abstract qualities with animate living things: colour, form, number, gender, partibility, and heat or coolness. When the uses of plants are motivated symbolically it is by means of these attributes. So it is in the exegesis of plant use that Chamba interpreters must consistently refer to these most abstract of qualities.

TREES

Particular tree parts are used in various rituals and cult performances. All cults are 'made' upon their particular leaves, and these leaves are the first elements of cult practice shown to initiates. Bunches of leaves may be left to indicate the identity of a cult protecting personal property or a field of growing crops. The motivation of associations between leaves and cults struck me as one of the main differences between accounts of ritual from Yeli and Mapeo (Chapter 1). Exegesis of these connections in Yeli, for which I am largely indebted to Dura, was reasoned in terms of resemblances between qualities of the leaves and cults; the Mapeo exegesis, explained by Titlɛsime and other elders, emphasised the conventional and, apparently, arbitrary choice of the leaf on which cults were made.

Most prominent among the leaves used in the cults are those of the shea butter tree and the ironwood, or false shea butter, tree. The similarities between these trees, and their leaves, are sufficiently close to permit pervasive motivation of their differences. In Chamba experience, both trees are found in and around the village and farm. They are equally fire resistant but likely to be gnarled and stunted where field burning is frequent. Both have long leaves. Here are summaries of the differences between the two trees recognised in Yeli.

kɔl   shea butter tree; the 'children' (i.e. shea butter kernels) from this tree were the source of cooking oil before the introduction of groundnuts. The shea butter was skimmed from the surface of water in which the kernels were soaked and processed by women. If a stalk of the shea butter tree is broken it secretes a white fluid like milk. A bunch of shea butter leaves stuck into the fence of a compound conventionally signals the naming of a girl. When all the leaves fall, the leaf bearing stems that remain resemble snakes. Snake bite cults are 'made' on shea butter leaves.

san   false shea butter or ironwood tree; although resembling the shea butter tree in many respects, the ironwood yields less oil. The leaves of the ironwood turn a vivid red and its trunk also has a reddish colouring. A bunch of ironwood leaves in the compound fence signals the naming of a boy. The ironwood leaf is that on which the leprosy cult is 'made', so custodians of this cult cannot burn its wood in their compounds.

The qualities that differentiate shea butter and ironwood trees simultaneously associate them with different genders and misfortunes. Its larger fruit ('children') and white sap support the identification of the shea butter tree as female. The redness of the bark and leaves of the ironwood suggest male identity. We might recall that the male mask is also red, and that red is the colour of the ochre coating of stones commemorating kills in the hunt. There are good precedents for considering red to connote masculinity. The skin of lepers is also considered to redden, so this makes the ironwood leaf an apt choice. But are there affinities between leprosy and masculinity? Leprosy is the attrition of the flesh during life, and we know that flesh and blood are a maternal contribution to the person. The first circumcised male, according to the Yeli tale of origin (Chapter 5), was a leper. Redness, masculinity and leprosy are potentially linked by multiple and recursive mazeways.

The feminine associations of the shea butter tree ramify in several directions. Shea butter, which is manufactured by women, is used to wax bamboo *lera* flutes. Shea butter has solid and liquid forms. The melting of the butter when heated is said to resemble the melting of clouds to produce rain. *Lera* music is played to beg God (*pɔb Nyama*) for rain. The master of the rains in Yeli is, of course, the chief whom we know to evoke numerous feminine characteristics by virtue of his election from the royal matriclan. It is more difficult to discern female characteristics in snake bite. Yeli informants explicitly discover the link between leaf and cult in the snakelike shape of the leaf-bearing stem of the shea butter tree. We might note, however, that snake bite cults are owned by matriclans, never patriclans, in both Yeli and Mapeo. Indeed, snake bite, along with stomach distension, are the paradigmatic afflictions of matriclan cults. The name of these cults is glossed as 'bears redness' (*ngwan ji*) because blood collects at the site of the snake bite. Identification of the snake with the penis might suggest that the victim of snake bite is in a position structurally analogous to the female container of blood. However, this supposition occurred to me too late to discover whether it might gain any plausibility from discussion with Chamba.

Mapeo practitioners do with leaves most of the things that Yeli practitioners do with them. Shea butter leaves (*tup ya*) and ironwood leaves (*bəng ya*) signify female and male at naming ceremonies. Mapeo elders use shea butter leaves in most of the cults concerned with snake bites and tend to include ironwood leaves in leprosy cults. However, they appear not to motivate these uses in the same way as Yeli informants. On the basis of research in Mapeo, I inclined to see leaves as completely arbitrary signs. No one had been able to explain to me why particular leaves were used for particular rituals.

This might be considered only a matter of defective research, but two considerations suggest something different. Mapeo Chamba may use shea butter and ironwood leaves in the same performative contexts as Yeli Chamba, but they also use them in contexts where Yeli Chamba do not and to which the Yeli exegeses could not be made to apply. Secondly, a major axis of the Yeli contrast depends upon identification of the colours of the trees. Chamba Daka and Chamba Leko colour terminologies differ in ways that make it impossible for Mapeo Chamba to make the same associations between the colours of animate and inanimate things as their fellow Chamba at Yeli (see below). Despite some consistencies between Mapeo and Yeli Chamba usages, it is therefore not possible to argue that the Yeli exegeses somehow correspond to a knowledge implicit in Mapeo. Other Mapeo practices as well as Chamba Daka colour terms preclude this.

Ironwood and shea butter apart, the leaf that features most often in ritual is that of the locust bean tree. This large tree produces long pods containing seeds that are made into a soup additive ('local Maggi' in Nigerian English); the pith between the seeds is sometimes eaten by children. However, the significance of the tree in ritual performances seems unrelated to its mundane use.

ləm, Leko; lɔm, Daka   locust bean tree; a bunch of the very small leaves of this tree, dipped into a calabash of water, is used to produce a fine shower of water to cool those taking part in rituals to do with cults or the relics of the dead. Water is also flicked from locust bean leaves during the rituals performed when Yeli Chamba have been approached to beg for 'dew' (i.e. rain). Locust bean leaves are used as stoppers for the 'skull' pots at annual commemoration of the royal dead at Yeli. In Mapeo, these leaves are regularly used to spray cooling water onto members attending cult meetings. The locust bean leaf is not a symbol of a particular cult in either of the two communities.

The locust bean leaf performs a specialised but quite commonly needed function. Other trees have more specialised and limited uses. Many of these concern the Chamba cults, and in three cases, as for locust bean, Mapeo and Yeli usages coincide.

ngwubma, Leko; kpi, Daka   the silk cotton tree; this tree produces pods containing capoc; sometimes its trunk is covered with pointed protrusions. The kapok-filled pods are used in the cult concerned with visual disorders (langa in both Leko and Daka). The pod, containing one of the protrusions, represents the symptoms for which the cult is responsible. Capoc is also suitable, according to Yeli sources, as a covering for the gravely burned or victims of smallpox. The pod is used as a container to carry salt to the hill to offer to the spirits which cause smallpox during kay batna (see Chapter 4). In Mapeo, the pod is used to conceal a relic of a dead person, usually a nail paring, for use in ordeals of innocence from complicity in causing the death (see Chapter 5).

Use of the silk cotton pod in the identically named sight cults of Yeli and Mapeo is similarly, and very specifically, motivated. According to different accounts, either the cotton pod is the eye of the sufferer and the sharp thorn the cause of pain there, or the brilliant white of capoc represents the whiteness of castes in the eye. In either case, the resemblance between the shapes of the pod and the human eye is important. Other uses of the pod respond to its white colour and connotations of coolness (as a dressing for smallpox or burns victims). No particular reason seems to motivate choice of the pod as a container for salt or a relic of the dead, although the pod is appropriate for use in the smallpox rituals by virtue of having no animal origin.

gbung, Leko; *dəsi*, Daka   the roneo palm; the sharp palm fronds are used in
the cult of *sara*, equivalent to *yaguman* in Mapeo, the patriclan cult of
Yambu/Jɛngnɛbba that causes and cures bodily swellings. The leaves
are appropriate because they resemble the pointed implements used for
lancing swellings. Another leaf used in the cult (*kuba*, Daka; *kan*, Leko;
probably a single type) is also pointed.

kisina, Leko; *gɛsi*, Daka   the savanna ebony; its leaves are used in the cleansing cult (*vɔm dagan*, Leko; *jup dagan*, Daka). Leko informants explain
its appropriateness by reference to its 'black' colouring which conceals
things: its leaves cover the place where a child is born in bush until a ram
can be sacrificed on the spot.

These five cases cover the majority of cases in which I know Mapeo and Yeli
leaf usages to be similar. Only shea butter and ironwood leaves are motivated as
symbols by contrast, and that only in Yeli. The two places share some criteria
of appropriateness that depend upon the resemblance between a leaf and a
feature of the world (palm fronds and points; the fine spray of rain from leaves
of the locust bean tree; the resemblance of the silk cotton pod to the human
eye). However, the lack of attention to leaf colour symbolism makes the
appropriateness of savanna ebony leaves purely conventional. Mapeo leaf
symbolism appears to be optional and when it occurs to be based in resemblance—a characteristic common to the motivation of most of the other
apparatus peculiar to particular cults. For instance,

nibri, Daka   a substance made from beeswax mixed with soot. This gummy
compound is used to enhance the resonance of drumskins and to seal
sections of gourd tube to make horns. In Mapeo, *nibri* is used in leprosy
cults (called *gina* and *kɔngla*). Its appropriateness depends on resemblance to leprous flesh: like the leper's body the wax cracks when dry and
hard. The substance also appears in the epilepsy cult (*la gənsɛn*); in this
case, blackness motivates the choice (recall that epilepsy can be glossed as
'falling into black').

It is probable that black wax is also used in the Yeli leprosy and epilepsy
cults, but I do not know with certainty. In both places, the leprosy cults are
made on ironwood leaves: appropriate in Yeli because of their redness and
merely conventional to the occasion in Mapeo. However, the Mapeo epilepsy
cult is equally conventionally made on shea butter leaves, an option which
cannot be encompassed by Yeli notions of appropriateness since the cult does
not concern women, nor snakes, nor whiteness. Mapeo Chamba also use
ironwood leaves when Yeli Chamba find them inappropriate.

gban tudna, Leko   a bush with large sticky pods; its seeds are burned to make
salty water (*ngwum wəl*). The pod's sticky liquid cures catarrh. The leaves
are inedible because they cause distension of the stomach: they are used to
make the Yeli version of the *nɔga* cult which causes stomach distension.
The Mapeo version of the identically-named cult employs ironwood
leaves.

Just as Yeli usage allowed the shea leaf to stand for female, or to stand for snake, but found it inappropriate to the condition of epilepsy, so the ironwood leaf may stand for male, or via redness for the condition of leprosy, but it cannot appropriately be used in the stomach cult of nɔga, as it is in Mapeo. Another leaf, with the specific external motivation of causing stomach pains, is brought into play. To generalise the characteristics of Yeli leaf uses (from materials in the Appendix): the shea butter and ironwood leaves can be used only where criteria of gender, colour or form crucial to the contrast between them are satisfied; if neither of these leaves is used, then other leaves must be appropriate in terms of colour or resemblance of form or effect. The Mapeo conventions differ: specialised uses are usually justifiable in terms of re-semblance of form or effect; leaf uses shared by numerous cults are purely conventional.

How might these differences be explained? Attrition of previous under-standing in Mapeo seems to be one possibility. By bringing a few anomalous uses of shea butter leaves and ironwood leaves into line, and by substituting a few specialised tree products for these, it might seem as if the Mapeo system could be given a symbolic overhaul. However, this project would still fail to address the crucial absence of congruent colour and gender contrasts between the paired shea butter and ironwood trees. This is not for want of gender contrast in Mapeo classifications of vegetable matter, as the ensuing discussion of medicines shows, rather it is because the colours and gender characteristics of vegetable matter cannot be correlated.

MEDICINES

When there is talk of medicine, or of 'medicine tree/wood' (*gan te*, Leko; *gɔn tim*, Daka), Chamba normally have in mind either the western drugs, powders and creams available (at times) from dispensaries, or the substances applied to patients during curative ceremonies by cult practitioners. Herbal remedies (literally 'tree root', *tim niksa*, Daka), of which some elders have specialist knowledge, have usually been tried before cult contagion or witchcraft are explored as causes of affliction. Such remedies can be administered for a small sum, but they are not medicine in the same sense as the medicine of the cult (*jup gɔn tim*; *vɔm gan te*).

The most important of cult medicines are called simply male and female medicine (*gan van* and *gan ken*, Leko; *gɔn lum* and *gɔn nu*, Daka). They are distinguished by form rather than colour. Male medicine (*Cissus quadrangula-ris*) is a succulent which grows in elongated fingers that are quadrilateral in cross section. The plant is found in many African medical systems. Chamba distinguish varieties according to size, each of which is appropriate to a different cult; to set up the cult a plant of the correct type must be procured. Its female counterpart is a round, onion-like bulb (one of the *Amaryllidae*), also recognised to have different types, which stings when applied to the skin. Both

plants are commonly found growing at the compound entrance of cult masters
and around cult precincts.

One or both of the medicines is blended with other ingredients, frequently
in a red (ochre) or white (beer lees) paste, for application to the patient.
Alternatively, the medicines may be inhaled or drunk to reach the site of the
affliction. These same compounds are administered to members in order to
fortify them during the meeting of the cults. Occasionally, I witnessed cult
members administer medicines without ceremony to their close junior kin for
minimal or no payment. If a youngster's offence is minor: a squabble with an
elder, failure to be obedient, or being inadvertent witness to some element of
cult practice, the automatic cult sanction considered to have been triggered by
the behaviour does not warrant a demand for full compensation (which the
senior matrikin would anyway be liable to pay). Full compensation is paid only
if the cult which has caught him or her does not belong to the sufferer's
matriclan or patriclan. Payment recognises proprietorship but is not instrumental to the healing process.

Under these circumstances, matrikin of the afflicted must assemble a reparation consisting of all the traditional Chamba foodstuffs (Chapter 3) in order
for curative ritual to be performed. In Mapeo and Yeli (but not throughout
Chambaland), some cults are said to 'catch' individuals (like snake bite cults)
but others 'follow the matriclan' (like *nɔga*, the stomach cult, and *jup* or *vɔm
dagan*, the purifying cult). In the latter cases, curing must be performed for all
closely related matrikin of the sufferer.

Male medicine is usually dabbed onto the body of the afflicted person: to the
forehead, the middle of the chest, shoulders, right arm and hand, left arm and
hand, right knee, left knee and the small of the back. Female medicine is
rubbed into the body. Either medicine may also be taken in a draft of beer (*nyə
gan te*, Leko; *son gən tim*, Daka, drinking the medicine wood), especially to
correct problems diagnosed to be internal. Additional mimetic actions are
required by the curative rituals of some cults (lancing of swellings in *sɔra* or
yaguman, removal of a pot from between the legs for swollen stomachs in
nɔga, purifying the compound in *jup* or *vɔm dagan*).

Neither in Mapeo nor Yeli are medicines invariably associated with particular ailments or consistently linked to the leaf on which the cult is made. No
informant was able to explain the association of medicines with particular cults
in terms other than convention. Although knowledge of how to make and
administer a medicine was an element of the later stages of induction to a cult,
initiates are not given general reasons why medicines are associated with one
cult and not another. Special medicine ingredients could be explained, but the
two gendered medicines are apparently related to particular cults only by
convention. Since there are numerous gaps in my knowledge of medicine, this
picture might change with further information. However, it seems that medicine use is far more variable than leaf use between Mapeo and Yeli.

If we take directly equivalent cults in Mapeo and Yeli, such as the 'male cult' (*jup lum*, Mapeo; *vɔm van*, Yeli), both concerned with snake bites, we find that the Mapeo variant uses 'female medicine' while its Yeli version uses 'male medicine'. There is a tendency for female medicine to be used in Mapeo snake bite cults more generally (also in *ngwan ji*, and in *karbang*, although the latter case is complicated since *karbang* is supposed to combine twelve cult medicines). Mapeo practitioners additionally use female medicine in at least some of the cults concerned with 'bad deaths' (*ja lɔk* and *kɔngla*, but there is, again, a complication in the latter case, since *kɔngla* is said to combine male and female medicines). Female medicine is administered as a stomach massage to encourage difficult births caused by *bɔntɔng*. Male medicine is variously used in different Mapeo cults: in combination with white paste it is applied to sufferers from the *nɔga*, stomach, cult; as an eye wash it is given to victims of the *langa*, eye, cult; male medicine is applied directly to the seat of incisions made either in bodily swellings, for patients of the *yaguman* cult, or in the inflated testicles of men caught by *je bɛl*. My Yeli data are slighter: female medicines are probably used in some of the cults concerned with 'bad deaths'; more definitely male medicine is used not only in *vɔm van*, but also in *vɔm ding*, another cult of snake bite, *kɔm vɔm yɛla*, concerned with stomach pains and blood in the sufferer's excrement, and *vara*, a cult which causes leg cramps.

Administration of medicines is more obviously linked to the disorder, since potions are either directly applied to the seat of localised disorders, or alternatively daubed on several parts of the body when symptoms are diffuse. Other elements of the curative ritual vary from technical procedures (eye washing, stomach massage, incision, the application of the ashes of ironwood leaves to lepers and burn cases, the confinement in the bush of smallpox victims who were doused with hot water) which are prescribed to act immediately upon the bodily condition of the patient, to mimetic actions like pot removal for victims of *nɔga* stomach disorders, or the planting of staffs in large beer pots to allow the widows of men belonging to *jup ya* to remarry (see Chapter 3).

It seems likely that more specific reasons would be found for the occurrence of most medicines other than the gendered pair. For instance, breech birth medicine is related to a tree type in Yeli (*wa su nyia*, see p. 40) because its shape is reminiscent of human limbs. In general, the precise composition of medicines is among the most effectively guarded of the secrets of the cults, and this affects how far this analysis can, or should, be pursued.

THE NATURE OF THINGS:
COLOUR, GENDER, HEAT, NUMBER AND FORM

The animate and inanimate things of bush share general properties of colour, gender, heat, number and form with human beings and the dead. By reference to these properties, informants discover analogies between different orders of being. In part, Yeli informants are able to do this more comprehensively than their counterparts in Mapeo because the normative hierarchy and specialisation of Yeli officials allows performers and performances to be related to one another, and to other orders of being, in terms of their differences. Yeli priests and their chief are more radically unalike than any pair of male statuses in Mapeo; therefore, rituals of communal importance can be referenced to the persistent characters and aptitudes of those who carry them out.

However, our perusal of the inanimate things of the wild suggests an additional difference in symbolising potential between the two places. Yeli informants were able to associate leaves with gender and affliction via the connecting idea of colour. Thus, the redness of the ironwood leaf was immediately evocative of leprosy and masculinity in Yeli, but these connections were much less evident to Mapeo informants. This difference corresponds to another between the conventions for naming colours in the two languages.

Colour-like terms that are neither compounds nor descriptive terms are few in both Chamba languages: there are three terms in Chamba Leko and four in Chamba Daka. More has to be said about the status and referents of these terms, but simply as a memory aid we might say that Yeli terminology is an example of the classic red/white/black African triad, and Mapeo terminology is the same but for the addition of a term that covers light shades of green, yellow and blue. Confining our attention to ritual concerns, we would find that in both places the simple triad of terms is used. The Mapeo term 'green' should, therefore, make no difference. But it does. The difference stems not from the uses of the 'green' term but from the equivalences possible in terms of the triad of terms which are rendered impossible with the addition of an extra term. For symbolic purposes three terms are better than four.

The distinction I have stated as black (*virgi*, Daka; *ding*, Leko) and white (*burgi*, Daka; *bid*, Leko) is more accurately described as a contrast between dark and white. I sometimes prefer to translate 'red' (*ji*, Daka; *yɛl*, Leko) as russet, because this is closer to the colour of its ritual exemplar. In Chamba Daka, but not Chamba Leko, *ji* may be held in contrastive relation with *jɛ*, 'greeny yellow'. All this could be represented in a diagram.

bid
burgi
WHITE

yɛl   RUSSET   GREEN   *jɛ*
ji   /YELLOW

DARK
ding
virgi

However, a diagram organised this way suggests that the terms, especially the four Daka terms, are organised around two contrasts. This is only part of the picture: in both languages, the terms in the basic triad may each be contrasted with one another (giving us three pairs which have unequal importance: dark/white, dark/russet and russet/white); the Daka series adds a contrast between russet and green/yellow. However, the green/yellow term is not found in any other contrast. Its sense, before a variety of artificially-coloured goods was imported, was restricted to descriptions of vegetable matter. *Je* is the colour of leaves and of bananas and of guinea corn plants in their early stage of growth. It tends to function as a term for moist growing things which redden and dry out with ripeness. 'Green/yellow' is unmarked in ritual; no dye is made to colour things *je*.

To elicit what we call colour, it is necessary to ask in Chamba what 'water' something has. Although there is no specialised term for 'colour', I am not aware of an indigenous theory associating colour with moisture. If we were to ask what colour clean water is, we would learn that it is without colour, just water. The use of the term for 'water' to mean colour seems to be a dead metaphor, but why this metaphor is used I cannot say. Eliciting the 'waters' of things we learn that all the darkest shades (of blue, green, brown, mauve or black) are covered by the term 'dark'. 'White' is for preference restricted to pure, brilliant whites. 'Russet' covers a range from light brown to deep crimson, that includes anything with redness; modifiers are often employed if the shade is other than a dull brick red. Modifying suffixes are used generally to express the degree to which things have these qualities of darkness, whiteness or redness. For instance, in Mapeo the suffix *pusum pusum* indicates slight darkness, whiteness or redness; *soyi soyi* is the suffix for a brighter red than blood; *tal tal* is the purest of whites; *zəka zəka* is a mottled black.

These visual qualities are also realised in ritual contexts by the use of dyes. The use of the three dyes is the closest an observer can come to witnessing unelicited pure colour operations. Each dye is conventionally made in one way only.

White: brilliant white paste is made from guinea corn: either guinea corn flour or the white lees taken from the bottom of the pot in which beer mash is boiled for the first time. In both languages this substance is called *kɛn*, or in full, *kɛn kum suma*, Leko, the '*kɛn* from the bottom' (of the pot). The languages share emphasising particles to express the brilliance of this whiteness: *bid tal tal*, Leko; *burgi tal tal*, Daka.

Dark: deep black paste is made by mixing soot, (*la lim sina*, Leko; *'isi sɛgum*, Daka, the residue of 'fire', *la* or *'isi*), produced by burning grass or scraped from the underside of a cooking pot, with shea butter. Black is usually understood to refer to intense black without the use of emphasisers.

Red: brick-coloured red ochre is made by mixing kaolin (*kasa*, Leko; *kut*,

Daka) with shea butter. The name of the substance is equally the name of the colouring agent. However, informants very readily identify *kasa* or *kut* as a substance like dried blood.

These three dyes are the closest Chamba come to a pure use of colour paradigms, but perceptions of colour remain closely tied to substances. The dyes are known by the terms for the substances which colour them: white is the colour of guinea corn flour, dark the colour of soot and russet the colour of caolin. An investigator seeking basic referents, especially of older informants, would find that these colours, or examples close to hand which resembled them, would be the ones pointed to. Thus, white might be exemplified in a gleamingly laundered robe, russet by pointing to a terracotta jar or to potter's clay, and dark by virtually any item of dark hue but preferably by black. Yet, for all that it seems Chamba teachers ostensibly resort to colour paradigms in order to instruct neophytes, the use of colour-like terms in speech is more fluid.

Colour distinctions involve all three contrasts within the triad: white and dark, dark and russet, and, less elaborately, russet and white. Although, the three dyes suggest themselves as virtual colour/substance paradigms, other spoken idioms make it less clear that we should privilege colour as a state. In Chamba Daka, black and red possess verbal forms which are lacking for the white and green/yellow terms. *Vitsi* is to darken something (transitive); *virgan* (intransitive) to become dark, for instance as a place does at late evening; *vit* is to be black. *Ji* (transitive) is to redden something. Clear informant preference for brilliant white as a paradigm suggests whiteness is an exemplary state, but darkening and reddening (the most labile poles of contrast) are equally tendencies or processes. To express a process of whitening, for instance in the greying of hair, Chamba Daka use the term *tɔman*, to be become ashen, derived from the word for ashes (*tɔma*).

HUMAN COLOURS

Because the Daka colour term 'green/yellow' is applied to nothing animate, colour judgements about people are restricted to the same three colours in both languages. Of the three contrasts potentially available, that between dark and red, with the dynamic potential suggested by the forms darken and redden, is the most widely employed. Superficially, human bodies are either dark or reddish (European bodies represent an extreme case of redness rather than whiteness in Chamba terminology). Whether traditional or not, contemporary aesthetics tend to value bodily redness over bodily darkness. To be very dark is to be unattractive. Change in body colour is more ambiguous. The body darkens during many illnesses, especially when emaciation ensues. Pregnant women find their bodies redden as they retain blood. However, leprosy is also a condition of redness. And a healthy moistness of the body is described as dark in Yeli (*ding pirik pirik*). Either reddening or darkening may be auspicious or inauspicious depending upon the desirability of the initial state that is changed.

Whiteness is apparent only as a component of the body: blood, skin and bone are respectively red, black and white. White is the colour of semen and of milk that nourishes blood retained by a woman to form a child. The creation of a child is often likened to making of pots, and the colour of red clay is a paradigm reference of the term I translate as russet. Pregnant women and newborn children are described as red. The human sources of life are red and white. In old age the blood is said to dry up, and greying hair becomes 'ashen'. Tightening and dessication culminate in the human relic of the white skull, which is preserved by coating it with russet-coloured ochre. The red/white polarity is re-established at the end of life, when skulls are contained in darkness in lidded pots as the foetus was earlier contained in the 'belly' of the mother.

Colour terms are used during life to describe human attributes. In Chamba Daka, someone with a red forehead (*nin ji*) is contrasted with someone with a black forehead (*nin virgi*) as respectively fortunate and unlucky people. Lightness and darkness on the surface of the body can only be contrasted as redness and blackness. In description of internal states, all three colours become available. *Tɛm ji tu*, a red-hearted person, quick to anger, is contrasted with a black-hearted, evil, person (*tɛm virgi tu*), and a good-hearted (*tɛm sɛmɛn*) or white-hearted (*tɛm burgi tu*) person, and also with a changeable person, possibly a witch (*tɛm baran tu*, spotted heart). When white becomes available neither red nor black have entirely auspicious connotations. Some of the colour terms in this analysis can be replaced by thermodynamic terms. Red-heartedness is close to hot-heartedness (*tɛm susu tu*), and good- or white-heartedness is very close to cool-, that is calm- or equable-heartedness (*tɛm 'ɔran tu*). Whether these usages are also metaphorical is not clear, since some informants claim that physical signs of witchcraft may be seen on the heart.

Where human subjects are concerned, the connotations of dark are predominantly inauspicious. Witches are black and nocturnal. To become blackened is to become dirty (*liga*, Daka; *lira*, Leko), and smiths are described as both dark and dirty. However, darkness is not wholly maleficent. Dark also connotes coolness, whereas illness is heat. The typification of the smith in terms of darkness recalls that he is the 'cool' man with a 'hot' job. More generally, the red/black distinction may stand for the male/female axis, most evidently in the colouring conventions of the Chamba mask. Nor is red colouring of the body necessarily auspicious. Snake bites leave red blotches on black skin, and we have seen that one of the snake bite cults derives its name, at least in local etymology, from this fact (*ngwan ji*, see Chapters 3 and 4).

By and large, red and black signify bodily condition and gender in Mapeo as they do in Yeli. Major differences occur in the application of colour terms to inanimate living things.

INANIMATE COLOURS

There is very close analogy between Yeli Chamba descriptions of the growth
and maturation of people and of guinea corn (Chapter 6). Guinea corn alters
colour during its growth: from a white shoot, to sprouts about an inch long
described as red, to a moist and growing phase described as black, then as the
lower leaves become dry and yellow (*yɛl nyɛm nyɛm*, a specialised compound of
red) it finally ripens and assumes its mature colour: either red or white. Colour
changes correspond to a developing analogy: from the whiteness of seed, like
semen, the plant reddens, like a foetus, then darkens and becomes pregnant, it
grows under the auspices of the chief's control over rain in an environment that
is dark and damp and cold. The heat of ripening, under the auspices of the
priest's harvest cults, sees the guinea corn hang down its head 'in fear of *vɔm*'.
Harvest is like circumcision, and because the heads of guinea corn are also
'heads' in Chamba, and the seeds are like eyes, is simultaneously analogous to
skull-taking.

The Mapeo description bears only a pale resemblance to parts of this
integrated scheme. The interwoven ideas of colour change (from dark to red),
which are analogous to changing ritual responsibilities (from chiefs to priests)
and changing predominant gender attributes (from feminine to masculine), are
systematically weakened. Growing corn is 'green' and not 'black'. Because
there is no chief, there can be no chiefly responsibility for the early growth of
the crop against which the priest's role at harvest might be measured. The
changing colour of the crop cannot parallel the shifting responsibility for the
crop from men to women because 'green' lacks human connotations. Guinea
corn is still said to become pregnant, but I have not heard harvest likened to
circumcision in Mapeo. There is no explicit analogy between the life cycles of
people and their staple crop.

Yeli associations between human conditions and vegetable products of the
wild are also weakened in Mapeo. In the Yeli scheme leaves may have any of
the colours of the basic triad, and so also may tree trunks and leaf stems. In the
case of the most important contrast, the leaves and trunk of the shea butter tree
are 'black' and the leaves and trunk of the ironwood tree are 'red'. The shea
butter tree exudes a white substance and produces large oil-bearing kernels.
The feminine and masculine properties of the trees correspond to conventionalised relation between colour and gender, including the black/red contrast
employed in colouring Chamba masks. In Mapeo leaves are 'green/yellow' and
therefore without human analogy.

Numerous other tree products are appropriate to some particular use in
ritual because of the connections made in terms of the colour triad. Leprosy is a
condition of redness; the leaves used in cults concerned with leprosy are of the
ironwood tree (red leaves on a red trunk) or the *nyɛdna* tree (black leaves
contrasting with a red leaf stem). Most leaves, in fact, are 'black'. A rare white

leaf is that of *te bira*, the white tree, which has cooling uses in ritual, and is also said to have a white trunk and leaf stem. The locust bean and the wild pawpaw, trees with black leaves on a white or whitish ground (*lɔm*, locust bean, has a trunk described as *bid zɔga*, a bit white; *lɛnga*, the custard apple or wild pawpaw has a white trunk), are both vehicles of coolness.

Because of the existence of an extra colour term, systematic exploitation of the analogies between colour, as a property of plants, and gender, or the attributes of ailments is impossible in Mapeo. Mapeo and Yeli share other sensible properties of tree products: the watery fruit of the wild pawpaw is here (as elsewhere in Africa) attributed medicinal properties associated with cooling; the locust bean tree has small leaves with which to produce a gentle spray of water. But these specific formal characteristics lack the potential to suggest pervasive patterning to the same degree as colour.

THE GENDER OF THE DEAD

All living things may be distinguished by gender. But what of the dead? Early in this book I noted male bias in the terms for the dead: in Chamba Daka the dead is a composite of skull and man; in Chamba Leko the person suffix in 'dead person' is understood to be masculine unless a female suffix is added. The implied sense of the masculine status of the inhabitants of the underworld was confirmed, unasked, by informants talking about the rhythmic clapping that takes place as a gesture of respect when, and where, the people of the underworld are present. Clapping, I was told, is always repeated in threes, with a short interval between bursts, even when it takes place in the women's cults. As elsewhere in Africa, three and four are respectively male and female numbers in Chambaland. This suggests that the more enduring state of being is masculine.

Old women dry out and become 'like men' before they die. When they no longer bear children they are permitted to do things that child-bearing women cannot do. Men also dry out and become 'tight'. The heads of both sexes become ashen, cold and white and dry. The direction of these physical changes presages eventual transformation into bone and skull. Skull is the prerogative of the patriclan, and the skulls of men and women may become mixed up we are told. Femininity is therefore a transient state related to moisture and fleshiness, unable to persist after death. Women propagate life by giving blood and milk, but even for them female characteristics are transient.

Although the underworld is usually described by close analogy to the world of people, with its farms, markets, roads and so on, I have heard no references to sexual intercourse or marriage occurring there. Sexuality, and menstrual blood, the externalised form of blood that would otherwise create life, have to be rigorously excluded from contact with the dead who are heated and angered by it. In relation to the living, the dead are cold. By virtue of the places in which they live, they are also associated with darkness. Dark coldness is one of the antitheses of the hot redness of blood.

This contrast between the states of the living and the dead tells us that the world of the living is especially distinguished not by masculinity but by the preponderance of female moisture and warmth through which living things are regenerated. Humans and animals reproduce in gender-related ways. Plants which produce leaves or fruits are normally described as feminine. Only guinea corn of the planted crops, the staple cultivated by men, is described so as to suggest that it is analogically masculine. Guinea corn, we may recall, is the pre-eminent example of whiteness. The bambara groundnut, the traditional women's crop in Yeli, is a red seed which grows below ground. The differences between men, donors of externalised white seed to their children, and women, donors of internalised red substance, are congruent with local descriptions of the gender-specific staples. In the reproduction of village and farm, men are predominantly associated with white and women with red; however, once the context shifts to that of the wild so also do the colour associations. In the bush, men are shedders of blood and women become associated with black (the colour of the female mask, witches, and the leaves and trunk of the shea butter tree).

PARTIBILITY AND THE SHEDDING OF BLOOD

Blood is always red and hot, but its further significance varies according to whose it is and where it is shed. Retained, female blood is the material of flesh; menstrual blood provokes the dead, spoils cults, and makes hunting fail should men come into contact with it. The man who sheds women's blood violently is liable to insanity without special ritual at the hunting shrine. The logic of containment of blood is common to human reproduction and to sacrifices made to gain fertility or to make offerings in matriclan cults (Chapter 7). Men are shedders of blood, but not within their farms or villages (where they are donors of seed). Blood-letting occurs in war, or in the hunt, or in sacrifice at the patriclan cults and shrines. Even circumcision blood is shed outside the village. Blood should not flow from other male orifices: when it does the man has been caught by a cult.

In Mapeo, the contrast between partibility and blood-letting, on the one hand, and impartibility and blood retention, on the other, can be pursued only to the extent of a distinction between patriclanship and matriclanship in general. In Yeli, the distinction is invested with hierarchical significance. The royal matriclan is kept intact in its graveyard; the chief's priest, ideally succeeding to his father's position, lays claim to his powers by cutting off his predecessor's skull before the flesh has rotted.

Logically, culmination of this contrast in statuses would seem to necessitate a feminisation of the chief relative to his priests. In the chiefdom of Sugu, closely linked to Yeli by traditions of origin and co-operation, the head of the chiefdom was indeed a woman. In Yeli, the predominant colour of chiefship is black. The chief favours the use of black cloth, and he controls the black clouds and thereby rain to enable the growth of guinea corn in the cool, dampness of heavy earth. The white guinea corn seed germinates in the black earth ('red' earth is not fertile) and puts forth white shoots that turn red by a process directly analogous to human conception. In order for ripening to take place, the chief's brief, to assure coolness, is superseded by the heat of *vɔm* which dries the place. The chief and his priests are made to behave analogously with parents—as if they were mother and father to the crop. Like a child, especially a male child, the crop passes from feminine to masculine tutelage as it matures.

By a different analogy to coldness, the chief is likened to the inhabitants of the cool, dark underworld. Because of this similarity, he is menaced, and may die, when boys are circumcised. Their hot blood, shed by the priests, falls onto the ground and threatens the coolness which makes him acceptable to the subterranean beings. Should the chief die, his death celebrations will occupy four days, like those for a woman, rather than the three days of a man.

Given the labile character of colourlike distinctions and their highly contextual links to gender, heat and number, it would be an error to claim that stable oppositions are established in terms of colour, or that colours are encompassed by one another through ritual. Images evoked by colour terms or colour substances are, or may be, loosely connected to one another. Different degrees of likelihood can be guessed for the mazeways through these associations that individuals or groups of individuals follow. Only in the very particular contexts can we guess how a colour analogy or the use of a colour dye is interpreted. None the less, a substratum of properties involving colour, gender, heat, number, form (and probably such attributes as sound and movement that I have not considered) is common to living things—human, animate, or inanimate—and to the dead. These properties allow the possibility of moving between orders of being by analogy.

Paths through the mazeways of associations may differ according to interest and context, and the full extent of the skein of relations may not concern those who pursue images down different paths according to their lights. However, I have suggested that Yeli informants find more paths converging than their Mapeo counterparts, and that this is so in part because they index the cycles of growth, sickness, maturity and decay of living things to their conceptions of political and ritual hierarchy, and in part because their reliance upon a classic triad channels animate and inanimate things into the same colour pathways.

9

THE NEW RELIGIONS OF GOD

A NEW POLITICS OF BELIEF

Monotheistic influences must have affected how Chamba speak of God. In both Chamba languages, the term for God is also that for the sun; but it is unclear what relation this implies between them: identity of God and the sun is denied by any Chamba to whom I have spoken on the subject.

In Chamba Daka, *Su*, God, is the same word as *su*, sun. Moon and month are both known by the composite term *su banan*, the suffix of which cannot be glossed. Sun and moon may be contrasted as *su nunan* and *su taka bɛ*: the *su* (or *Su*) of daytime and night-time. Some informants would make these light sources respectively male and female, hot and cold. That the term for sun is probably cognate with the description *su su* for extreme heat must encourage the plausibility of this contrast. Conventional ideas linking gender with colour might also seem appropriate, since maleness could attach to the redness of the sun and the female character of the moon coheres with the darkness of night.

Traditionalists insist that creation, and in the final analysis all that occurs in the world, happens as God wills. How far, and if so for how long, this dogma has been influenced by Muslim or Christian opinion is impossible to say. Certainly, God is commonly invoked in traditional performances. Before sacrifices at cults, the cult master may proclaim, *Su an tɛ, wurumbu bɛn sɔ*, 'God is here, the dead below the ground'. Such spatialisation of human between-ness is consistent with other elements of Chamba outlook; light and heat are contrasted with dark and coldness. Although prayers beg (*pɔp*) God for rain or fertility, and although his name may be spoken in oaths to assert veracity, sacrifices are made only to the dead. God has no use for beer or sacrificial animals.

Chamba Daka speakers seem to have suffered no uncertainty in deciding that *Su* was the appropriate term to translate what they took other Muslims and Christians to mean by God. Christians may use the phrase *Su n daran*, God above, to refer to the God of the trinity; while Muslims prefer the simple *Su*,

other than whom there is no God. But there is complete agreement that God is
Su and not the dead, *wurum*. Chamba Leko usage has a more chequered
history. There are grounds to suppose that the Leko term for the sun, *nyam*,
served as the term for God, much as did its Daka counterpart. Moon and
month are called *so*, apparently cognate with the Chamba Daka, *su*. Chamba
Leko terms encourage association of the creator God exclusively with the sun
(as God is pre-eminently associated in Chamba Daka also). However, recent
Bible translations into Chamba Leko have preferred *Vɛnɛb*, the singular form
of the term for the dead in Balkossa dialect, as a word for God. A Chamba priest
has written an article justifying this usage in terms of his understanding of
Chamba conceptions of God onto which the newer Christian idea is to be
'grafted' (Bernard, 1982).

Whatever word they use, nowadays most Chamba see themselves as
members of monotheistic world religions. Christianity and Islam appear
to have swept all before. Some older men are thought, by the more devout,
to be lax in their religious practices, and a few well-known life histories
involve reconversions from Christianity to Islam, or more rarely vice versa, but
there is no evidence for the emergence of a normatively syncretist religion,
nor any strong Chambaisation of world religious traditions. The precise relation between Chamba religion, Islam and Christianity varies from place to
place, but everywhere the traditionalist element of the population consists of
those marginal to contemporary currents. Some traditional festivals continue
to be observed, even to thrive (like *jup kupsa* in Mapeo), but many who
participate in these ceremonies have little interest in Chamba religion outside
the annual communal festival. The demise of traditional religion seems
assured.

There are many reasons why this should appear to be the case. Islam and
Christianity both came as religions of conquerors, and the circumstances
under which Chamba converted continue to be pertinent to perception of the
new religions. Chamba talk of themselves as relatively recent converts. This is
undoubtedly true of Christianity; Islam has been known to them since the early
nineteenth century and probably longer. The local debate over Muslim conversion hinges upon a distinction drawn between adoption of some outward
signs of conversion, in particular localities and by certain people and probably
expediently, and the genuine renunciation of traditional practices to embrace
the new religion. As often as not, the most devout Muslims argue most forcibly
that Chamba conversion to Islam is a phenomenon of the British colonial
period and later.

Taken together, the relative marginality of Chamba to colonial interests
(whether German, French or British), the apparently recent date of Chamba
conversion to Islam or Christianity, and the status of the ethnic carriers of the
two faiths, seen through Chamba perceptions of the interplay of political
interests between Fulani, European and themselves, have meant that religious

change has occurred abruptly when measured against many other areas of Nigeria or Cameroon. Religious change has been part and parcel of the social and political upheavals that have followed from Fulani jihad, a succession of colonial regimes and administrative statuses, and the inclusion of Chamba in states about to complete three decades of formal independence. Doubtless, conversion has stemmed also from personal faith, but the observer more easily detects the significance of the context within which religious affiliation has become self-conscious and contested.

Other explanations of the slight resistance of Chamba religion in the face of the world faiths might question the potential of its beliefs to remain plausible under challenge. Even to pose a question in these terms we must accept a context in which a people called 'Chamba' had a 'traditional' 'religion' that involved states of 'belief'. To have gone so far is to have heavily prejudiced any response, for the emergence of this intellectual context is part of the answer to the initial question.

In terms of the intellectualist thesis, proposed by Robin Horton (1975), a movement of the search for explanatory coherence from microcosmic to macrocosmic elements in the traditional explanatory system ought to correlate with an expanding network of social relations. When conversion to a world religion has simultaneously been a means for people to increase their social range, separating intellectual plausibility from social purpose, or even arguing the difference between them, may be dubious. Whatever the case, this new context reveals how unelaborated are any macrocosmic ideas Chamba may have shared. Movement from microcosmic to macrocosmic dimensions was impossible short of adopting radical innovation on existing ideas or outside religious inspiration.

The terms in which masks, cults and men might be imagined to share characteristics of the dead, the wild and the human, depended upon no specific beliefs about a creator God and recognised no intermediary, godlike agencies between God and the local dead. The decline in the significance and otherness of the bush, and the erosion of importance of matriclanship (especially once Christians and Muslims contested the matrilateral inheritance of moveable property), meant that the cogency of ideas about the wild rested on a fragile practical basis. Chamba ideas of the dead, which straddled distinct translations of spirits and ancestors, were easily subject to classification as belief in evil spirits. Overall, the lived coherence of these Chamba notions was closely related to peculiarities of Chamba terms and the links that could be intuited between them. The new religions arrived in Arabic, Fulfulde, Hausa, English and French but rarely, and then only for short periods, did either of the Chamba languages function as medium of a world religion.

Ganye Local Government, with its created 'traditional' chiefship and its periodically changing systems of local administration, has been the object of contemporary Chamba struggles for influence and power. The question of an explicit response to change in self-consciously Chamba religious terms has remained academic. The desire to forge intellectual tools consciously from the materials of tradition would have necessitated a political self-confidence that was denied to the relatively marginalised, disunified and small Chamba population. The powerful agencies of Europeans and Fulani could only be confronted on the ground of their own traditions of religious worth. Fragmented and dominated by the Fulani during the early colonial period, the Chamba were able to assert themselves in local political contexts only by joining the religious traditions which formed part of the dominant cultures. So, it seems as if factors both intrinsic and extrinsic to Chamba religion tended jointly towards its marginalisation. Given that Chamba self-assertion required conversion to both Islam and Christianity, attempts to mobilise an ethnic argument in support of aims presented as collective could appeal to one of the two new religions only at the risk of division. But neither could the ethnic argument appeal to 'traditional' religion upon which the elites were obliged to claim they had turned their backs. Politically and intellectually it is difficult to see how any Chamba could have risen to prominence, other than in the most restricted sense within his own community, without becoming a Christian or Muslim. None did.

The dances, music and masks have lent themselves to enacting an ethnic identity within the national states in which modern Chamba now seek their place as Chamba Christians and Chamba Muslims (see Fardon, 1988). They are markers of cultural distinction and tokens of historic identity. The prominence of these performative elements of Chamba 'tradition' requires no verbal exegesis of local participants nor, for that matter, any decision about the Chamba language in which explanation should be sought. For members of the Chamba elite these symbols have been largely voided of their earlier connections with daily concerns. They finesse the problem of answering quite what being Chamba might historically or culturally mean. The ethnic argument can support relations between Chamba of different regions and countries, but only if it is able to stand independent of the division between Christian and Muslim, and apart also from any too specific interrogation of the highly varied religions, cultures, even languages of the component communities of the present day Chamba. By coming from villages, whose remoteness from the modern centres can be read also as temporal distance, elements of Chamba artistry can enact ethnic difference.

Pockets of traditional religion are to be found enclaved within villages or concentrated in more remote settlements. But stirrings of interest in the creation of a Chamba Culture Centre in the administrative headquarters of Chambaland suggest a realisation of the diminished size and uncertain future of these.

ISLAM AND THE JIHAD

The objectives of the Fulani jihad will remain a source of contention so long as events which took place at the beginning of the nineteenth century continue to loom so large in current politics. Was the jihad a movement of religious idealists or a bandwagon joined by a motley crew of freebooters in search of wealth and power? Probably something of both. In Chamba eyes, especially Muslim Chamba eyes, it was more the latter than the former. Contemporary Chamba see the Fulani invasion of their homelands as an attempt to wrest power from them and to reduce them to the status of slaves. They prefer to insist that Chamba did not convert to Islam before the twentieth century and that most Chamba stood out against the invasion in their hill-fastnesses or compelled Fulani to recognise Chamba political rights to regulate their own communities.

The picture that emerges from the earliest travellers' reports and from what has been pieced together of Fulani politics is more complex. In the first place, while Chamba informants talk as if the nineteenth century was the time of a confrontation between Chamba and Fulani, it is clear that Chamba had not emerged as a clearly bounded ethnic identity, and that the local communities to which Chamba owed their allegiance before the jihad were frequently at loggerheads (see Fardon, 1987, 1988). Furthermore, the Fulani chiefdoms were infrequently able to sink their differences, and unity of purpose was achieved between particular chiefdoms only in the short term. Every crystallisation of Chamba/Fulani relations was local and transient.

Communities of eastern Chamba, including Mapeo and Yeli, were least well-equipped to withstand the deterioration of local security in the early nineteenth century and possibly in the late eighteenth century as well. In the extreme east, the establishment of the cordon of Fulani chiefdoms along the Rivers Faro and Deo early in the nineteenth century led to a virtual evacuation of the plains by the Chamba Leko chiefdoms. Perhaps a majority joined Chamba-led raiding confederacies which were to colonise areas of the plains below the River Donga as well as the Bamenda Grassfields. Others sought refuge in the Alantika Mountains, directly the west. As Chamba renounced control over the plains, so the Fulani were able to press further south, usually in the wake of Chamba raiding parties, which had themselves assumed a multi-ethnic composition. In a short time, Chamba communities found themselves entirely encircled by Fulani chiefdoms and clients.

Although they recognised rough territorial boundaries, the nominal sub-chiefdoms of the Adamawa Emirate do not seem to have concerned themselves with establishing strongly-centralised governments over these territories. The chiefdoms developed centres around the palaces of the Lamidos with courtly organisations. On the peripheries of the chiefdoms were slave villages directly under the control of the Lamido or one or another of his officials but, beyond this, the Fulani seem to have treated their territories as repositories of exploitable resources both human and material, although the line between the regions controlled and exploited was not fixed. There was an interest in assuring safe passage to traders and to pastoralists, which meant that those who were not members of the Fulani chiefdom and its integral communities had either to be persuaded into passivity or their capacity for nuisance clearly localised. The nominal territories were carved up between court notables who were considered to represent the communities for the Lamido.

Since this system persisted so long into the colonial period, it is difficult to trace the fortunes of the nominal fiefs. Relations between Fulani and Chamba were highly changeable. Representatives of the Lamidos might try to exact regular tribute from the communities in their charge, but they appear frequently to have failed in this task or to have considered the attempt imprudent. As the century wore on, the Fulani found themselves engaged in campaigns further south against local peoples and against other Fulani chiefdoms; presumably these richer pickings would have led them to neglect the, by now impoverished, areas nearer to home. In the intermittent interest they showed in the territories they claimed, Fulani overlordship may rather have resembled its colonial counterpart. One can imagine Fulani officials, like colonial officers, hatching administrative initiatives only to find that a war elsewhere, or a lack of resources, enabled little more than a holding operation. Even when Chamba did pay tribute to one of the chiefdoms, they do not seem to have been assured protection from slave raiding by the very people to whom they paid tribute or by a predatory neighbour of their patrons.

From late in the nineteenth century we find evidence of Fulani attempts to routinise their control over Chambaland. The chief of Dalami, a Chamba chiefdom of the central plain, became a broker, forwarding to Yola the levies of corn and livestock he exacted from Chamba communities remaining in the plains. His village was a mixed settlement of Fulani and Chamba, and his installation is said to have been by winding on a turban in Yola. In the southern Chamba chiefdom of Sugu close alliance with the Fulani of Koncha is recalled, expressed in mutual gift-giving. From the Koncha perspective, the same relation implies Fulani conquest of Sugu. In the mid 1920s, a British observer noted that the chief of Sugu performed daily prayers, but we do not know how much earlier outward signs of Islam had been adopted (Migeod, 1925).

Early travellers' reports and oral traditions suggest that most of the mountain plateaux remained outside even nominal Fulani control until the colonial period. To members of the various expeditions that traversed the area between the early 1880s and the demarcation of the German–British border some thirty years later, there appeared to be clearly discernible differences between areas where Fulani were abroad, and often established in small hamlets or else in quarters of Chamba villages, areas where Chamba lived in apparently cowed condition on the peripheries of the chiefdoms, and other areas of 'free pagans', where there was no Fulani presence or control. In the last case, even outward show of Islam was absent, although some things considered its trappings might have been adopted in the form of gowns or koranic charms. Nowhere is there evidence to suggest abandonment of Chamba religious practices even when arrangements with the Fulani involved outward show of conversion on the part of the chief. Early syncretism continued until the more effective imposition of a colonial system of administration when the British assumed responsibility for the core area of Chambaland.

COLONIAL OCCUPATION

Chambaland saw a number of colonial false starts; indeed, it saw little else. German penetration really occurred only in the last decade of the nineteenth century, and was followed by about a dozen treks by German officers through the region, of varying duration and extension, during the first decade of the twentieth century (Moisel, 1912, Maps D2 and D3). Administration began to be consolidated on the eve of the First World War, when the Kamerun colony was lost to France and Britain. The vast majority of the Chamba area then passed into British hands under the terms of League of Nations' Mandate Orders, in 1923 and 1932, that were later to be the basis of a United Nations' Trusteeship Agreement in 1946. Not until the 1930s did the British devote sufficient resources to the Mandate to assure regular administration.

A World War again reduced administration to the barest minimum, and the colonial presence was not restored to its 1930s level until the 1950s. By that decade, the days of Trusteeship were clearly numbered and, under the impetus of a succession of U.N. Visiting Missions, steps were taken to prepare the area for independence. The task of determining the fate of the Trust Territories on the independence of Nigeria and Cameroon briefly focused attention on the problems of local administration. Even then the importance attributed to the southern part of the British Cameroons Trusteeship, and the greater political activism there, tended to deflect interest from the north.

From the point of view of religious change, a couple of features of the colonial period need to be remarked. Since the colonial presence was so slight, the main beneficiaries of colonial rule were a number of Fulani chiefdoms, of somewhat dubious traditional pedigree, which became the principal administrators of the Chamba area. The appointment of one of their number, the District Head of Nassarawo, as Lamido of Yola in 1926 was the opportunity administratively to place most Chamba within the Yola Emirate. Colonial administration thus succeeded where the Fulani had failed during the previous century, and Chamba found themselves routinely administered through Fulani with the authority of the colonial presence overseeing the relation. In local perceptions, Chambaland became a region of the staunchly Islamic Adamawa Emirate. Thanks to their role as mediators of European authority, Fulani influence over the appointment and deposition of Chamba Village and District

Heads was substantial. The current association between Islamic faith and suitability for chiefly office was encouraged from the 1920s, and even then represented a continuation of the policy of requiring conversion of allied Chamba chiefs during the nineteenth century. Only in the relatively actively-administered decades of the thirties and fifties were steps taken to enhance the independence of Chamba chiefs from Fulani within the administrative system, and the first set of reforms had scant effect because of the intervention of the war.

The second point of note is that Christian missionary activity, both Catholic and Protestant, was a relatively late starter; the earliest initiatives were made at the end of the twenties, and the forties was the decade of greatest expansion. Probably by design, Christian missionary activity tended to be concentrated in communities which had retained greatest independence from the Fulani. Thus the Protestant mission began in the Gurum chiefdom, the staunchest bastion against the Fulani, while the Catholics established themselves in Sugu and then in Mapeo. Missionary endeavour seems to have steered (or been steered) clear of the northern mountains or plains where Fulani influence had been strongest.

PROTESTANT AND CATHOLIC MISSIONS IN NIGERIAN CHAMBALAND

Margaret Nissen's official history relates that the establishment of the Sudan United Mission in the chiefdom of Gurum, among the 'Chamba tribe proper', was taken because Donga (a chiefdom founded by emigrant Chamba south of the River Benue) had been the site of one of the earliest S.U.M. mission stations (Nissen, 1968: 198). Initially, the British Branch of the church invited Mr. and Mrs. Fleming (he a New Zealander, she a Scot and one-time assistant to Mary Slessor) to open their station at a place called Gandole, within the Emirate of Muri, and inside Nigeria rather than the Mandate. The subsequent move to Gurum, east of the Shebshi Mountains within the Mandated Territories, followed the Flemings' realisation that more Chamba were concentrated there. This account suggests an early propensity to view Chamba tribally. Despite differences of language or dialect, history and culture at Donga, Gandole and Gurum, a Chamba propensity to convert was thought to link them. Muslim interest in Gandole was certainly much stronger than in Gurum, Nissen refers to the 'little interest' of Gandole people in Christianity before the 1960s (Nissen, 1968: 207). Resistance to the Fulani, and therefore to Islam, ought to indicate fertile Chamba ground for the gospel. Gurum, in these terms, was exemplary.

The Gurum mission was installed in 1929 (Nissen, 1968: 199), with the assistance of the Chief of Daksam (a market village in Gurum chiefdom) who had encountered mission influences when carrying taxes to Numan, an early site of S.U.M. endeavours in Nigeria (see Engskov, 1983). Mr. Fleming set about organising construction of a dry season road to link Gurum with Numan and, in 1932, began the construction of a mission house. He and his wife became 'proficient' in Chamba, and they produced 'a Primer, the Gospel of Mark, a combination Catechism and Songbook, and a collection of Old Testament Stories' (Nissen, 1968: 200). These volumes are still the most substantial published literature in Chamba Daka. The Flemings were to stay in Gurum until 1942, content to make slow but solid progress. A school and dispensary were opened to attract Chamba students and patients. Students who had attended the school for some time were sent as teachers at the invitation of villagers. Baptism was apparently withheld from those who had not completed seven or eight years of religious instruction. Fleming's values were stern; he appears briefly in British colonial records as the author of a 1935 letter on the problem of Chamba wife-stealing in which he suggests somewhat draconian measures, including imprisonment and flogging, for men 'stealing' the wives of fellow villagers (3058; Letter of 26.11.35). The Resident found his suggestions 'not very helpful' (*ibid*, note).

By 1947, almost twenty years after the decision to establish a mission at Gurum, only thirty-four Christians had been baptised (Nissen, 1968: 203). That year, the Church area was taken over by the Danish branch of the mission, and policy changed in several respects. The British missionaries had been 'members of the Church of England' or 'of Baptist persuasion' and had baptised only adults. The Danish Lutherans were to change this and to abandon the attempt to proselytise through the vernacular. By learning Hausa, Chamba converts would have access to the whole Bible and enter 'fellowship' with other Christians of Northern Nigeria, especially those within the Adamawa Church with its strong foothold among the Bachama in Numan. Hausa was also introduced into the Gurum primary school, where education had previously been in Chamba. More catechists were sent into the villages to work, and a large church was built in Numvan, a village in Gurum, as a central place of worship for Chamba Protestants (Nissen, 1968: 203–4).

An indication of the rate of conversion to the Lutheran church can be gained from figures supplied by missionaries for inclusion in annual reports the British were obliged to submit to the United Nations' Trusteeship Commission. Interpretation of these figures is complicated by our ignorance of all the considerations that might have influenced those who compiled them and by changes in terminology in the reports of different years. In 1946, the S.U.M., with a declared expatriate staff of two (catechumens were excluded from staffing figures), claimed a hundred and fifty 'converts'. This number greatly exceeds the thirty-four baptised Christians reported by Nissen for 1947, but the level of commitment implied by conversion is unstated. The report of the following year, coinciding with the reversion of the mission to the Danish Lutherans and the opening of a new mission north of the Gurum station at Dashen, records a doubling of staff and fourfold increase to 615 'converts'. But Nissen dates the first three baptisms in Dashen to 1948 (Nissen, 1968: 409).

S.U.M. figures then follow a path of gentle increase reaching 934 converts in 1949.

Returns for 1953 and 1954 (repeated in 1955 and 1956) fall sharply—to 105 and 130, although staffing had risen to five and seven. Simultaneously, the description of the missionised Africans changes from 'converts' to 'adherents'. Between 1957 and 1959, however, the S.U.M. returns a series of, slightly different, numbers of 'adherents' all around the level of three and a half thousand, suggesting a resumption of the growth curve recorded during the late 1940s. It appears that between 1953 and 1956, the S.U.M. compilers reacted to the change in terminology, from 'converts' to 'adherents', by tendering figures for baptised Christians (see especially 1955 Report). The dramatic increases of the later 1950s represent reversion to the older practice of returning figures for people showing some unspecified level of interest.

Interpreted this way, the figures tally with local accounts of church development as steady if unspectacular during the years of the Trusteeship. Those who could be deemed to show interest in the church, either through its extension activities in education and health, or by church attendance, were a little under five times more numerous than the baptised Christians when the Flemings departed; by the late 1950s they outnumbered baptised Christians twentyfold. The proportion of baptised Christians would have risen steadily once children were born into the households of parents married in church. Given a population in Yelwa, the district in which the S.U.M. was most active, of about 22,000 in 1958, and allowing that some Protestants lived in Nassarawo District, the S.U.M. claimed about 10% (in the roughest terms) of the Chamba population as 'adherents' in some sense.

The S.U.M. church became the Lutheran Church of Christ in Sudan before adopting its present title of L.C.C.N. (Lutheran Church of Christ in Nigeria) in 1954. A large church has been erected in Ganye, the administrative centre of Chambaland, to meet the needs both of Chamba Lutherans and of their co-worshippers from other ethnic groups living in Ganye. This church has supplanted both Numvan and Dashen as the pre-eminent site of Protestant worship.

Before the independent Nigerian government took control of all schools, Lutherans typically opened new areas under the tutelage of evangelists in whose wake came schools, dispensaries, maternity clinics and stations for the treatment of leprosy. Classes for religious instruction were organised in forty-one villages in 1955. A great part of the effort involved was expended by local men who had been trained as evangelists, many of them, after 1951, at Dashen in the northern part of the area to be administered eventually from Ganye. Education, health and religious instruction thus tended to come as a package often carried by Chamba men.

In 1955, Lutherans were in receipt of £311 in British government aid to run a junior primary school in Gurum which was attended by 120 boys and girls.

Further small grants were made towards dispensaries in Gurum and Dashen, and a leper colony was run by the church in Gurum (Colonial Office Report for 1955: 126). Three years later, the church was running three Junior Primary Schools, and the number of classes for religious instruction had risen to sixty-nine. The Chamba literate elite emerging from this expansion of the church, and of church-run education, was to give voice to Chamba grievances about their administrative position *vis-à-vis* the Fulani and also to supply the majority of Chamba elected to representative office from the late 1950s. Perhaps because responsibility was devolved more rapidly onto local men, Lutheran rather than Catholic Chamba were in the vanguard of ethnic self-assertion.

The Roman Catholic Mission entered Chambaland about a decade after the Protestant S.U.M. The missionaries active in Chambaland were members of the Irish Province of the Augustinian Order, an order without previous missionary experience (Hickey, 1984: 75). Berchman Power (1976: 35-9) recalls receipt of permission from the colonial authorities to found a second Catholic mission station among the Chamba in April 1940. Catholic missionaries in Sugu chiefdom were busily engaged in the construction of the first mission when the exploratory party passed through. Mapeo was chosen as site for the new mission after the Village Head invited them to build a school (Power, 1976: 36). Receiving provisional authorisation to build in Mapeo, the missionaries decided to erect buildings rapidly before the authorities had a chance to change their minds (Power 1976: 39).

St Mary's in Mapeo was founded in February 1941, and seven students began their studies in 1943 (Dalton, 1961: 34). By 1960 there were thirty students living under the roof of the Father 'quidam a parentibus missi, quidam a parentibus fugitivi, quidam orbati parentibus, quidam gyrovantes' (sent by their parents, fleeing their parents, orphans, or going the rounds). The mixed bag clearly posed problems. In 1944, they were speaking nine different languages. If burdened with work the boys fled, but if the Fathers relaxed their discipline the boys became 'otiosi et inutiles' (Dalton, 1961: 35). Chamba recall the regime to have been strict. It proved possible for the missionaries to carry out the first three baptisms of boys in Mapeo during Pentecost in 1946.

Figures of 'adherents' submitted for inclusion in reports on the Trusteeship to the United Nations return Chamba Catholics together with Margi, Fali, Higi and other peoples of the northern area of Northern Cameroons. However, given the slightly earlier date of the two Chamba missions, it seems likely that a majority of those 'adherents' enumerated (eighteen in 1946, 246 in 1948, rising gradually through 325 in 1952, 950 in 1954, to 3550 in 1955 and 6000 in 1959) were Chamba. Allowing for the vagaries in interpreting both these and the Lutheran figures, it seems the missions enjoyed about the same rate of success in the Trusteeship period. The greatest difference between the two sets of figures is that the Catholics submitted a number of adherents about twice that for baptised Christians, while for the Lutherans this factor rose to about twenty.

The Catholic contribution to education and health was more extensive than that of the Lutherans. Even allowing that some Catholic activities took place outside Chambaland, it seems likely that expatriate staffing usually ran at about twice or three times the level of the S.U.M. By 1958, in addition to Junior Primary Schools (the figure of fifteen includes those outside Chambaland), the Catholic Mission also ran a Senior Primary School at Mapeo. Its government grant of almost £14,000 for capital and recurrent expenditure was far greater than anything received by the S.U.M. Additionally, the mission sisters ran the health centre (four beds) and maternity home (twelve beds) built by the government in Sugu, where the mission had established a Girls' Boarding Senior Primary School in 1956. Both the Catholic and S.U.M. missions ran several leprosy clinics.

From policy, the Catholics preferred to maintain greater numbers of expatriate missionaries in the field to instruct and lead worship. The advent of Nigerian or Chamba Catholic priests to take their places has been relatively recent, and priests and sisters from abroad have continued to predominate numerically over local men and women. The Lutheran church, by contrast, had begun ordaining Chamba pastors as early as 1955 (Nissen, 1968: 202). Despite the evident ability of some of the Catholic Missionaries in Chamba Daka, the only flirtation with the vernacular as a medium of Christian doctrine appears to have been the publication of a Catechism in 1951 in the Mapeo dialect of Chamba Daka. Its author, Malachy Cullen, a versatile linguist among the earliest Mapeo missionaries, was certainly a competent Chamba speaker, although his text uses an idiosyncratic orthography. For different reasons, Lutheran and Catholic missions both abandoned Chamba language for religious instruction in favour of Hausa. The Lutheran decision coincided with the transference of the Chamba church to the Numan area; Catholic reluctance to endorse use of the vernacular appears to stem from more pervasive anxiety about potential fragmentation of the church.

The expansion of Islam in Nigerian Chambaland is much more difficult to infer. Cullen's notes on the Mapeo mission, written in the early 1940s, indicate a competition between Islam and the Catholic church for the allegiance of Mapeo youths (Cullen MS). Nissen records a Muslim convert among the earliest pastors of the Dashen church (Nissen, 1968: 212). Koranic and western schools were opened at roughly the same period and competed for pupils. The introduction of a school fee for western education could temporarily shift the balance in favour of the koranic schools (e.g. Nissen, 1968: 208, on the early period of the Dashen school).

Many of the competing considerations of the period remain germane today. The Fulani were firmly ensconced in the colonial indirect administration and local courts of Chambaland until the late 1950s. Conversion to Islam might be the precondition of appointment to office or to the court, or marriage into a Muslim family, or commercial transactions with Muslim entrepreneurs. Conversion potentially opened a network of helpful co-religionists, or at least it could be made to seem thus. On the side of the Christian missionaries were two countervailing and related arguments. Education might open opportunities for advancement which bypassed Fulani control. Literacy was the *sine qua non* for seizing these chances. Moreover, opposition to Fulani, which in many areas was a tradition, could be expressed through conversion to a competing religion and adoption of an alternative culture of western manners, book-learning and Christianity. Caught between these trends, it seems that many older men, who preferred the status quo, tried to resist schooling their children which involved the loss of their labour power.

THE CHAMBA SEPARATIST MOVEMENT OF THE 1950S

The influence of Christian missions became highly visible to British colonial officials when Chamba began to agitate actively for the right to administer themselves. Reports of the organised protest that British officers dubbed the Chamba Separatist Movement give a snapshot view, albeit from a particular vantage, of the forces in play at the very end of the colonial period (Fardon, 1988: 276–80). Leaders of the Chamba Separatist Movement were concerned to protest to the British, and thus focus the attention of the U.N. upon what they felt to be the underdeveloped state of the Chamba Native Administration. They voiced grievances that administration was dominated by Fulani, that pressure was brought to bear on Chamba to convert to Islam and that basic services and communications were not provided on an appropriate scale. The main centres of the movement were mission stations: Gurum and Sugu; leading roles were played by adherents of the Lutheran, Gurum, mission, as a resume of events reveals (NAK Files 3058 and C. 778).

In January 1951, four or five 'youths' had paid a visit to the British Resident at Yola to ask that the Chamba be made independent of the Fulani District Head of Nassarawo and granted a Chamba chief. Simultaneously, reports were submitted by the same Fulani chief claiming that the chief of Gurum was 'fostering' this movement. To understand the grievance we need to recall the major features of the existing administration. Under this set-up, the Chamba Subordinate Native Authority, composed of five districts, was a part of the Adamawa Native Authority with its headquarters at Yola. This, as I have already explained, seemed to many Chamba an expansion of the Adamawa Emirate under British sponsorship. By 1950, one of the districts of the Chamba Subordinate Authority, called Nassarawo, was three times more populous than the largest of the other four (Sugu, Binyeri, Gurum and Yebbi). Hamman Tukur, the Fulani District Head of Nassarawo, was also Wakilin Chamba, that is to say president of the the five districts, and the linchpin in relations between Chamba District, and the British Resident and the Lamido of Adamawa, both based in Yola. In effect, he had become responsible for the administration of the whole of Chambaland in the British Trust Territory. The British sent an official (Rickford) to investigate developments on the ground.

It transpired that a Christmas celebration had been held at the Gurum mission to which the Chamba District Heads had been invited along with leaders of the mission. At a 'tea party' held afterwards, pro-Chamba independence speeches were made, and the delegates were invited to express a unified demand for independence to the District Officer on the next occasion that he toured. The chief of Gurum is reported to have encouraged the movement privately, while saying that he would have to disagree with its aims officially. He must have felt himself caught between the British, the District Head of Nassarawo with the support of Yola, and the demands of the mission party in his own chiefdom. Gang Kuba, then chief, had been appointed in 1936 on the dismissal of his predecessor for embezzlement. He was to suffer the same fate himself, as well as a year in prison, six years later in 1957.

Rickford ordered the chief of Gurum to cease his support for Chamba separatism and to warn the mission group in Gurum to do so also. An invitation to the District Head of Yebbi to support the movement was to be withdrawn. The reporting British officer felt that the mission Chamba were not sufficiently numerous to be a force on their own; although, he stated, the mission at Gurum had seven hundred converts, only about twenty were active in the movement. Europeans at both Gurum and Sugu missions were said to dissociate themselves from the movement; however, his judgement appears to have been at fault in the former case. He went on to identify three ringleaders and five principal followers in the agitation. The first-named of the eight, Dama of Mbulo, described as a teacher, is probably the Mallam Dama who was one of the first converts to the Protestant church when the missionaries arrived in the late 1920s. This remarkable man is said to have given up the chiefship of Daksam, a village in Gurum, and renounced three of his four wives in order to become an evangelist. After 1945, he moved to Mbulo, north of Gurum, to continue his evangelical and educational work (Nissen, 1968: 202, 208).

The remainder of the supposed agitators (Dogo of Daksami, Bemute, a teacher of Numvan, Dasin Daudu of Numvan, Gangabani of Pindore, Billa of Daksami, Visumenso of Gamu, Janguri of Numvan) appear to have been employed by the S.U.M. either as school teachers or as evangelists. Three were resident in Numvan, the mission's centre in Chambaland, and another in Daksam. Some had spent two years at the mission training centre in Numan. The Numan link featured in another aspect of the event, since a Bachama from Numan, a Sergeant Major Jonah of the Middle Zone League (an organisation campaigning for the formation of a central Nigerian state able to escape northern Muslim domination), had toured mission stations as a 'sort of S.U.M. visiting teacher' in October and November of the previous year. His encouragement was credited with catalysing the Chamba movement.

The leaders of the protest were predominantly young, literate and Christians. At around fifty years of age, Mallam Dama, if he was the leader, was probably older than the other agitators. He was prominent in a further development which kept the movement before British attention. On tour in March 1951, S.J.A. Cassidy found himself approached by between a hundred and a hundred and fifty 'adherents' of the S.U.M., led by Mallam Dama, whose spokesman, called Daniel, was identified as an attendant at the mission-run dispensary in Gurum. The group wanted to contribute, their spokesman related, to the discussion about amendments to the constitution and local administration. They could not voice their views through their village heads and chiefs because a reprimand had already been administered to the chief of Gurum by the British, and they were threatened with punishment. Cassidy noted that the chief of Gurum, who felt personally insulted by having to announce publicly the warning given him by the previous investigating officer, had become antagonistic to the demands of the mission group. These were much as they had been earlier in the year. The Chamba wanted a Chamba chief since they had never been conquered by Fulani; they wanted an administrative officer to be posted in the area, and roads, schools, wells and dispensaries to be built. But the material demands were secondary to their desire not to 'live longer under the Fulani'.

From the Danish pastor, Jeritslev-Hansen, who was to retire in 1953 after working in the area since 1947, Cassidy learned that Chamba disquiet was related to discussions about a new Nigerian constitution, since they felt that without independence from Yola they would be unrepresented. Hansen treated the investigating officer to a 'tirade' about the activities of the Fulani in general and Lamido of Yola in particular, as well as a 'sermon' on the need for the Chamba to unite. He and his followers, Hansen explained, were ignorant of the new constitution since the local newspaper, *Gaskiya*, was Muslim and they did not read it. Cassidy recommended that the provincial representative be sent to explain matters, though noted that it was 'unfortunate' that this man also was a Fulani.

Cassidy needed to send the Resident in Yola another letter, this time from Sugu where he was visited by twenty-five past and present students of the Roman Catholic mission school. They had accepted an invitation from Gurum to join the Separatist Movement despite a warning from the Catholic priest that doing so would lead to their dismissal. Their demands, voiced by a Mallam James, were virtually identical to those heard in Gurum, but specifically included the Chamba grievance that the Native Authority employed only Fulani in Chamba District.

Chamba agitation effectively focused the attention of administrative officers, but without achieving substantial effects. When the District Officer, W.H. Paul, sat down in September 1951 to compose a report headed *Chamba District Affairs* his recommendations were that the administration should be thoroughly 'Chambaized' and he pointed to the defects of previous attempts at reorganisation which had served to entrench Fulani domination. However, little immediately came of his ideas other than an order to the Fulani District Head of Nassarawo to limit his activities to his own district. It was not until 1955 that a second report, by D.S. Sorrell, proposed again that a Chamba Federation should be created, and that it should be organised so that Chamba were administered by Chamba, rather than by Fulani. After 1955, one demand had been met and a touring office was stationed at Jada 'when available'.

In 1958, the United Nations' Minorities' Commission was visiting Adamawa Province, and an extensive report was prepared for submission to them by the Assistant District Officer. P.S. Crane voiced the opinions of the emerging Chamba, Christian elite—he calls them the 'articulate Chamba'—who resented being called 'slaves' by Fulani, and who saw their chiefs as Fulani 'tools' encouraging the Muslim faith, and using district councils and electoral colleges to assure the election of 'Yola nominees to the Federal and Regional legislatures' (Crane, 1958: 10). They felt discrimination to operate at every level of the system:

> They resent the attempts made by the N.A. to make Islam the 'official religion'. It is difficult for the Christians to obtain work in the roadgangs because they refuse to work on Sundays. There is also great difficulty in obtaining permission to build churches and open classes for religious instruction, and Moslem propoganda is continually pressed in more subtle ways. The unfair allocation of places in N.A. Senior Primary Schools to the exclusions of candidates from the Mission schools is another justified cause for complaint.
> (Crane, 1958: 10—copy annotated by its author)

SEPARATION AND AFTER

The first Chamba nominee to the Federal House of Representatives—M. Abubakar Gurumpawo, elected to represent the Southern Adamawa Trust Territory between 1954 and 1959—was a Muslim who stood for the Northern Peoples' Congress party, which was closely identified with northern Muslim interests. His election had been via a series of electoral colleges, rather than through a popular franchise. In 1959 another Gurum man was returned. Philip Maken, a prominent Christian, stood on an Action Group ticket, in Christian Chamba eyes an alternative to the Muslim-dominated N.P.C. He was headmaster of the Gurum Mission school and two years previously had failed to be elected as the first District Head of Yelwa.

Following the deposition of the Gurum chief, and the retirement—under a cloud of suspicion concerning tax matters and accusations of apathy—of the District Head of Yebbi in the same year, the British had decided to amalgamate Gurum with the very small district of Yebbi to form Yelwa. The first chief was chosen by delegates from the two constituent districts after, as a report euphemistically puts it, they had been 'addressed by the Lamido' of Yola, who had promised to build a new headquarter's town at Yelwa (Crane, 2 February1958). In 1961, Philip Maken became the second Chief of Yelwa District, of which Gurum was the largest part. In addition to all this, he was chairman of the District Council of Gurum Church (Nissen, 1968: 199). After setbacks to his career under the military governments which succeeded the First Republic, he returned to the political fray to stand unsuccessfully as gubernatorial candidate of the Unity Party of Nigeria (successor to Action Group) for Gongola State during the Nigerian Second Republic.

Philip Maken belongs to a branch of the Gurum chiefly family: his father, Gang Sa, had succeeded to the chiefship of Gurum at the death of his brother, the long reigning Gang Maken, in 1924. Twelve years later he was deposed on accusations of embezzlement (Crane, *ibid*). Philip Maken took his name from his father's older brother. Judging by the attendance of some of their children at mission school, both Gang Sa and his successor Gang Kuba may have been broadly sympathetic to the S.U.M. However, the chief of Gurum presumably had numerous children; in a report of 1935 he is reputed to have kept twenty-eight wives (3058 Chamba Wife Stealing, note of 6.11.35). Philip Maken's broader appeal, shown by his 1959 electoral success, derived from old and new sources: education, youth, understanding of the broader Nigerian context, his position as a Christian leader unlikely to become another Chamba client of the Yola Fulani, and his membership of a well-placed family.

Dominic Mapeo, a Catholic from Mapeo and one-time teacher and schools' inspector, briefly achieved ministerial rank in the last government of the First Republic. His later career included spells as a commissioner in Northeastern State, and appointment to the post of Waziri (Prime Minister in local English translation) in the traditional administration of Ganye Local Government Authority. Before his death in 1983, he received the Nigerian Order of Merit. Like Philip Maken, Dominic Mapeo was elected on a popular franchise with support built initially from his local community but also tapping broader Christian and Chamba sentiment. Unlike Philip Maken, he did not start with the advantage of a chiefly pedigree.

Dominic Mapeo claimed that he resisted considerable coercion to convert to Islam on his appointment to the office of Waziri of Ganye. A tendency for popular votes to return Christian candidates for office while appointive positions are filled by Muslims has become almost institutional. Dominic Mapeo's successor as Waziri of Ganye, who has recently made the pilgrimage to Mecca, had been an ordained pastor of the Lutheran church since 1962, and that was still his status when, in 1977, he gained the Chairmanship of Ganye Local Government on a popular vote during the run-up to the restoration of civilian rule. There are few exceptions to the unwritten rule that Christians are not given office in the traditional system of administration. The first, and so far only, Chief of Ganye, is a convert from Catholicism and all the present District

Heads in Ganye Local Government Authority are Muslims (having converted from Christianity in some cases). Both Philip Maken at Yelwa, and the only other Christian District Head in Sugu, were removed from office.

This is not to say that discrimination has systematically worked against Christians. Muslims might claim the opposite of employment in schools and local administration where Christians predominate. Chamba Muslims and Christians share many aims within Gongola State across the religious divide. For insiders and outsiders alike, it is not easy to predict what will become of this uneasy balancing act between religion and ethnicity. The danger of religious polarisation, far more than ethnic separatism, preoccupied those to whom I talked about such matters in the run-up to the creation of Nigeria's Third Republic.

PROTESTANT MISSIONS IN CAMEROONIAN CHAMBALAND

A minority of Chamba Leko speakers, including those in the chiefdom of Yeli, had been placed on the French-administered side of the international border by the agreement dividing British and French Mandated Territories after World War I. These Chamba were depleted by occasional waves of emigration to Nigeria: the largest movements, during the 1920s, populated the plains north of the border with Chamba Leko speakers; intermittent, smaller, movements have occurred in more recent decades. The general isolation of this fragment of Chambaland, effectively cut off for much of the year from Cameroon by a river system to the immediate west, is one cause of the movements. But equally important, according to local accounts, is the fact that Fulani dominance went virtually unchallenged in the administration of this part of Chambaland. Although the Fulani chiefdoms existed only as vestiges of their former scale, they were granted virtual autonomy in administration by the French and, from the Chamba perspective, their use of this power was exploitative.

Missionaries did not enter Chambaland in North Cameroon until the 1950s. The earliest mission complex was built in the chiefdom of Balkossa, like Gurum a place with a history of resistance to the Fulani. According to the present American pastor at Balkossa, before the arrival of missionaries there about a dozen Chamba had converted to Islam following the arrival of the son of a Balkossa woman who had married a Nigerian Muslim. Although there was an early attempt at evangelisation in 1953, with the placing of a catechist south of Balkossa, this individual was 'chased out' by the Lamido of Tchamba. A Balkossa Lutheran Mission, with an American pastor, was established around 1958 and converted some Chamba Muslims to Christianity. The mission had been invited by a long-reigning chief of Balkossa, and such success as it enjoyed was probably due to the benefits anticipated from the establishment of a school. Previously, and even presently, many Cameroonian Chamba can gain access to education only by moving to neighbouring Leko communities in Nigeria. The earliest language of instruction in the mission school was

Fulfulde, the northern Cameroonian lingua franca (Edward Mueller, personal communication, 1987).

During the 1980s the Balkossa mission established a Samba Literacy Centre devoted to the publication of the gospels and primers in Chamba Leko. Unlike earlier attempts at translation into Chamba Daka, these materials employ a script which marks vowel quality, tone and vowel length. The mission's expansion, including the building of a chapel in Yeli, has relied on methods shared with the early Lutheran S.U.M. in Nigeria. Catechists have been trained and local pastors ordained creating a network of Christian congregations within the Chamba villages. This network is denser the closer one comes to Balkossa, while Chamba villages further from the mission centre appear to be predominantly Muslim. The commitment to proselytisation in the vernacular has its only counterpart in the earliest years of S.U.M. establishment in Nigeria.

MAPEO

With this much local background behind us, we can return to the two villages that have featured in my account. I earlier described the three-cornered set of my relations in Mapeo: my immediate neighbours were Muslims; my network of younger, professional (i.e. non-farming) friends was predominantly Christian; the people with whom I spent most time were traditionalists. The views of these different parties towards one another were constantly volunteered.

Members of the small community of Muslims with whom I lived maintained dense relations among themselves, focused upon their collective prayers at the small mud-walled enclosure that served as their mosque. The oldest men were of the first generation of adult converts to Islam who had been initiated into Chamba cults after circumcision. In comparison to the traditionalists, their lives were restrained and private. None of them, to the best of my knowledge (and the signs are not easy to disguise), either brewed or drank guinea corn beer, which is the normal accompaniment to Chamba male socialising. This effectively cut them off from more than passing contact with the traditionalists or the Christians for whom drinking was the accompaniment to relaxed conviviality. For the Muslims such behaviour was raucous, uncontrolled and liable to lead to argument, while squandering economic resources. Their views echoed the case frequently stated against entrusting Christians with positions in the 'traditional' system of District and Village Headships.

Jup, the Muslims claimed, were both dirty and dangerous, in strong contrast to the elaborate and public washing preparatory to their own prayers, which were without malice. The vehemence of their condemnation probably related to the initiation of older men into the cults prior to their conversion to Islam. Without exception, their own fathers had been traditionalists, and in some cases among the great *jup tu bu* (men of the cults) recalled in popular memory. The older Muslims denounced *jup* but did not deny their efficacy.

The younger, second-generation Muslims did participate in communal dances, but—except in this—also tended to keep themselves apart.

Most of the Natup Muslims were also interrelated through common membership of a patriclan (Yangur); the remainder were, none the less, co-residents. Conversion of the present Muslim community had been a process lasting about twenty years. One major step in this had been the invitation to a Fulani mallam to live among them. At least one man from a different Mapeo hamlet had come to build alongside his co-religionists in Natup. He died before my first fieldwork, although the unroofed buildings of his compound were still standing. Some of the children of this man, like many children of other Natup Muslims, were Christians. Their father's conversion had occurred after his oldest children had entered education at the Mapeo mission school. The religious affiliation of later children had been more contentious. The oldest son and daughter of his first wife were Christians before their father became a Muslim. A second son of this wife converted from Islam to Catholicism, and this decision is recalled to have occasioned a family dispute in which the Catholic priest had intervened. Of three sons by a co-wife, the first was Christian and the younger two Muslims. Split religious affiliations in this family rested on the outcome of a tussle between father and oldest son, a prominent Christian, for the religious loyalties of the younger children. By and large, the religion of the girls depended on that of their husbands, although their marriages, in these cases, do not seem to have occasioned changes of religion.

Examples of diverse religious affiliations among closely related men were common in Natup. In another case, the older brother, probably around sixty years of age in the mid-1970s, of a sibling set remained a traditionalist, his slightly younger brother was a Muslim. However, the sons of both were Catholics. While the son of the traditionalist took some part in traditional celebrations, the Catholic son of the Muslim altogether absented himself from them. A more predictable pattern seemed to crystallise in the decade between the mid-1970s and mid-1980s, largely because of the demise of the senior generation of adherents of Chamba religion. In the mid-1970s, the oldest men had almost all been traditionalists. Ten years later, the oldest generation was a mixture of Muslims and traditionalists, and it was clear that the latter were not able to induce their sons to follow their religious practices. After the earlier period of transition, when members of the same family might belong to three different religions, it seemed that a norm of sons following the religions of their father was being established. Since the sons of traditionalists were, by and large, independent from them, the demise of the traditional religion was already achieved. Time would do the work of attrition on the remnants of the last generation involved with the esoteric aspects of the Mapeo cults.

Without exception, men I met in the mid-1980s whom I had known ten years earlier maintained the religion (Muslim, Catholic or Chamba) they had practised when I lived in Mapeo. Although there had been conversions of older men only a few years before my first visit, none that I heard of had occurred subsequently. Together these observations suggest that the memberships of the different faiths were stabilising after an earlier period of change. Natup was not the only Muslim community in Mapeo, although it was the one I knew best. Members of both world religions were to be found in all the main hamlets, although there was a tendency for Muslims or Christians to predominate in particular hamlets or areas within them. Another concentration of Muslims was to be found at the extreme eastern end of the village, where the Village Head had his compound. The hamlet in which Christians constituted the highest proportion of the population was a relatively new site that had been established during the 1950s in close proximity to the mission and church.

Informants, whether Christian or Muslim, recalled that Islam and Christianity had made roughly contemporary inroads into Mapeo. Both sought to minimise the influence exercised by Fulani in conversion to Islam in Mapeo. However, there are indications in oral traditions concerned with the vexed issue of the village headship, that at least nominal conversion had been a strategy in the attempt to gain office during the colonial period. Christianity had tended to capture converts through the schools. Thirty to forty years later, the ages of the oldest Christians reflected the fact that the first baptisms in Mapeo had occurred in 1946. Cullen records the presence in Mapeo of young converts to Islam just after the foundation of the Mapeo mission. However, the conversion of the older men I knew appeared to have been slightly later, and many became Muslims during the 1950s and 1960s, after their sons had become Christians. It is likely that earlier converts had left Mapeo, or lived in the hamlets I knew less well. Although it is difficult to be certain, it seems that the post-independence decade had been a particularly active time of conversion of mature traditionalists to Islam. Once the lines between the religious communities had been drawn by the end of the 1960s, affiliations appear to have stabilised. Those men who had not converted tended to remain traditionalists to their deaths, although their sons could not be retained within the traditional religion.

Traditionalist reactions to the phenomenon of Mapeo Chamba Muslims were strongly voiced, and seemed to appeal to an older paradigm of Fulani/Chamba relations that was homologous with the distinction between Islam and *jup*. Chamba Muslims were said to have become Fulani (*bit Puli*), using the verb that denotes shape-changing or sudden transformation in state. I scarcely heard it said of Christians that they had become *Nasara* (Europeans).

At least two contrasts are involved. Christians, at least Mapeo Catholics, have remained drinkers of local beer, although this was beginning to change on my visit in 1984 when two bars selling the bottled product had been set up. By 1987 economic hardships had led to the closure of the bars, and a number of senior Christians had taken a principled stand against alcohol. This was generally received with sympathy as reaction against one of the grounds on which discrimination against Christians was said to have been practised. In general, Christians are not perceived by their traditionalist elders to wish to withdraw from commensality. Common beer drinking is more than a social habit, it is also a token of trust, since the weapons of sorcery are usually imbibed by victims in the gift of a calabash of beer.

As drinkers of local beer, Christians are generally willing to organise the traditional wake at the death of their elderly relatives. The certainty that their funerals would be adequately provided with beer is claimed by many traditional elders to be a compensation for the knowledge that their sons will not follow them into the esoteric stages of cult activity. It is difficult to overemphasise the centrality of drinking together as a form of shared conviviality or the frequency with which references to alcohol are made in statements conveying the attitude of the different religious camps to one another.

Beer is also important to Christian participation in the public phases of traditional ceremonies, particularly the celebrations of harvest time which are rapidly assuming a local reputation as the distinctively Mapeo variant of Chamba culture. Since the harvest festivals are supposed to have no capacity to inflict illness, many Christians are found among the drummers and horn players (as they are, on other occasions, among *lera* flute players). Here, the degree of involvement seems to correlate with the status of the Christians. The 'white collar workers', teachers and civil servants especially, usually limit their participation to beer brewing and dancing. Among the Christian cultivators, a graduated scale of involvement depends upon personal decisions about the compatibility between particular performances and Christian belief, as well as on the degree of pressure exerted by their elders. Catholic Christianity has demanded a less complete withdrawal from Mapeo public ritual than has Islam. Because of its association with education and, in some instances, with political influence, there have been compensations for the elders for what they feel as their loss of authority over their sons. A second contrast between the Christians and Muslims, involving notions of collusion, is directly related.

From the perspective of the traditionalists, to become Muslim was to collude in Fulani dominance. Since Europeans had been seen, to an extent, as a counterweight to Fulani, to become Christian did not involve collusion, at least not the same collusion. Fulani were the traditional enemy; despite the colonial period, Europeans did not come to replace them in Mapeo traditionalist demonology. The date of the establishment of the Catholic Mission was also important. The first generation of Catholic converts, while containing some notable personalities, had not been particularly large. By the mid-1970s, the oldest Christian converts were probably in their late forties or early fifties, the bulk of the converts was much younger. Christianity was still seen as a young man's religion. Despite resentment that Christian doctrines had stopped young men paying to become cult initiates, Christianity was associated with education, and education was the route to success outside the village economy, especially in government offices and education. The most successful Mapeo man, Dominic Mapeo, who had gone on to hold Nigerian government office, was an early Christian convert. Even if all his actions were not uniformly applauded, the fact of success was considered prestigious, and he was often referred to as the 'real chief' of the community by members of all religious traditions. His death in 1983 is said to have occasioned the largest ceremony ever seen in Mapeo.

Not only were Christians not said to have 'become Europeans', they were not even said to have 'become' Christians. The verb *bit*, used of conversion to Islam (to become Fulani) was not used of Christians. Perhaps the immediacy of transition implied by the verb *bit*, to change into, did not seem to apply to the Christians whose religious leanings were considered to stem from a long process of education and especially from literacy. Traditional elders remarked that Muslims converted first and learned afterwards, while Christians had to convert from childhood to learn to be Catholics. The choice to convert to Islam appeared open to elders, although they claimed not to countenance it; conversion to Christianity was out of the question. This was not only a matter of education but of potential status reversal. By remaining traditionalists, the elders could lay claim to knowledge outside the grasp of younger men. If they converted to Catholicism they would find themselves neophytes.

Ways of referring to members of the two new religions were rather different. Muslims could be called Fulani, or it could be said that they 'greeted God' (*dɔm Su*). The term Christian had itself entered Chamba; alternatively Christians could be said to 'make prayer' (*nak adua*). This usage combines the older idiom of making, as in *nak jup*, to make *jup*, with the Hausa loan word *addua*, prayer, applied to a Christian rather than Muslim prayer.

Religious conversion was intimately tied to notions of ethnicity. Although Chamba do not appear to have become Fulbe-ised, that is to have adopted Fulani identity in the way that this occurred among peoples dominated by the Fulani in Cameroon, conversion to Islam clearly seemed akin to ethnic change to Chamba. An intimate nexus between Islam and Fulani identity had been forged during the jihad. Because 'becoming European' was not seen to be an option, other than metaphorically, Christianity was able to appear as a counterweight to the Muslim Fulani in political affairs. During the height of the Chamba Separatist Movement, Christianity must have offered Chamba a less problematic identity than Islam. For older informants, especially Mapeo Muslims, there was still potential contradiction in being at once Chamba and Muslim, and they took every opportunity to stress their innocence of collusion in Fulani political aims. My impression is that the village perspective is no longer shared in the towns. Adherents of Chamba religion are hardly to be found there, and Chamba Muslims and Christians must define their religious and ethnic affiliations in relation to the current threat of national polarisation in religious affiliations.

Christians now reaching an age which traditionally would have conferred elderhood are discovering ambiguities in what had seemed to be the most coherent of identities: modern, educated, Christian and Chamba. The routes to village pre-eminence are effectively closed to them, at least they see it this way. They can neither expect to be given traditional nor administrative local offices. Their paths to fortune involve the jobs for which education is prerequisite, and policies which affect the availability or accessibility of such posts are largely beyond their control. As Nigeria faces austerity after the oil-rich years, the number of educated men and women far outstrips the capacity of the state to create the employment they seek. Many are discovering their 'traditional' culture.

There is a growing feeling of the value of Mapeo Chamba identity. A few Christians have begun to take part in the exoteric public dances of their patriclan cults as a token of belonging. Polygyny is becoming an issue for some: their wealth and position demand that they take second wives, but the church withholds communion from them if they do so. Many of them still have fathers, and all have classificatory senior kin, who are involved in cult religion. They seem uncertain quite how they are going to become elders in their turn, what model should inform their behaviour. The Christian alternative offers no clear counterpart to Muslim elderhood.

To an extent, the three communities are closed by their cultural differences and preference for the company of their co-religionists. Religion tends to go along with other features which make people companionable or not. The Christian schoolmasters and functionaries discuss areas of concern to them, while traditionalists maintain a round of social engagements largely dictated by the exigencies of cult meetings, funerals and beer brewings. The Muslims cluster around their prayer area, converse, work and pray. Younger men who are Christian farmers, rather than tailors, catechists, bicycle mechanics or functionaries, are more likely to maintain an ambiguously half-hearted interest in cults, these are boys with traditionalist fathers who have not excelled at school or not been given the opportunity to apply themselves to schoolwork. Muslim youngsters tend to have Muslim fathers and be that much more distanced from the religion of the cults because of abstention from beer. However, state control of education means that religion and literacy in English are not as closely correlated as they were. Christianity is no longer prerequisite to a western-style education.

Distinctions become accentuated during the major annual celebrations. Traditionalists organise their main celebration at *jup kupsa*, when eating the new season's corn inaugurates the Chamba New Year (Chapter 6). Their songs, dance and drinking are shared by Christians, who contribute local and bottled beer, and justify participation by appeal to the common consensus that *jup kupsa* is a collective performance (*langsi*) but not dangerous (*giran*). The Muslim attitude is complicated by the fact that *jup kupsa* is the occasion for over-indulgence in beer drinking to celebrate the new plenty. Younger Muslim men take part in the dance, which is also an occasion to meet girls; and many of the wives of Muslim men also dance. Older men might be expected to be among the horn players, and risk lampooning on this account by their traditionalist contemporaries, so they remain at home or watch proceedings from a judicious distance.

The major Christian celebrations of Christmas and Easter combine church services with beer distributions. Male friends contribute beer and a fowl to meetings held in the better-appointed compounds where they eat and drink. Although the context is different, the huddles of eating, drinking, conversing men are not so distant in tenor from a traditional cult meeting. Women are excluded from the men's groups, but some beer is usually provided to elders who drop by. New Year and Independence Day are treated in the same way.

The Muslim festival at the end of the month of fast combines prayer with preparation of food (often rice, which is not highly thought of by sorghum-eating traditionalists), and the killing of one of the larger animals: a sheep or cow. The food distribution may include non-Muslim neighbours in hamlets where Muslims and non-Muslims live closely together. The Muslims have more cordial relations with their Fulani co-religionists, at least on this occasion, than do the other two groups, but even for them friendship is mixed with caution.

Religious affiliations also become visible during death celebrations when major differences are evident between Muslims on the one hand and the Christians and traditionalists on the other. Graveside prayers are offered for some older men by their Christian children, but subsequent stages of funerals retain their traditional character. Muslim burials are devoid of traditional funeral ceremony. During the 1970s the age structure of Mapeo was such that deaths were either of the elderly, who tended to be traditionalists, or of minors or of young women in first childbirth. In the latter two cases, the type of funeral depended upon the religious affiliations of the father. In the attitude that the religious communities take to one another's public expressions one hears an echo of the older expectation of cultural difference between patri-clans—and, occasionally, even the ridiculing of difference in privileged abuse. Localisation enhances this sense of *déjà vu*.

Religious affiliations became associated with residential separation during the gradual process by which Mapeo hamlets shifted from earlier hillside locations towards the present road. The newest hamlets are predominantly associated with one of the new religions. Within older hamlets, some areas have come to be the preserve of Muslims, like the part of Natup in which I lived. The associations are far from clear cut. Some men prefer to remain on the sites of their father's compound, rather than move to be with their co-religionists. Many Christians have moved to the hamlet of Sabon Lai, established close to the Mission compound, but just as many have not done so. The upshot is a settlement pattern still thought about primarily in terms of the ownership of hamlets by the patriclans which founded them but which, on closer inspection, reflects numerous considerations of clanship, religion, access to the road, and personal compatibility. None the less, the localisation of co-religionists adds plausibility to the tendency of Chamba speakers to slide between the perspectives of patriclanship, locality, cultural difference, ethnicity and religious difference—which are interrelated as types of distinction.

Emphasis on relations of commensality focuses a contrast between Muslims and both Christians and traditionalists; other perspectives would encourage other views. Muslims and Christians together represent themselves to be on the side of modernity in contrast to traditionalists, whom they claim to live in the past. According to contemporary Mapeo informants, early missionary teaching associated *jup* with the works of the devil and banned attendance at its rituals. Some early converts were forced to revert to Chamba religion under the influence of their fathers. Mapeo Muslims associate the underground beings of Chamba belief with troublesome spirits, *ginajobu*, a compound with plural suffix formed from the same Arabic root as our borrowed term djin. Both Christians and Muslims call Chamba religionists by the deprecatory term *dɔ*, pagan; once this word referred disparagingly to non-Chamba strangers. Stigmatisation of traditionalists' esoteric practice has become more evident during my recent visits when some Muslims and Christians have begun to pick upon qualities of *jup* most reminiscent to them of witchraft. They turn to their own advantage general associations between *jup* and sources of menace that traditionalists have long exploited (see Chapter 3). As a consequence, traditional secret practices are increasingly described as a source of evil.

Christians and Muslims share other attitudes which they consider modern. They do not wish their properties to be divided on the lines of Chamba partible inheritance; their preference will be for inheritance by their sons. They cannot, therefore, accept inheritance from their own maternal uncles, since this would imply endorsement of their sister's children's future lien on their own property. I have often listened to men describe the iniquity of their nephews inheriting the fruits of the labours of their sons. A more general symptom of changing attitudes to kin is that younger Muslims and, to an even greater extent, Christians who have left the village for secondary and later education, are uncertain about the extension of kinship terms outside their own matriclans and patriclans. Since so many of these relations are instantiated in performances, the demise of traditional funeral and cult observances is likely to accompany a withering of the ramifications of Chamba clanship.

Whatever their differences among themselves, Mapeo Chamba continue to evince shared antipathy to Fulani political schemes. This was shown most dramatically in 1971 when the installation of a Fulani to a District Headship, of which the previous incumbent had been a Chamba, culminated in armed action by predominantly Mapeo Chamba men, quite regardless of religious affiliation. Imposition of martial law was followed by the detention of some men in prison for several years. If anything, Chamba Muslims have to be more strenuous in their denials of complicity in local Fulani plots for ascendancy, and their accounts are vehement in the assertion that Islam was introduced to Mapeo at roughly the same time as the establishment of the Catholic Mission and independently of direct Fulani influence. Between the members of the two world religious communities in Mapeo an extreme discretion is practised. The traditionalists are the mouthpiece of most opinions expressed about Islam, Christianity and their relative merits. A sense of Mapeo and Chamba solidarity is voiced against the increasing religious antagonism expressed elsewhere in Nigeria. Mapeo men point to the religious pluralism of their immediate families and to their shared belief in a single God as defences against polarisation. Between the mid-1970s and mid-1980s the frequency with which such views were volunteered to me mounted apace with the threat they were felt to hold at bay.

YELI

As the source of misfortunes and epidemic diseases, and the place of origin claimed by many Chamba, Yeli maintains a prestige out of proportion to its size or practical significance to other Chamba. Yeli is not in the same country as most of Chambaland, and the fact that so few Nigerian Chamba have been there probably allows more imaginative leeway to their notion of it as the authentic source of Chamba-ness. Conversion has further diminished the already small reservoir of participants in traditional performances. Of three Yeli hamlets in Cameroon, one is predominantly occupied by Chamba Muslims who take no further part in Chamba rituals. The chief's own hamlet is the site of a small chapel attached to the Protestant Mission in Balkossa, which is attended by the younger men both of that hamlet and of the third, very small, neighbouring hamlet of Gbandiu. Some of the younger men take part in traditional religious observances, largely at the behest of their fathers. Most claim that as their fathers die they will abandon a participation which is anyway restricted in the main to the exoteric public aspects of performance. This suggests that the performative aspects of major celebrations will outlast their esoteric practices and importances.

The recent initiative of the Balkossa mission to translate the Bible into Chamba Leko had not, by 1984, made an impact. Services were generally held in Fulfulde using available translations in that language. Unlike Mapeo Chamba, virtually all Yeli Chamba also speak Fulfulde. The aged chief of Yeli, whom I had known throughout my fieldwork, died in 1986. His replacement is said to support Chamba religious performances materially while taking no part in them himself. Although I was not able to return to Yeli in 1987, rumours of

The chief's new palace in Ganye (1987).

an association between the failure of rain to fall in a small locality of Nigerian
Chambaland adjacent to the border and the death of the last traditional chief of
Yeli were widespread.

RELIGION, LANGUAGE AND POWER

Yeli and Mapeo are relatively remote from the main centres of local administration. Nigerian Chamba communities closer to important new centres (District Headquarters like Jada, Sugu, Yelwa, Kojoli, Toungo and Mbulo or the
Local Government Headquarter at Ganye) have witnessed even greater atten-
tuation of interest in traditional religion. Of the new and growing administrative centres, only Sugu, and to a lesser extent Mbulo, are sites of
pre-colonial Chamba chiefdoms. Nnakɛnnyare-speaking Chamba, whose
dialect is expanding as a Chamba lingua franca of the administrative centres,
are predominantly Muslim or Christian; in their accounts of the contemporary
scene, Chamba religion is associated with sub-tribal groupings of Chamba
Daka speakers, with geographical remoteness or with old age. Since they
assume an ongoing homogenisation of Chamba language, a gradual improve-
ment in communications aided by road building and descent of the last
Chamba hill communities, and that the old will die, Nnakɛnnyare Chamba
foresee Chamba religion dying also. In the meantime, their attitude is ambiguous. Islam and Christianity are political constituencies; Chamba traditional
religion is not, although Chamba ethnicity is a political consideration. The
present chief of Ganye (first occupant of a position created in 1971), as well as
his four senior 'traditional' councillors, are Muslims. However, the full
traditional council has a statutory Christian representative. Moreover, this
'traditional' council has gradually lost its powers to the (frequently reshuffled)
local government organisation staffed by functionaries responsible for specific
duties: education, health, forestry, works, agricultural development and so
forth.

In the civilian elections of the Second Republic (1979 and 1983), Chamba
predominantly voted for parties that were not identified, as was the National
Party of Nigeria, with northern, Fulani, and Muslim interests—such as the
Great Nigerian People's Party (led by the Kanuri Alhaji Waziri Ibrahim, a
minister in the first civilian government), and the Unity Party of Nigeria (led
by the veteran Yoruba politician Chief Awolowo). In both elections, Chamba
returned predominantly Christian representatives, repeating the outcomes of
local governmental elections since the resumption of civilian rule. The return
of the military, and the allocation of administrative offices has likewise produced a predominantly Christian personnel.

The present situation is delicately poised. In the forty years since the
beginning of British Trusteeship after World War II, the organisation of local
and national politics has changed with bewildering frequency. In the face
of this uncertainty, Chamba response has usually been compromising and

The chief of Ganye's musicians.

cautious. The reaction to overt confrontation in 1971 was a salutory reminder of the penalties at the disposition of the state. Local struggle over control of administration, as well as access to the Nigerian economy and state, has been embedded in a matrix of Muslim/Christian relations. Chamba religion has become stigmatised as an impediment to, often competing, Chamba efforts to claim national resources.

In part, I have emphasised the political and economic concomitants of conversion because states of conviction are difficult to demonstrate, but political factors also weigh large in the accounts of most of those to whom I have talked. Chamba incorporation into the nations of Cameroon and Nigeria was on unpromising terms: domination by the Fulani was initially abetted by colonial adminstration; a late onset to colonisation—followed by statuses in mandated and trust territories—retarded the pace of change; Fulfulde, German, English, French and Hausa have been the languages of the state and, rare interludes apart, of religious instruction also. By the time an emergent Chamba elite agitated for self-definition and separatism a new dialectic of claims to power and knowledge had begun to eclipse older conceptions grounded in the differences between clans, political communities, and ethnic and religious categories of the nineteenth century. It remains to be seen whether members of another generation—in their turn—will feel any compulsion to relearn conceptions on which their grandfathers felt compelled to turn their backs.

Postscript 1990. Controversy continues to surround appointments to the Ganye traditional council. The new Waziri has been dismissed and two Fulani appointed to titles. One of these is the son of the last Wakilin Chamba and he has revived his father's title. The issue is highly emotive: some Chamba suspect a new Fulani or Muslim intrigue, others (including the chief) argue that the development of Ganye has been retarded by failure to enlist Fulani money, expertise and influence.

In Mapeo, a Muslim Chamba successfully brought a court action against fellow villagers for playing *jup* by his compound. They have been heavily fined and complain the Fulani judge failed to understand that as part of *jup kupsa* the performance was harmless.

10

GOD AND THE DEAD: LOCATING THE UNKNOWN

A POLITICS OF KNOWLEDGE

Anthropologists' theories of local knowledge, so I argued in the first chapter, come prepackaged with recipes for the kind of order they are designed to detect. Each recipe requires instructions for what to do with informants' accounts that either do not fit, or appear insufficiently incisive. These are dealt with in ways that can be ranged between the argument that certain features are simply too obvious for informants to find them worth saying—at one extreme—to various reasons why certain things are unsayable in principle—at the other. Accounts of knowledge and their shadow accounts of ignorance are mutually defining.

If organised accounts of knowledge demand that ignorance be systematic, then analysis cannot fail to be a political act. The coherently ignorant must be excluded from some specific knowledge, or systematically not paying attention to something germane to the knowledgeable; in either case, the why and how of the relation deserves explanation. True of the relation between ethnographers' versions and those of their informants, the proposition that claims to knowledge entail judgements about ignorance also holds of the accounts of different informants.

The general problem has taken particular shape in this volume because in two Chamba communities, only a few miles apart, practices that appeared similar to the outsider were interpreted differently by those who carried them out. At least some informants' views could not be transposed from one place to the other. Moreover the relation was asymmetric rather than incommensurate: Yeli accounts of ritual intellectually encompassed Mapeo versions—they said all the Mapeo version said and more. Only under special circumstances might we anticipate that Mapeo doubts about significance would displace the greater certainties of Yeli. Since local judgements made Yeli the fount of authentic Chamba-ness and the ancient ritual hegemonist of the region, both Mapeo and Yeli men were more likely to persuade themselves of the correctness of the Yeli account. A close fit obtained between what was taken to count as knowledge and what was taken to count as power.

Despite differences of language and political organisation, in many other respects Mapeo and Yeli versions were virtually identical. Is what they share Chamba culture? Contemporary Chamba see themselves as a people, tribe, or ethnicity, but the self-definition emerged over a long period in the face of extensive differences of language, political and social organisation (Fardon, 1988).

CULTURAL PLURALISM AND CULTURAL EMPIRICISM

Rather than setting myself the necessity to discover some essence in Chamba culture, I have preferred to present ritual through the interpretive practices of its practitioners. Another approach would *define* at the outset the entity I wanted to be able to *recognise* in local terms. Moreover, it would do so by rendering marginal the most important commentators—the performers themselves. However, I have claimed only that I ought to start here; questions of informants' disagreement and silences, not to mention their capacity to produce versions that help the ethnographer recognise his subject, all beg explanation.

I do not know what culture 'is'. Methodologically, I treat it as the capacity to do and say particular things. Chamba doubtless do and say some things in the same way as their neighbours, or maybe the majority of West Africans; other tasks of saying and doing are quite differently accomplished in different parts of Chambaland, or by the same people in different contexts. The more a capacity is shared the more we are likely to apply a metaphor of depth to it—on the argument that its very shared quality makes it difficult to frame or reflect upon it. As a general rule, when Yeli and Mapeo Chamba share the capability to handle tasks of ritual in a particular way, such capacity can be related to ideas about sociality that they also share.

PEOPLE, MASKS AND CULTS

The most important Chamba discriminations, given my interests here, are those between three types of agency: God, the dead, and the wild ('things of the bush'). Reasoning things out, local exegesists usually arrive at one of these terms and stop: the attempt at explanation has gone about as far as it can. People, masks and cults, however, are more complex agents; potentially each is composite.

People are composites of maternal substance, paternal spirit and identity, and God-given breath. Age and gender affect the balance of these qualities and determine appropriate ways of acting upon people: to modify their normal state or redress an abnormal condition through performance. The matrix—substance, identity, breath—can also be imagined through qualities of the wild, the dead and the human. This composition is most visible in the Chamba mask: a skull to which animal attributes are added that completes a costume worn by a person. Similar qualities are attributed to Chamba cults in which human agents harness the powers of the dead and the wild. Much of the book has concerned the multi-layered and complex ways in which these resemblances (summarised here far too neatly) are realised as Chamba go about their tasks. If, by and large, Mapeo and Yeli Chamba discover the same images and associations, it is because they share common institutions and vehicles as the contexts and cues for imagination: double clanship, friendship, cult organisation, masking and so forth. Neither is the cause of the other; rather the institutional contexts and people's understandings of them are aspects of a single phenomenon. If we wish to call this Chamba culture, it has to be with recognition that not all Chamba share it, and that it probably applies also to many non-Chamba. In short, it is not an ethnic attribute. Furthermore, because understandings are elicited by cues and contexts, they have a degree of autonomy from one another. In comparative Chamba terms (see Fardon, 1988), it is quite possible for attributes associated with the context of patriclanship to wax in significance while those associated with matriclanship wane.

DIFFERENT INTERPRETATIONS

Most of the major differences in exegesis between Mapeo and Yeli concern the range of events that can be submitted to a consistent scheme of explanation. I have sought to explain the differences by reference to history and organisation, and to language.

For contemporary informants, the present organisation of Yeli has to be understood in terms of a historical scenario involving indigenous patriclans, who had always lived there regulating the land with their cults, and an immigrant royal matriclan, accepted by these people because of the control it was able to exercise over rain, epidemic disease and locust infestation. On the basis of this understanding of the past, distinctions can be drawn between: indigenous, land-owning, patriclan cult masters, and the immigrant, royal matriclan with its *lera* flutes and capacity for ritual regulation of the environment. In terms of the east/west axis, the priestly peoples may be envisaged as eastern Chamba Leko speakers, while the chiefly clan is contrasted in terms of a western origin from areas where Chamba Daka was spoken. Differences between elements, selectively preserved and put to the service of a communal regulation, allow the constituents of the chiefdom to make contributions to the whole in terms of their special aptitudes.

A sociological understanding of public performance (who has the right to do what) in Yeli is at the same time a symbolic coding, because of the way in which social agents are conceived. The chief and his assistants are encharged with cooling crops, animals or women; they confer qualities that are also qualities of matriclanship. Treatment of royal bodies in Yeli is an exemplar case of the retentiveness of matriclan interest in substance. The priests' cults heat the land in order to ripen crops; their power derives from the shedding of blood in sacrifice and the partibility of their bodies. The qualities of priestly potency are shared with patriclanship. Through a play of contrast, and analogy between contrast, Yeli exegesists are able to encompass the different roles of chief, priest and smith as hierarchical expressions of coherent and pervasive distinctions that also invest clanship, gender, space and so forth.

Mapeo informants' versions of settlement history are more contentious. Their refugee community was swelled by immigrants who arrived from different places. In detail, the order of arrival is contested, as is the political organisation which existed at different periods. Attempts by elements of various clans to install notional hierarchy, on one or other of the available Chamba models for doing so, failed. There are no counterparts to the rituals of communal welfare performed in Yeli. Yeli itself was feared as the source of misfortunes, and its intercession was required to avert misfortunes over which Mapeo Chamba could not themselves exercise control. In this social and historical context, and on this understanding of what the social and historical context was, ritual actions are still interpreted by reference to those who carry them out, but these agents are envisaged, especially in the context of patriclan rituals, to be discharging discrete patrimonies. Ritual practices are motivated by the idea of difference alone; the differences are not envisaged to be part of an encompassing order in which each aptitude finds its place. By performing in its own way, each clan reproduces the fact of its difference.

Such tendencies in Mapeo Chamba religion are reinforced by the predominance of the cult over all other forms of religious activity. Secretive by definition, and open to initiates only on the basis of one of the links of extended clanship, the dominance of the cult system accentuates the tendency for knowledge to become particular and fragmented. The ethnographer's situation of partial knowledge is shared by his informants. In Mapeo, even the greatest cult masters have not 'seen all' and do not 'know all' that happens in the *jup*. Mapeo Chamba read the diversity of patriclans in their community as akin to a diversity of ethnic cultures.

Incomparability is not claimed of affairs that concern different matriclans. Unlike patriclans, matriclans are not considered culturally, even ethnically, distinct; on the contrary, their cultures are thought fully commensurable. As a correlate of this, in Chamba experience motivation of ritual practice is more consistent within matriclan, than patriclan, cults. Moreover, hierarchical relations obtain in Mapeo neither between matriclans nor between matriclans and patriclans. There is no counterpart to the position and distinction of the royal matriclan in Yeli.

In Mapeo, ritual practices are most readily comprehended in terms of their immediate sociological circumstances. Performance of rituals in general, or particular people's participation in them on specific occasions, are readily explained as rights and prerogatives, as markers of engagement or simple presence, or as indices of individual or collective prestige. I have demonstrated this for routine cult meetings, for the attendance of cults at funerals and for the cycle of harvest festivals. For Mapeo informants, the sense of a performance is often equivalent to its perceived effect in sociological terms. Unlike its Yeli counterpart, the sociological account in Mapeo does not connote a complex articulation of properties and qualities of the world that are indexed to the human agents (such as priests, chiefs and smiths) of the rituals. Difference in Mapeo more often denotes competition.

Situating the Mapeo and Yeli exegesists in this fashion, remains close to their own sense of the contexts from which they explain things. Differences between these contexts explain why understandings in one place cannot be translated wholesale to the other, albeit parts of them might apply to both.

Performance on the basis of these diverse understandings tends to reinforce already distinct images of place and history. Imagining themselves to be repeating a script handed down from an earlier, more illustrious period, Yeli Chamba describe their present efforts as an attempt to sustain the old centre against the encroachments of diminishing size and prestige as well as inducements to younger men to abandon traditional practices. Circumstances in Mapeo are both similar and different. The sheer number, particularity and cost of cults reflects competition between clans in terms of cult ownership that is said to have occurred in the past. On a reduced scale, elders can still keep most, but not all, of these cults supplied with sacrifices and the requisite round of convivial beer-drinking events. But Mapeo elders' sense—that the relative prestige of clans depends closely upon such observances—is shared by a diminishing proportion of the village population. The resistance of older traditionalists to attitudes towards their religion that range from disinterest (on the part of most younger villagers) to stigmatisation (by some adherents of world religions) has a number of sources: belief in the efficacy of *jup* performances and the prestige that accrues within the circle of adherents are important considerations. But the simpler fact is that they see no alternative: Islam is closed to them by antipathy to the Fulani and by their reluctance to abandon beer drinking, as their rather orthodox Mapeo co-religionists would expect; Christianity seems the religion of young and literate people unlike themselves. Either conversion would trade their seniority for the position of neophytes.

Differences of history and organisation—and the local appreciation of both of these—pervasively affect the explanation of ritual in Mapeo and Yeli, but I have argued that differences of language are only occasionally important and then in specific ways. The Chamba Daka dialect spoken in Mapeo and the Yeli dialect of Chamba Leko are entirely mutually unintelligible. However, the two places are historically related by a skein of movements of people, ideas, institutions, goods and so forth. Various degrees of bilingualism have existed in the past, particularly after the immigration of Leko-speaking clans to Mapeo. Presently, several Yeli men get by in Chamba Daka because they have lived in Nigeria, or worked there, or married Chamba Daka-speaking women. There is evidence of a prolonged exchange of concepts and words between the Chamba languages. These are not the kinds of words that appear in linguists' questionnaires of basic vocabulary; shared vocabulary here is virtually nil. But I have noted throughout the book how similar are terms and idioms used in Chamba Daka and Leko to describe features of rituals, or some key kinship statuses, or many specialised features of the natural world. Moreover, these shared terms are often the most difficult to gloss other than in a Chamba language. For instance, Chamba share a linkage between terms that relate spider, skull, death, corpse, and the dead, albeit the roots differ in the two languages. Such mutual connotation is impossible to retain in English (or indeed Fulfulde) translation.

Some differences of language are significant; colour is my best example. Mapeo and Yeli Chamba use the same triad of coloured substances in rituals. However, Chamba Daka has four basic colour terms and Chamba Leko only three. In the three-term system direct analogies can be drawn between states of vegetable matter (either red, black or white) and human states: involving moisture and dessication, colour coding of gender, or colour as a marker of stages in human development. Thus, Yeli Chamba can draw an extended analogy between changes in colour both during the growth and ripening of the staple guinea corn crop and during processes of human reproduction, maturation and death. In Mapeo, the same parallels cannot hold because a second term for hue (approximately light 'green/yellow'), with a traditional sense restricted to the state of vegetable matter, vitiates associations between animal and vegetable living things made via the colour triad in Chamba Leko.

As important as demonstrable language difference is the supposition that terms without known etymology in Mapeo dialect will transpire to be of Leko origin. This assumption has as much to do with perceptions of history and relations of power as with linguistic evidence. Terms that Mapeo Chamba assumed would be known to Yeli Chamba (for instance several cult names) were frequently unknown to them. Moreover there had been traffic in the other direction that went unstressed: demonstrable Chamba Daka loans in Chamba Leko, including the names of at least two adopted cults, were recognised by Yeli informants and correctly glossed, but not taken as evidence of pervasive influence, as Leko loans in Mapeo would be. This was despite the dogma that the Yeli chiefly family was of Daka origin—that the chief was properly known by a Daka title, and that his oldest *lera* songs were in Chamba Daka language. Daka loans in Leko were interpreted as evidence of occurrences in the past that had no bearing on the current state of relations between the two languages and the people who spoke them. Leko loans in Daka, however, were interpreted as evidence for presently pertinent cultural influence. Although an outsider might judge the linguistic traffic between Leko and

Daka relatively balanced, for the anthropologist it is significant that Chamba do not construe it thus.

Language accentuates differences between the interpretative styles typical of Mapeo and Yeli by encouraging different ranges of motivation (as in the case of colour) or by itself becoming an element of the recognised historical and political disparities which encourage people to seek different exegeses. What other factors might account for the variations in interpretative conventions that I have discerned? Time and scale seem two likely factors. To take time first: if different rates of change had occurred in Yeli and Mapeo, it might be argued that a tradition of exegesis disrupted in Mapeo had persisted in the less 'open' setting.

On the face of it, there is evidence to support such a view. Although both places are somewhat remote from major urban centres and poorly connected to them by road, Yeli is worse placed than Mapeo. At least, that is the case if we look at Yeli and Mapeo in their own national contexts. However, many individuals from Yeli, and from other Cameroonian Chamba communities, have moved over the border either permanently or temporarily: for education, employment, to evade Fulani dominance, to marry, to find fertile land, or for any one, or combination, of these and various other reasons.

The dates of establishment of missions on the two sides of the international border would also suggest that the pace of change has been quicker in Mapeo than in Yeli. Mapeo is a mission centre, Yeli only has a chapel attached to a mission in Balkossa. Mapeo has schools, Yeli has not. Educated Catholics from Mapeo have made an impact within contemporary politics, education, business and the church that is far more substantial than anything achieved by their Protestant counterparts in Yeli.

However, the average ages of active adherents of the traditional religions in the two places are very similar. Moreover, thanks to its larger scale, the sheer number and frequency of traditional rituals in Mapeo far exceeds that in Yeli. The proposition that different exegeses are to be explained by an erosion of understanding in Mapeo that did not occur in Yeli misses a critical feature of the difference. Given that Mapeo did not evolve a hierarchy of offices considered to possess distinct prerogatives and aptitudes, the Yeli account can never have been applicable to Mapeo circumstances. Finally, it seems as likely that competition from world religions with developed theologies would enhance, as erode, self-conscious attention by Mapeo exegesists to the justification of their rituals.

An appeal to scale is equally difficult to sustain. Although Mapeo is a far larger community than Yeli, an argument from scale must take account of the quality of relations between the components of the local population. For instance, antagonistic relations between its component patriclans, rather than simple scale, explain the truncated symbolic motivation of rituals in Mapeo compared to their counterparts in Yeli.

Members of interpretative associations develop exegetical styles concurrently with an understanding of their history under the very circumstances that these understandings are designed to encompass. Despite formal similarities between rituals in Yeli and Mapeo, the sense made of them in one community cannot be transposed to the other. Meaning, in a sense that can be reattributed to agents who enact it, cannot be inferred from form alone (compare de Heusch, 1985 for the opposite approach). A random sample of the counters of Chamba explanation (covert knowledge, masquerades, marked attitudes towards breech births, stories of shape-changing bushcows, special aversion to leprosy or smallpox, etc.) can be identified over much of West Africa and beyond. But this distribution can be interpreted in different ways: either to suggest a timeless Africa-wide symbolic grammar or as the traces of the divergences and developments that such counters have undergone historically. The two projects have not always been separated. But if the latter guides our understanding, then the contrast between Yeli and Mapeo offers some indication of the many ways in which slippage of the sense of pervasive elements in African cosmologies has occurred historically.

The makers of meaning in Yeli and Mapeo continue to affect the internal consistency of their symbols by anticipations they entertain about design. The symbolically self-conscious produce symbolically motivated performance; reflecting upon their performances, they rediscover the motivations that went into them. All things being equal, symbolically self-conscious behaviour reproduces itself through the consciousness of social actors. The obverse obtains also (as in motivation of leaf uses in Yeli and Mapeo rituals). By reliance on formal similarity, to the neglect of local exegesis, analysis risks blindness to currents of historical change. Thus, revitalisation of the contrast between shea butter and ironwood leaves in Mapeo—to bring it into line with Yeli—would have to involve new conventions of exegesis or a revision of practices. But the assumption that Yeli motivations somehow applied in Mapeo (albeit they could not be stated there) would preclude noticing either possibility.

BEYOND CLOSURE

Since the publication of Evans-Pritchard's classic account of Zande thought, anthropologists have tended to describe African religions as logically closed sets of presuppositions, resistant to change because they encompass so much of social life and possess such a variety of irrefutable secondary elaborations. For Robin Horton, African religion was to be distinguished from western science by its relative closure (Horton, 1967). Evans-Pritchard had earlier argued in compatible terms that Zande try to explain more, not less, than westerners. The famous accidents—those falling granaries and unfortunate encounters with elephants—lose their accidental character seen through Zande eyes. African systems of thought digest events and produce conceptual order. But how warranted would be the assumption of such certainty in the Chamba case?

Chamba exegeses, I have argued, are relatively closed in terms of some fundamental presuppositions but open or indeterminate in others. Competing explanations for occurrences, like deaths in Mapeo, are rarely resolved but temporarily shelved or, as we are suppposed to believe of academic problems, superseded when people lose interest in them. Comparative evidence, moreover, suggests rapid and radical change in all facets of Chamba ritual and understanding during the last century. Strong hypotheses of either closure or stability seem to fly in the face of the evidence.

Rather than certainty, some Chamba presuppositions lead to the necessity of men's ignorance: in both senses I distinguished in introduction—not knowing (and being perfectly aware that they do not know), and not paying attention to. Mapeo elders do not, I argue, pay attention to systematic symbolic motivation; it does not seem important to them. Much of the time they do not know what many of their fellow villagers do in their rituals. Secrecy, payment for membership in cults, grades of revelation, and so forth all require others who do not know. Not knowing, or not paying attention to, are crucial to the concept of knowledge. When the covert has little content, 'not knowing' carries the burden of defining it.

That Mapeo elders ignore some types of symbolic motivation has been part of my argument contrasting Mapeo and Yeli variants of rituals. That they cannot know all the rituals of their community is a consequence of the way the cult system works. But beyond both these specific uncertainties, is another broader and shared area of doubt. For death, and to a lesser degree the bush, are crucial to Chamba notions of efficacy, and circumscribe the possibilities of knowledge in principle. Death is the area to which explanations tend, but having talked themselves there informants cannot say much specific on the subject, except that they cannot with certainty know. Something central and crucially important is yet elusive and unknowable. And this is part of the Chamba version of the human condition.

The intuited resemblances between death, skull, forebear, subterranean being, spider, corpse—things that are 'one thing'—are the reason for so many things being as they are: patrikin being reincarnated, cults working, people dying or becoming sick, Europeans possessing technical knowledge, seers suffering beatings and so on and on. But quite how these connections should be defined, and just what subterranean beings are like, are questions beyond human capacity. The dead remain a crucial, instigating unknown.

The principled limitations of knowledge are critical to the experience others have of the world that ethnographers attempt to describe. By writing away different levels of ignorance, ethnographers risk transforming a practical getting-on-with-life into a falsely coherent philosophy of life (Hountondji, 1977; Fernandez, 1965). The certainties that earlier anthropologists projected onto African systems of thought may have reflected their own certainties about the nature of the world in which they lived. The criteria of charitable

interpretation change (Gellner, 1970). In a different age, certainty and deter-
minacy may be less fashionable. They may come to smack of smug
knowingness.

I have argued that we can attempt to describe limitations our informants
sense in their own knowledge. These limitations are not everywhere the same,
and we can make plausible attempts to explain the variety, and self-conscious-
ness of understanding. This is to suggest, not that local exegesis is irreproach-
able, but that our statements about other peoples' knowledge should address
the circumstances under which an informant might proffer something similar
to our statement. If this is unlikely, the reader deserves more than the rather
unspecific gesture towards limited local self-understanding that often serves as
the anthropologist's interpretative carte blanche. We may inevitably invent
what we set out to describe; but we can try to invent collaboratively.

APPENDIX 1:

DO DIFFERENT EXEGESES REFLECT ONLY RESEARCH METHODOLOGY?

It may seem more appropriate to dismiss at the outset the likelihood that my results are determined only by the way research was conducted. It is unfair to pull out the rug under a reader who may have come this far in good faith. Unhappily, this likelihood can only be considered sensibly once the reader knows what results are being claimed and with reference to what kind of evidence. At the most obvious, short of having researched as I did, I would have no problem to address. In all probability, other researchers would have found their attention engaged by other problems. But how much more ought to be conceded to participant effect? Prolonged soul-searching is liable to become self-justification, so I shall append only a brief note to the references to fieldwork in the main text.

I arrived in Nigeria in 1976 as a postgraduate student. After living in Ganye for about six weeks, I moved to Mapeo and remained there for a year. The remainder of my twenty months research was spent living in, or visiting, other Chamba places, and included a further short stay in Mapeo as well as three visits to Yeli and three months in a western Chamba chiefdom called Gurum. My grasp of Chamba Daka improved during my residence in Mapeo and, by the end of my time there, I was researching in the vernacular. Once I left Ganye, I did not use (and could not have afforded) the services of a regular translator, but from time to time English-speaking friends kindly helped me clear up confusions and failures to comprehend what was said to me. Much of my time in Mapeo was spent with older men: attending cult meetings, funeral wakes and other celebrations. During the year, I devoted more time to this topic than any other. However, when I came to write my doctoral thesis, I had not formulated the problem posed in this book.

I did not return to West Africa for six years. My main fieldwork in Yeli occupied six months of a nine-month trip to Cameroon in 1984. The remainder of my time was spent in Bamenda, but I was able to make a couple of visits to Mapeo. My application for funds to carry out that research contained an early formulation of the subject of this book, which occurred to me while writing a book on Chamba history, reading in order to teach a course in the anthropology of religion, and listening to the reaction of anthropologists to the account I have proposed of Mapeo ritual. I never learned to conduct my own research in Chamba Leko. By the end of a six-month stay, I could manage some rudimentary conversations, could translate transcribed materials with assistance and had compiled a vocabulary for comparison with terms I knew in Chamba Daka. Problematic terms had been considered at length. I was far more observer of, than participant in, the Yeli scene. I attended rituals but had no role in them. I did not find myself swept up in a round of cult meetings and kinship obligations as I had in Mapeo. Without the daily help of the chief's son, my friend from 1977 Bouba Bernard, with whom I lived, I would have been unable to carry out the research at all.

Our private language for discussing the research became a compound of French, Chamba Daka and Chamba Leko. The three-cornered relation between the two Chamba languages and a European language necessary for translating the research experience became abundantly clear at this time. The advantages I did have in Yeli were that I was not a complete stranger, for I had known the chief and Dura since my earlier visits, and that a number of people, including Bouba, his father the chief, and Dura, were able to speak Chamba Daka, although probably less easily than I did.

Between 1976 and 1978, and again in 1984, I took every opportunity to visit Chamba places other than Mapeo or Yeli, usually with someone known to the community or on the basis of formal invitation or casual meeting, in order to conduct interviews. In 1986, I was able briefly to carry out exploratory work among the southern neighbours of the Chamba Leko, the Pere. This added to my sense of a skein of similarities that extended beyond Chambaland. A visit to Ganye and Mapeo during six weeks of 1987 was especially significant because I was accompanied by Raymond Boyd, an experienced descriptive linguist, and we were able to begin the work of compiling a lexicon of Chamba Daka.

These were the occasions on which I collected the materials that have gone into this book. The potential biases are several. Since I participated more fully in Mapeo ritual, both in the sense that I took more part and in the sense that I researched in Chamba Daka, it does seem predictable that I gathered more materials on practical organisation. However, the absence of some kinds of symbolic exegeses I was later to find in Yeli still seems anomalous. I did not overlook this aspect; early in my research, I anticipated finding materials that could be analysed on the lines of Victor Turner's Ndembu studies or Mary Douglas's work on classification, since these were the parallels in my reading before 1976 that seemed relevant once I understood the broad character of Mapeo cults. I have, moreover, had opportunities to check my findings on later visits. Some of my evidence (for instance of the diversity, numbers, expense, multiple ownership and so forth of the cults in Mapeo) is relatively easily verifiable and likely to be consistent for different observers.

The more arcane symbolic materials come from the community where I spent less time and was less well equipped linguistically. I did have the invaluable assistance of Bouba Bernard. But Bouba is a Christian who earlier had distanced himself from the traditional religion. When I knew him in 1977 he refused even to drink beer. In 1984 he still played little role in the traditional festivals but was responsible for preparing contributions, especially of beer, to be made by his father. The old chief, whose sight had become poor, knew he was not far from death. This, in part, accounted for Bouba's interest in understanding the elders' religion while the opportunity still existed. None the less, he was constantly surprised by replies received to our enquiries from his father, the chief, Dura the priest and other older members of the village which challenged the sense he had learned of the irrationality and superstitious nature of 'pagan' belief. His Christian faith was not challenged, but he became excited by the logic that informed the ideas of his elders. Without Bouba I could not have carried out the research, but with respect to traditional religion he was my interlocutor, discussant, co-worker but not my informant.

Had I known in 1976, when leaving for Nigeria, with little more than scant and frequently inaccurate notes from the colonial period to go by, the kind of book I would finish thirteen years later, I could have organised research differently with a view to documenting my points more fully, recording conversations and so forth. I have never used a tape recorder as a research tool—not by design but because my equipment broke early on during my two longer periods of fieldwork. Especially during research in Mapeo, I used virtually no interviews. Over a year's worth of discussions during rituals, beer drinks, rambling fireside discussions and so forth could not have been recorded. Most of my Mapeo material is not very appropriately attributed to a single source, since I heard similar opinions on many occasions. Attribution to a time, date and speaker would give a spurious formality to conversation. In the absence of recordings, I have refrained entirely from the attempt to reconstruct verbatim conversations.

The decade or more that goes into the making of most monographs—with accompanying biographical development, as well as theoretical and methodological change in the broader disciplinary context, to say nothing of the changes happening to those about whom one writes—produces the complex inner temporality of a monograph.

APPENDIX 2:

NOTES ON CHAMBA CULTS

These incomplete materials are included as an indication of the range of Chamba cults. Ownership of cults is frequently contentious. I include owner-ships that came to my attention; but there are surely versions of some cults of which I am unaware. I have not included a few cult names about which I otherwise know nothing.

bəntəng

Ownership and cost: patriclan *jup* predominantly owned by clans of northern origin—Lira, Lib, Jab (all presumptively Bata or Bachama), Siri (Yangur), Wɔsan (Leko), Bəng, Gang di nε (at Lengdo), Kɔ. Initiation costs two fowls. Additionally, a goat and a white cockerel have to be supplied when it performs at the wake of a clan member.

Symptoms and comments: causes difficulties in childbirth, deformity at birth and broken bones. The name of the cult is supposed to be an ideophone of the distinctive gong beat accompanying the dance. For the origins and perform-ance of the cult see main text.

Leaves and apparatus: guma or gima (*Ficus sp?*) and locust bean leaves. In performance the cult is led by *lera* flutes and a double hand-bell. A pestle, spear, shield and sickle are wielded by dancers. The mask appears in the Yangur version. The main cult object is made from a large calabash, filled with earth, containing a smith's hammer and relics of the dead. The package is sewn in local cloth. A female medicine is administered by massage to the belly of a woman undergoing difficult childbirth.

gina

Ownership and cost: ownership restricted to *dəng kun* and San. The entrance fee is two fowls.

Symptoms and comments: the cult is concerned with leprosy—from *kinan* leper (and collapsed rectum according to some). Black wax (*nibri*) is one of the symbols of the cult.

ja lɔk

Ownership: one version only in Mapeo.

Symptoms and comments: causes epilepsy, madness (and leprosy?)

Apparatus: ashes and black wax are used as symbols; cure is administered with female medicine.

ja rɔ

Ownership and cost: pre-eminently a patriclan cult owned by clans predominantly of western origin: Kpe, Tiran, Dəng, Daga. Also owned by *dəng kun*. Entrance fee is small (two chickens?).

Symptoms and comments: madness; the cult name may be an ideophone for the ranting of the insane. Claimed to be related to *ja lɔk* but tones of *ja* differ.

Leaves: shea butter and locust bean leaves.

je bɛl

Ownership and cost: Only Lam patriclan in Tisayeli.

Symptoms: enlarged testicles or collapsed rectum.

Leaves: shea butter and locust bean leaves; cure involves male medicine and incising testicles.

jɛm

Ownership and cost: most matriclans and patriclans own versions of the women's cults. The following have women priests (*jɛm gang bu*): *kɔngla kun*, *su kun*, *kɔm tur kun*, *dang kun*, and the patriclans of Lira and Gban. A single chicken is given for performance of curative rituals. Entrance payments are low except for women priests, who must donate goats.

Symptoms and comments: cessation of menstruation in young women, failure to conceive, blood in urine, failure of hunting, black smut on sorghum.

Apparatus: small hoes accompany women's songs at wakes (see main text); the hidden cult (*jɛm 'oran*) resembles a men's cult with small metal rattles and a sickle. The cult is especially associated with women's crops: bambara groundnuts, melon seeds (*jɛm sina*) and a small tuber (*jɛm sagum*)—see description of *jup kupsa* in main text.

jup bin bono

Comments: initiation is into the constituent cults which 'close the road' to drive out disease. Combines the apparatuses of: *sɛndu*, *kɔngla*, *langa*, *ngwan ji*, *yaguman*, *gina*.

jup dagan

Ownership and cost: Yam, Tiran, Dəng, Kpe, and Daga patriclans. When children fall sick, a goat must be given to this cult by any man who has committed adultery with their mother.

Symptoms and comments: especially causes pneumonia, belly ache, vomiting, but also other diseases, in children of adulterous women and stolen wives. May also cause these women difficulty in childbirth. Additionally used to purify compounds of breech birth. Derived from *dag*, to make light or clean.

Leaves and apparatus: *gɛsi* (savanna ebony?) and locust bean leaves. Instruments include gourd horns, iron rattles and statues. Performs at wakes and annual remembrances of clan dead.

jup Jang

Comment: generic term for the dancing cults with gourd horn that are supposed to be of Leko origin. Since these cults do not cause affliction, they have no initiation fees. (See *jup kupsa*, *jup nyɛm*.)

jup kupsa

Ownership and cost: in Mapeo belongs to Jang, Dəng, kɔm kun, kɔngla kun, dəng kun, Wɔsan, Lira, San as well as to many others outside Mapeo. No fee. Repeated as *jup kupsa gɔgan* (see main text).

jup lum

Ownership and cost: kɔngla kun, kɔm kun, ngwana kun, yɛt kun. Solely matriclan cult. Entrance fee of two goats, four chickens, but no beer.

Symptoms and comments: causes snake bite. Derived from *lum*, male suffix.

Leaves and apparatus: shea butter, locust bean and *kan* (?) leaves. Apparatus includes large iron rattles, a gourd horn, small male stick figure, stones, skull of water monitor, stones, palm fruit husks. Female medicine is applied.

jup nyɛm

Ownership and comments: in Mapeo belongs to Dɛng, Gban, Jang, San, Yanguru, Wɔng. But ownership is disputed; a number of recalled matriclan owners no longer perform. Begins the harvest (see main text). Repeated at *jup nyɛm gɔgan*.

jup nu

Ownership and cost: belongs to dəng kun, kɔm kun, yɛt kun, San, Dəng. Entrance fee of four chickens, worn-out hoe, new calabash.

Symptoms and comments: impotence in men. Public symbol is phallic pole. Derived from *nu*, female suffix. (See main text for ritual.)

Leaves and apparatus: ironwood leaves. Medicine calabash, phallic poles. Medicine made from various 'roots'.

jup ya

Ownership and cost: *dəng kun*, *jam kun*, *kɔm kun*, *yɛt kun*, Dəng, San, Yangur, Lira, Jang. Entrance fee of a goat and five pots of beer, then a goat and six pots of beer, plus two chickens.

Symptoms and comments: causes sickness in either or both partners to a sexual relationship involving a married or widowed woman. Derived from *ya*, leaf. Especially associated with wakes and *jup kupsa* (see text).

Leaves and apparatus: shea butter leaves and *jup ya 'isi* (type of flowering grass). Red, white and black stones, two staves (one coloured red and one black), large iron rattles, 'five pot' during performance at wakes.

jup ka

Comments: belongs to the priests, *ngwan*, of Jang patriclans. Claimed to be represented by the smallest horn in the priest's *jup dagan* horn band. Cleanses breech births and assists difficult births. Prerogative of priestship. Some derive it from *ka*, grandmother.

kamsa

Ownership and cost: Yam, Lam, Gban, Wɔng patriclans. Entered for one chicken and one pot of beer.

Leaves and apparatus: large and small rattle sacks accompany songs during the night of wakes of members of owning clans; also large and small horns and drums and iron rattles. Pointed leaf (*kuba*) also used in *yaguman*.

Comments: madness, a condition which is dramatised in daytime performance at wakes.

kang yili

Comments: belongs only to *kɔm kun*; its public symbol is a stick with feathers in the top; causes sore throat and/or headache.

karbang

Ownership and cost: matriclan cult of *dəng kun*, *jam kun*, *kɔngla kun*, *kɔm kun*, *su kun*, *ngwana kun*. The most expensive of cults: three sheep, two goats, twelve chicken, twelve pots of beer.

Symptoms and comments: snake bite accompanied by head or back ache. *Karbang* is supposed to combine the medicines and apparatuses of twelve cults (see main text for rituals).

Leaves and apparatus: shea butter leaves (from the snake bite cults), *jup ya 'isi* (from *jup ya*), *buri* (?), fruit of *kɛm sim* ('monkey beer', *Ximenia americana*). Gourd horn, bullroarer (from *langa*), arm bones lashed in rope and dyed red, 'female back' of dead cult masters also dyed red, small brass statue of aged woman, mouth pieces of gourd horns (from *ngwan ji*). Medicine from the constituent cults is mixed with chicken blood and the scent gland of the civet cat (*mɔt*).

kɔngla

Ownership: *yɛt kun, su kun, kɔm kun, kpe kun*

Symptoms and comments: causes leprosy and epilepsy. Name derives from 'elephant'.

Leaves: ironwood leaves; both male and female medicines.

la gənsɛn

Ownership and cost: *yɛt kun* in Mapeo and other matriclans elsewhere. Entrance fee of three sheep, two goats, four chickens, no beer.

Symptoms and comments: causes leprosy and epilepsy. *La* might derive from the verb to sleep and *gənsi* from to circle. Some informants relate this etymology to sleepwalking and falling into the fire. Others argue a Leko origin.

Leaves: shea butter leaves and black wax (*nibri*).

langa

Ownership and cost: matriclan cult of *dəng kun, kɔm kun, nɛ kusum bɛ kun*. Entrance fee of one goat and two chicken.

Symptoms and comments: causes problems with sight, including eye casts. *Langa* is also the name of the iron bullroarer; some claim it to be an ideophone of whirring.

Leaves and apparatus: specially associated with the pod of the silk cotton tree (*kpi kimli*), which is the public symbol of the cult. Also shea butter and locust bean leaves. Thorn in pod represents aggravation of eye; only other apparatus is a bullroarer. Male medicine is administered as an eye wash.

luri

Comments: women's cult concerned with failure to conceive.

nɔga

Ownership and cost: *nɔga disa* belongs to *dəng kun, jam kun, gang van ji kun, kɔngla kun, ngwana kun*, and *yɛt kun*. It costs four chickens. *Nɔga burgi* belongs to *dəng kun, ngwana kun*, and *yɛt kun*. It costs a goat and four chickens.

Symptoms and comments: stomach distension and cramps (see main text for discussion).

Leaves and apparatus: ironwood and locust bean leaves. Apparatus consists of single or paired statues coloured red, iron rattles, quill-pierced gourd, stones, terracotta turtles and horns, three gourd horns (with a small fourth for 'owl' *nɔga*). Curative ritual involves removal of pot from between legs and application of male medicine.

ngwan ji

Ownership and cost: matriclan cult of *dəng kun, jam kun, kɔngla kun, kɔm kun*, and *su kun*. Entrance fee of three sheep, two goats, four chickens.

Symptoms and comments: snake bite accompanied by red blotches on the skin. Some informants gloss the name as 'bears redness'.

Leaves and apparatus: shea butter leaves; apparatus includes the mouthpieces of gourd horns (included in *karbang*); female medicine is applied.

ngwan kɔblin

Comments: apparently a version of *ngwan ji* owned only by *dəng kun*. Same fee as *ngwan ji*.

ngwɔm

Ownership and cost: matriclan cult of *dəng kun, su kun, kpe kun*. Initiation fee includes a goat and chicken.

Symptoms and comments: causes snake bite and nose bleeds. Local etymology derives name from *wɔ mi*, old woman child. A brass statuette of an old woman occurs in the cult apparatus.

Leaves: shea butter leaves and female medicine as for other snake bite cults.

puga

Comments: causes intolerable itching of the skin. Made on ironwood leaf.

sɛndu

Comments: cult that leads *jup bin bono* with its gourd horn.

sunsun

Ownership: belongs to *jam kun*; entrance fee is two goats and four chickens.

Symptoms: snake bite.

Leaves and apparatus: shea butter and ironwood leaves; performed with small rattle sacks. Supposed by some to be of Verre origin.

təmsi gam

Comment: a cult belonging to the Wɔng patriclan which is now defunct in Mapeo. Caused bow legs. Name derives from sheep's horn, and the apparatus contained terracotta sheep.

tɔlɔng

Comment: cult belonging to *yɛt kun* that causes epilepsy and leprosy. Named after a large straight-horned antelope or unicorn.

Leaves and apparatus: ironwood leaves. Apparatus includes double and single statues.

vara

Comment: cult causing back pain.

wa jab

Comment: cult belonging to *yɛt kun*.

vo

Comment: cult belonging to *kɔm kun* that causes lightning strikes. The name derives from the term for thunder. Apparatus includes undulating iron rod representing lightning.

ya guman

Ownership and cost: the patriclan *jup* of Yam clansmen throughout Chambaland. Joining fee of two chickens, but entrance is highly restricted.

Symptoms and comments: causes bodily swellings filled with pus that must be lanced for an application of male medicine to be made. *Ya* is generally accepted to mean leaf; *guman* is said to be from *gum* meaning potash. Mapeo informants claim that this is a description of a soup, meant only as a nonsense name to reveal nothing about the cult. Nnakɛnnyare-speaking Chamba derive their *ya bumɛn* from leaf and calabash.

Leaves and apparatus: pointed leaves such as palm fronds (*dəsi*) and *kuba* (?). Apparatus includes stones, iron point, gourd horn (rituals described in text).

yagra

Comments: cult belonging to *kɔngla kun*, *kɔm kun*, and Gban said to cause emaciation.

YELI *VƆMA*

My Yeli notes are even less exhaustive than their Mapeo counterparts and yet more subject to strictures about possible error.

dɔna

The name means elephant. The cult is equivalent to *kɔngla* in Mapeo and is responsible for leprosy. The associated leaves of ironwood and *nyɛdna* (probably *Haemastaphis barteri hook*) are both red coloured and evoke the colour of leprous skin. Ironwood leaves are burned at a crossroads and the patient is covered with the ashes. Payment is in chickens only, since the grease in goat's flesh connotes the excessive grease in the body of the leper.

go bɛl

'Pulls rectum'; possibly eqivalent to *je bɛl* in Mapeo.

kamsa

Equivalent to the identically named cult in Mapeo.

kɔm vɔm yɛla

'Red cult of the Koma'; responsible for diarrhoea with blood. Associated with leaves of *nyɛdna* (red fruit and leaf; see *dɔna*), and *bɛgum bɛgum* (?). Uses male medicine.

la gbira

La is fire, but I could not discover an etymology for *gbira*. Like the Mapeo *jup* of *la gənsɛn*, the cult is concerned with epilepsy. The part etymology is again explained by the propensity of epileptics to fall into fires.

langa

Identical to *langa* in Mapeo and also concerned with disturbances to sight. Associated with the pod of the cotton tree *ngwubma*. Main apparatus is an iron bullroarer.

nɔga

Identical to cult of this name in Mapeo; causes swollen stomach and cramps. In Yeli, the onset of symptoms is said to be slow and typically accompanied by yellowing of the eyes (probably hepatitis symptoms). In Yeli, *nɔga* is a euphemism for menstruation. As in Mapeo the cult has two forms: *nɔga kena*, female *nɔga*, and, *nɔga disa*, owl *nɔga*. Unlike Mapeo, associated leaves are of *gban tudna*, a bush with sticky pod. Brewed leaves are said capable of inducing symptoms of *nɔga*. Apparatus includes the pierced calabash representing stomach pains also found in Mapeo.

ngwan ji

Snake bite cult that is presumed to be of Chamba Daka origin and to have a Chamba Daka etymology. Equivalent to *ngwan ji* in Mapeo. As in Mapeo made on shea butter leaves.

səra

The term, which is without known etymology, is accepted to be the Leko language equivalent of the cult that Mapeo Chamba call *yaguman*. Like the Daka cult it causes swellings with pus which have to be lanced. One version of the cult belongs to the Jɛng patriclan, considered the Leko equivalent of the Yam patriclan among Chamba Daka speakers. Two other versions of the cult are said to be owned by the Chief of Yeli (called *səd Yɛla*) and by various matriclans. Its leaves are probably identical to those in Mapeo: *gbunga*, the roneo palm, and *kan*, another pointed leaf presumably equivalent to *kuba* in Mapeo. Maize cobs are also used as public protective symbols to represent the point of the iron lance head used to pierce swellings. The apparatus includes the iron lancing tool. This is said to be placed secretly inside a pot which covers the head of the corpse of an initiate. The tool is removed before the corpse is buried and secreted in the clothes of one of the cult practitioners. A similar practice in Mapeo was supposed to involve a gourd horn mouthpiece.

te dinga

'Black tree or wood'; the hunter cannot find game, or if he shoots animals they do not die. Returning home he cannot find the path. All is blackness. The cult leaves are of *te bira*, white tree (probably a *Combretum* species). The whiteness counteracts the problem of darkness.

val kena

'Death wife'; the corpse is laid on a pole and wrapped with 'soft' then 'hard' mats. The bundle is lashed and the free end of the rope measured around the waist of a woman sat by the corpse. This portion is cut off and retained for burial at *val batna*. Anyone who sees the rope and has not lost a spouse will die. Associated leaves are of *kə'əna* (probably *Anogeissus schimperi*) which used to be worn as a sign of menstruation before women wore wrappers. Members of this cult remove the three hearth stones of a dead woman.

vara

No etymology; the affected person does not eat and his face darkens. Associated leaves are of *gama*, a large and spreading tree from which water is said to run if the bark is pierced. Symbolises plenitude.

varaa

No etymology; responsible for cramps in the feet or legs which prevent the afflicted person from walking. Associated leaves are from locust bean (*ləm*), and *kan dəng dəng* (?). Male medicine is administered.

vɔm ba'a

Not now present in Yeli, but said to cause the birth of deformed children.

vɔm dagan

Daka origin and etymology: equivalent to *jup dagan* in Mapeo. Catches the children of adulterous women (as Mapeo). Typically, the child's stomach swells rapidly. The mother's lover is obliged to make a full reparation to the husband. Its leaves are of *kina* (West African ebony). The apparatus includes a small, spherical clay pot with a hole. Water from this pot is put onto the afflicted person with an iron tool. The cult is also associated with the gourd horn bands of the harvest ritual, especially the largest of the horns. The small clay pot may also be used as a musical instrument by blowing across its hole.

vɔm dinga

'Black vɔma'; associated with snake bites and nose bleeds. Uses male medicine.

vɔm kila

'Turtle *vɔma*'; causes hard lumps on the body. Its apparatus includes small terracotta turtles, turtle skeletons and shells.

vɔm ninga

Ninga is said to derive from a verb to drive out. This is a rite of the harvest time, also associated with *vɔm dagana*. It is apparently equivalent to *jup bin bono*, the cult closes the road, in Mapeo.

vɔm nyia

'Tree trunk *vɔma*' is equivalent to *jup nu* in Mapeo. Like that cult it is concerned with male impotence. Rites and apparatus, of which I know, are identical to the Mapeo version.

vɔm van

'Male *vɔma*' is the literal equivalent of *jup lum* in Mapeo and like that cult is concerned with snake bite. The cult is made on leaves of the shea butter tree. The male medicine is of a large type.

vɔm za'an

A harvest ritual held before the new guinea corn is eaten. Similar to *jup kupsa* in Mapeo.

yɛb sa

'Lightning', equivalent to *vo* in Mapeo. Apparatus and symbols include red flowers, twisted roots, and undulating iron rod.

yagət wa

'Dog child'; pains in a woman's lower stomach prevent childbirth. The apparatus includes small terracotta models of dogs.

REFERENCES

Published works

Barley, Nigel (1983) *Symbolic Structures. An Exploration of the Culture of the Dowayos*. Cambridge: Cambridge University Press.

Bennett, Patrick (1983) Adamawa—Eastern: problems and prospects. In I. R. Dihoff (ed.) *Current Approaches to African Linguistics 1*. Dordrecht: Foris Publications.

Bernard, Bouba (1982) Is God *veneb* or Yaama?, in Philip A. Noss (ed.) *Grafting Old Rootstock. Studies in the Culture and Religion of the Chamba, Duru, Fula, and Gbaya of Cameroon*. Dallas: International Museum of Cultures.

Bourdieu, Pierre (1977, originally 1972) *Outline of a Theory of Practice*. Translated by Richard Nice. Cambridge: Cambridge University Press.

Boyd, Raymond (1989) Adamawa-Ubangi. In J. Bendor-Samuel (ed.) *Current Trends in Linguistics: State of the Art Reports: the Niger–Kordofanian Congo Language Family*. The Hague: Mouton.

Chilver, E. M. (1967) Paramountcy and protection in the Cameroons: the Bali and the Germans, 1889–1913. In Prosser Gifford and Wm. Roger Louis (eds.) *Britain and Germany in Africa*. New Haven and London: Yale University Press.

Colonial Office (1947–59) *Cameroons under U.K. Administration: Annual Reports*. London: HMSO.

Dalton, Rev. A. (1961) Historiola missionis nostrae in Nigeria, *Missionalia Augustinia* (Curia Generalizia, Roma), pp. 34–37.

de Heusch, Luc (1985) *Sacrifice in Africa. A Structuralist Approach*. Translated by Linda O'Brien and Alice Morton. Manchester: Manchester University Press.

Douglas, Mary (1975) *Implicit Meanings. Essays in Anthropology*. London, Boston and Henley: Routledge and Kegan Paul.

Engskov, Ernst (1983) *Adamawa Province. Reflections on Gongola State*. Translated by Ninna Engskow. London: Root Publishing.

Fardon, Richard (1985) Secrecy and sociability: two problems of Chamba knowledge. In Richard Fardon (ed.) *Power and Knowledge*. Edinburgh: Scottish Academic Press.

Fardon, Richard (1987) African ethnogenesis: limits to the comparability of ethnic phenomena. In Ladislav Holy (ed.), *Comparative Anthropology*. Oxford: Basil Blackwell.

Fardon, Richard (1988) *Raiders and Refugees. Trends in Chamba Political Development, 1750–1950*. Washington: Smithsonian Institution.

Fardon, Richard (forthcoming a) Alliance et ethnicité: aspects d'un système régional de l'Adamaoua. In Françoise Héritier-Augé (ed.), *Les complexités de l'alliance*. vol. 4 Paris: Editions Archives Contemporaines.

Fardon, Richard (forthcoming b) The Highlands. In Arnold Rubin and Marla Berns (eds.), *Arts of the Benue Valley*. Los Angeles: Museum of Cultural History.

Fernandez, James (1965) Symbolic consensus in a Fang reformative cult, *American Anthropologist* 67:902–27.

Fernandez, James (1986) *Persuasions and Performances. The Play of Tropes in Culture*. Bloomington: Indiana University Press.

Feyerabend, Paul (1975) *Against Method. Outline of an Anarchistic Theory of Knowledge*. London: Verso.

Fortes, Meyer (1987) *Religion, Morality and the Person. Essays on Tallensi Religion*. Cambridge: Cambridge University Press.

Frobenius, Leo (1913) *Und Afrika Sprach*. Volume 3. Berlin: Vita Deutsches Verlaghaus.

Frobenius, Leo (1925) *Dichten und Denken im Sudan*. Volume 5. Jena: Eugen Diedrichs.

Frobenius, Leo (1987) *Peuples et sociétés traditionelles du Nord-Cameroun*. (A translation, by Eldridge Mohammadou, of the chapters of Frobenius [1925] concerning Cameroon.) Stuttgart: Franz Steiner.

Gellner, Ernest (1970, originally 1962) Concepts and society. In Bryan Wilson (ed.), *Rationality*. Oxford: Basil Blackwell.

Gilsenan, Michael (1976) Lying, honor, and contradiction. In Bruce Kapferer (ed.), *Transaction and Meaning*. Philadelphia: Institute for the Study of Human Issues.

Hickey, Rev. Raymond (1984) *Christianity in Borno State and Northern Gongola*. Ibadan: Claverianum Press.

Horton, Robin (1967) African traditional thought and western science, *Africa* 37(1):50–71, 37(2):155–87.

Horton, Robin (1975) On the rationality of conversion, *Africa* 45(1):219–35, 45(2):373–399.

Hountondji, Paulin (1977) *Sur la 'philosophie africaine'. Critique de l'ethnophilosophie*. Paris: Maspero.

Kuhn, Thomas (1962) *The Structure of Scientific Revolutions*. Chicago: International Encyclopedia of Unified Science. 2nd edition, enlarged 1970.

Lewis, Gilbert (1980) *Day of Shining Red: an Essay on Understanding Ritual*. Cambridge: Cambridge University Press.

Meek, C. K. (1931) *Tribal Studies in Northern Nigeria*. Volume 1. London: Kegan Paul, Trench and Trubner.

Migeod, F. H. W. (1925) *Through British Cameroons*. London: Heath Cranton.

Moisel, Max (1912) Maps of Kamerun: D2 Schebschi Gebirge; D3 Garoua. Berlin: Dietrich Reimer.

Nissen, Margaret (1968) *An African Church is Born. The Story of the Adamawa and Central Sardauna Provinces in Nigeria*. Denmark: Purups Grafiske Hus.

Polanyi, Michael (1958) *Personal Knowledge*. London: Routledge.

Power, Berchman O.S.A. (1976) Our mission beginnings, Part IV. *News Letter of the Order of St. Augustine, Province of Ireland*, 11th February, pp. 35–39.

Shweder, Richard A. (1984) Anthropology's romantic rebellion against the enlightenment, or there's more to thinking than reason and evidence. In Richard A. Shweder and Robert A. Levine (eds.), *Culture Theory: Essays on Mind, Self and Emotion*. Cambridge: Cambridge University Press.

Soyinka, Wole (1981) *Ake. The Years of Childhood*. London: Arena.

Strathern, Marilyn (1985) Kinship and economy: constitutive orders of a provisional kind, *American Ethnologist* 12(2):191–209.

Turner, V. W. (1968) *The Drums of Affliction. A Study of Religious Processes among the Ndembu of Zaire*. London: International African Institute and Hutchinson.

Unpublished references

(other than those held in the Nigerian National Archives)

Crane, Peter (1958) *Histories of Gurum and Yebbi Districts*, Typescript. Ganye: Local Government Headquarters.

Cullen, Fr Malachy (1944) *Notes on the Mapeo Chamba: origin, custom, juju*. Manuscript. Yola Catholic Mission. (Previously kept in the Mapeo Catholic Mission.)

Mueller, Pastor Edward (1987) Letter to R. Fardon, August 22nd.

NATIONAL ARCHIVES, KADUNA, NIGERIA

I have referred to materials in two files from the *Yola Profile* in Chapter 9. The letter-number citations are those under which they are catalogued in Nigeria.

3058 *Chamba marriage—wife stealing*
Fleming (1935) Letter on wife stealing in Gurum (annotated).

Welch (1936) *Report on Chamba marriage and wife stealing.* Letters on the same subject.

C.778 *Chamba Federation. (1) Separatist Movements*

Paul (S.D.O), Letter to Yola Resident February 1951.

Rickford (Touring Officer), Reports to S.D.O. February 1951.

Cassidy (Touring Officer), Reports to S.D.O. March 1951.

Paul (S.D.O.), Letter to Yola Resident *Chamba District affairs*, September 1951.

Resident, Letter to Permanent Secretary, September 1955.

Sorrell (A.D.O.), *Report on Chamba Federation*, June 1955.

Crane (A.D.O.), *The Chamba Subordinate Native Authority*, statement prepared for the visit of the U.N. Minorities Commission to Adamawa Province in February 1958. (There is another copy of this document in Rhodes House, Oxford.)

(Correspondence continued in File C.932 which could not be located in the Kaduna Archives in 1977.)

INDEX